Rhetoric for a Multicultural America

Robert Cullen
San José State University

Allyn and Bacon
Boston • London • Toronto • Sydney • Tokyo • Singapore

Vice President, Humanities: Joseph Opiela
Series Editorial Assistant: Mary Beth Varney
Executive Marketing Manager: Lisa Kimball
Production Editor: Christopher H. Rawlings
Editorial-Production Service: Omegatype Typography, Inc.
Composition and Prepress Buyer: Linda Cox
Manufacturing Buyer: Suzanne Lareau
Cover Administrator: Jenny Hart
Electronic Composition: Omegatype Typography, Inc.

Library of Congress Cataloging-in-Publication Data

Cullen, Robert.
    Rhetoric for a multicultural America / Robert Cullen.
      p.   cm.
    Includes bibliographical references and index.
    ISBN 0-205-28219-9
    1. English language—Rhetoric. 2. Ethnic groups—United States—
Problems, exercises, etc. 3. Pluralism (Social sciences) Problems,
exercises, etc. 4. Readers—Pluralism (Social sciences)
5. Readers—Ethnic groups. 6. College readers. 7. Report writing.
I. Title.
PE1408.C76   2000
808'.042—dc21   99-23610
                                                      CIP

Printed in the United States of America
10 9 8 7 6 5 4 3 2 1   04 03 02 01 00 99

Text credits appear on page 303, which constitutes a continuation of this copyright page.

For Gerry and Jerry

Contents

Preface

WHY A MULTICULTURAL RHETORIC?

You have never read a "multicultural rhetoric" before. What should you expect now that you are about to begin? I can give you a good idea by explaining the title, *Rhetoric for a Multicultural America*.

The possibly unfamiliar word "rhetoric" means, first and foremost, that this book is concerned with the art of effective communication; its purpose is to help you become a better writer. The word also indicates that this book belongs to a group of textbooks called rhetorics, as opposed to handbooks, workbooks, or readers/anthologies. This means that you'll find many suggestions to improve your writing but only about a dozen essays and no punctuation rules or guidelines for footnotes.

The word "America" in the title is used to encompass not only the fifty states, but also Puerto Rico, for example, and American Indian nations, and Washington, D.C.; in addition, the book recognizes that ideas and languages and writers and students can all cross national boundaries, and as you read, you will spend an occasional moment in Mexico, at the Canadian border, and even on the island of Antigua.

The tricky word in the title is "multicultural," because this term has been used in so many different ways in recent years. My notion of multiculturalism is broad and inclusive. To me, it does not simply mean multiracial or multinational or multiethnic, important as these concepts surely are. I intend *multicultural* to embrace many kinds of diversity in American society—ethnic, to be sure, but also regional, religious, economic, sexual, and more. I call America "multicultural" rather than simply "diverse" to emphasize that the many subgroups within our society are dynamic and profoundly important social forces. It makes sense to me to think of deaf culture, for example, or gay culture as much more than the presence of deaf or gay people in our society. And it makes sense to study writing with a keen awareness of such cultural contexts. This book will help you do that.

As you can perhaps see all around you, American colleges and universities often reflect the diversity—indeed the multiculturalism—of our broader society; they bring together people who differ in age, background, economic class, gender, religious belief, ethnicity, dialect, political ideology, and many other ways. Many campuses can also boast of students visiting from other countries, as well as of recent immigrants. For this reason, and because even students from America's least diverse campuses will inevitably work in a multicultural society, all education should take diversity into account. But diversity is especially important in writing classes, where students often work together closely, discuss controversial issues, and learn how to communicate effectively in a new and sometimes intimidating environment.

This book, then, is built on the premise that the multicultural nature of American life—both on and off campus—is of vital importance to how we write. Rather than pay lip service to diversity, it puts it squarely in the foreground. Here are some of the features of this text that set it apart from business-as-usual rhetorics:

- an extended discussion of American dialects/languages and their relationship to college composition, including sections on Ebonics and Spanglish
- a survey and critique of the Western rhetorical tradition that produced today's composition classes, with special attention paid to the role of women throughout that history and to the role of rhetoric in the United States
- coverage of issues of student authority in the classroom and in academic writing generally
- an introduction to "women's writing," also known as *écriture féminine*

- a discussion of sexism in language
- attention paid to how and when bilingual and bidialectal students can use their second languages or dialects in college writing
- discussion of aggression in language, including hate speech and libel
- readings by a highly diverse group of writers
- short quotations by dozens of nonmainstream writers

Rhetoric for a Multicultural America also has plenty of down-to-earth advice on writing, gathered from my twenty years of teaching composition. The book offers practical tips on planning, writing, and revising student papers. Even the most traditional methods introduced, however, are presented in a multicultural framework. For example, the discussion of age-old figures of speech such as metaphor and irony is balanced by a countercultural figure of speech called Signifyin(g). Writers held up as models include some "classic" writers and representatives of a broad spectrum of contemporary authors.

The aim of the book, then, is to teach effective writing strategies in a decidedly multicultural context, the only realistic and sensible context for an America entering the twenty-first century.

OVERVIEW

The book is divided into two main parts. Part 1: Bedrock Strategies for Writers covers the kind of information students are most likely to need most urgently, namely, how to plan, write, and revise an essay. Part 2: Rhetoric in Cultural Context emphasizes cultural contexts such as history, gender, students' authority over their writing, and the linguistic diversity of the United States.

Part 1: Bedrock Strategies for Writers

Chapter 1, Names and Labels, addresses fundamental issues of how writing works—how learning and language are related, how words reflect value judgments, how words can be used as weapons. It also covers definitions, denotation versus connotation, and issues of "politically correct" word choice. The readings for Chapter 1, by José Antonio Burciaga, Roger L. Welsch, and Patricia J. Williams, discuss language and meaning in relation to naming, in-groups, and politically incorrect humor. Like every chapter, Chapter 1 contains two Writing Breaks—quick activities designed to integrate your writing and your reading—and ends with Discussion Questions and Writing Assignments.

Chapter 2, Bedrock Strategies: Invention and Organization, covers the first two essential steps of the writing process, generating and organizing ideas. It reprints several examples of brainstorming sessions and presents a multicultural version of Burke's Pentad, a powerful intellectual tool you can use to generate interesting ideas to write about. The chapter also presents some basic strategies for paragraph-level and essay-level organization, along with special advice on organization to students from other cultures. The two readings in Chapter 2 focus on creativity; the excerpt from Roger von Oech's *A Whack on the Side of the Head* provides all-purpose boosts to creativity, while the interview with Sonia Sanchez explores the sources of a feminist poet's art.

Chapter 3, Bedrock Strategies: Imitation, Writing, and Revision, begins with a discussion of the importance of imitation in learning how to write, even in a diverse and rapidly changing society like ours. (Both the first Writing Break and the activities at the end of the chapter provide guided practice in various kinds of imitation.) The next two sections cover various aids to writing and revision—nuts-and-bolts advice about the various ways writers get their work done. The last section before the readings introduces schemes and tropes with a multicultural twist, using a discussion of the black English linguistic device called Signifyin(g) to illuminate more traditional figures of speech like metaphor and irony. The chapter defines these rhetorical devices, illustrates their usefulness, and provides activities to help you incorporate them into your own writing. The two readings for Chapter 3 provide a strong contrast of styles. Jesse Jackson's speech, delivered to a massive crowd on the thirtieth anniversary of the March on Washington, is highly structured and uses many of the rhetorical devices covered in Chapter 3; Jamaica Kincaid's "In History" also examines the meaning of a significant historical event—European discovery of America—but her essay is best suited to contemplative reading. Questions on these readings will help you identify the ways the writers are matching their language to their differing audiences and purposes.

Part 2: Rhetoric in Cultural Context

Chapter 4, Rhetoric in Historical Context: An Introduction and Critique, provides what may be the world's quickest summary of 2,500 years of Western rhetorical history. Rather than list every important event or thinker, the chapter focuses on a handful of key ideas: the strong connection of today's composition classroom to the origins of rhetoric in ancient Greece; the position of women throughout the rhetorical tradition (including the recent regendering of that history/herstory); and the importance of rhetoric in defining moments of American history such as the founding of the nation and the abolitionist movement. The readings for this chapter, Michael Kelly's "Running On" and Hendrik Hertzberg's "Big Talk," analyze the rhetoric of the 1996 U.S. presidential campaign, illustrating how the rhetorical tradition is at work not only in classrooms, but in the broader culture as well.

Chapter 5, Authority and Gender in Student Writing, extends the gender theme from Chapter 4, looking at gender issues in contemporary writing and relating them to the issue of authority in writing. "Authority" is a matter of whose speech and writing a school or a culture acknowledges, values, and promotes. Chapter 4 describes some of the barriers women historically had to overcome to be heard; Chapter 5 recognizes how challenging it remains for students to become authoritative writers and discusses the roles of gender, class, and ethnicity in this process. As always, the abstract ideas are balanced by practical applications, such as how to choose pronouns and how to find striking quotations by women. Chapter 5 also introduces the idea of a women's rhetoric, or *écriture féminine*, and provides an example of such writing by Gloria Anzaldúa, "Speaking in Tongues: A Letter to 3rd World Women Writers."

Chapter 6 is about dialects and composition. It summarizes essential information about dialects and casts American diversity in a positive light. Dialects and Composition then discusses Ebonics (also known as "black English") and Spanglish. The second half of the chapter uses dialect learning as a metaphor for acquiring the academic vocabulary and style students need to succeed in college. The readings for Chapter 6 return to the issue of black English/Ebonics; readings by Eldridge Cleaver and James Baldwin feature strongly contrasting opinions, while the article by Fawn Vrazo compares the debate over Ebonics to a similar cultural struggle concerning the Scots dialect in Scotland.

ACKNOWLEDGMENTS

A portion of my research and writing was supported by a sabbatical leave from San José State University. At Allyn & Bacon, Joe Opiela showed faith in this book from a very early stage and helped me make innumerable improvements through successive drafts. Mary Varney provided prompt, cheerful, and highly competent assistance in matters ranging from schedules to permissions. Susan Simmons at Omegatype Typography, Inc. expertly guided the book through the editorial-production process. A cadre of reviewers steered me away from several blunders and made numerous excellent suggestions; thank you, Patrick Bizzaro, East Carolina University; Faun Bernbach Evans, Chicago State University; Jeanne Gunner, Santa Clara University; Paul Heilker, Virginia Tech; Fran O'Connor, Nassau Community College; Alison Warriner, California State University, Hayward; and Randal Woodland, University of Michigan, Dearborn. I am especially thankful for the patience and encouragement that my family and friends offered in endless supply throughout the long process from research to publication. Above all, I wish to express my gratitude to my wife, Liz Silver, without whom I could never have written this book.

■ Part 1

Bedrock Strategies for Writers

1

Names and Labels

Language is not just an instrument that humans wield, but rather the very medium through which human identity, thought, and action emerge.
—JOHN SCHILB

We live in a world of language as much as in a world of things, and in this world of language, no act is more important or powerful than the act of naming. Many of us identify ourselves, for example, with a number of labels—student, mother, Republican, lesbian, Hoosier, Buddhist, sculptor, Nisei, Chicana—words that name the groups we belong to; some of these labels may be of modest importance to us, but others speak to the very essence of who we are.

The significance of naming goes far beyond the terms we apply to ourselves: our language influences how we perceive and understand our world. Think, for example, of what the word *horse* might mean to a very young child; she might have a few extremely basic ideas about horses—for example, that they are large animals that can be found on farms or ranches and can sometimes be ridden. Then imagine the child growing up to be an expert on horses, familiar with Appaloosas and pintos, Clydesdales and Morgans, Thoroughbreds and trotters. For such an expert, the language and the ideas merge like dancer into dance: knowledge of horses is tightly bound up with the words that name horses, and in a very real and important way, a person who knows a forelock from a fetlock and a haw from a hock sees a different animal from the rest of us. To give you another simple example, I've known snow all my life—I grew up in Denver—but when I took up skiing recently, I had a completely new experience of snow and thus acquired, almost unavoidably, a new language to describe it: corn snow, hard pack, mashed potatoes, Sierra cement, champagne powder, death cookies.

If naming affects our perception of simple physical things such as horses and snow, imagine how important it is when people discuss controversial or abstract subjects such as "masculinity," "disabilities," "high crimes and misdemeanors," "civil disobedience," or "bias." It's a wonder sometimes that humans can communicate at all, and when we communicate best, it's usually because we have been careful and accurate with the names we attach to people, things, and ideas.

This chapter uses the idea of names and labels to explore several facets of college writing. It shows how many aspects of writing, not just the use of proper names, can be seen as kinds of naming, and further, that virtually all learning depends on *language* learning. Moving from such framing ideas to highly practical matters, the chapter will help you learn how to write and use definitions, to discern the difference between descriptive and evaluative language, to understand denotation and connotation. The chapter also looks at naming and labeling in cultural context, defending "political correctness" and studying how names and labels can be used as weapons, for example in libel and hate speech.

Near the end of the chapter, you will find essays by José Antonio Burciaga, Roger L. Welsch, and Patricia J. Williams. These essays explore the sometimes uneasy relationship between labels, culture, and group membership. The chapter concludes with discussion questions about these readings and further suggestions for thinking, talking, and writing.

⊠ FEATURED PAPER TOPICS

Here are two paper options that are closely linked to the ideas in Chapter 1. The first calls for a personal essay; the second is more academic and analytical. Read further in the chapter before you begin writing, but keep these topics in mind—especially if your instructor has assigned one or both.

- Write a short essay in which you explore the meaning of one or two names or labels that are important to you. These could be family names, nicknames, or words that describe your membership in some group.

- Write a short essay in which you investigate the denotation and connotation of one or two important words or phrases in American English today. A few examples are *Hispanic, Third World, welfare, neurotic, sexual harassment, native, queer, homeless, poverty line, class, angel, Middle Eastern, dysfunctional, Nuyorican, vegan, Asian, Oriental,* and *macho/machismo.* You may wish to consult a college dictionary, textbooks, news stories, Internet resources, or the *Oxford English Dictionary*—a special dictionary in your school's reference section that shows the history of words' meanings. You may also wish to interview family, friends, and classmates to see how they would define and use your term(s). Note that differences, disagreements, ambiguities, paradoxes, and changes in usage or meaning will be more interesting to discuss than universal agreement. Your essay need not try to identify a single correct meaning.

WORDS AND MEANINGS

Writing as Naming

Observe the magic of naming at work in the passage below, as novelist Amy Tan creates a family out of thin air, as it were:

> But just to set the genetic record straight, Kwan and I share a father, only that. She was born in China. My brothers, Kevin and Tommy, and I were born in San Francisco after my father, Jack Yee, immigrated here and married our mother, Louise Kenfield.
>
> Mom calls herself "American mixed grill, a bit of everything white, fatty, and fried." She was born in Moscow, Idaho, where she was a champion baton twirler and once won a county fair prize for growing a deformed potato that had the profile of Jimmy Durante. She told me she dreamed she'd one day grow up to be different—thin, exotic, and noble like Luise Rainer, who won an Oscar playing O-lan in *The Good Earth.* When Mom moved to San Francisco and became a Kelly girl instead, she did the next-best thing. She married our father. Mom thinks that marrying out of the Anglo race makes her a liberal…. (From *The Hundred Secret Senses*)

Look at how much naming, how many different kinds of naming, are going on here. First, we have the various names Tan assigns her fictional family, including the contrasts between the Chinese names Kwan and Yee and the stereotypically "American" names like Kevin and Tommy. Illogical as it may be, just conjuring up specific names like these seems to make characters real. After all, how can Louise Kenfield have a name if she doesn't exist? Next, we have her daughter's name for Kenfield, Mom. Even with this simple word, Tan makes a choice, for the narrator *doesn't* say "mother" or "ma" or "mama," any of which would change the atmosphere of the passage and our first impression of the mother–daughter relationship. Beyond this, the passage brims over with proper names, which Tan and her characters use to define their world. Place names like San Francisco and Idaho make the setting specific. Other proper names like *The Good Earth* and Jimmy Durante (a performer with a very large nose) and even Kelly girl are cultural markers, familiar landmarks of the American scene— or more accurately, we may say that these names *were* cultural icons, for they help place Kenfield in a particular generation. The passage is also concerned with how Kenfield defines herself: she considers herself a liberal because she married a Chinese immigrant and even describes herself with a food metaphor, "American mixed grill, a bit of everything white, fatty, and fried." Finally, we can consider Tan's choice of adjectives as a subtle type of naming, as when she characterizes Oscar-winner Luise Rainer as "thin, exotic, and noble"—a nice contrast, by the way, with "white, fatty, and fried." Tan begins to define who Kenfield is by arranging all these names around her.

> *An order given in battle, an instruction issued by the master of a sailing ship, a cry for help, are as powerful in modifying the course of events as any other bodily act.... You utter a vow or you forge a signature and you may find yourself bound for life to a monastery, a woman, or a prison.—Bronislaw Malinowski*

Tan is a professional writer, of course, but college writing is not so very different from the novelist's art. "Composition" is not just a matter of recording ideas, of writing down thoughts in acceptable academic formats. No, composition is invention, discovery, creation; it's seeing your world and choosing how to name it.

Names and Knowledge

A word is a bridge thrown between myself and another. If one end of the bridge depends on me, then the other depends on my addressee.—Mikhail Bakhtin

It *is* possible to think in purely nonverbal ways. Nonverbal thought might include musical or visual creation, spatial thinking, mathematical calculation, and perhaps philosophical or logical thinking that is purely symbolic. Most of our thinking, though, involves language in one way or another—necessarily so if we want to communicate any ideas we can't draw or act out in pantomime. Language is not just packaging, not just a delivery system, but rather an integral part of our mental experience. Language plays an important role in memory, emotion, and reason. This is often true even of a "mindless pleasure" such as daydreaming, but it is especially important in college reading, writing, and learning.

Although your college experience will be much richer and more varied than rote memorization of terminology, what you learn could be measured by your ability to name things correctly or understand precisely what various names mean. What is meant by *mimicry, homeostasis, villanelle, Bauhaus, luciferase, Fauvism, transcendentalism, phoneme, neoclassical?* If you know all these already, go straight to graduate school. If not, stick around and learn the lingo of your chosen field. Chapter 6 expands on this notion of learning academic "dialects"; it will suffice for now to understand that your learning in college, whatever your major, will involve learning new concepts *plus* new vocabulary. The vocabulary will not only name objects, but will extend to processes, operations, historical eras, theoretical models, and "schools" or movements within a given discipline.

Where does writing come in? For one thing, writing demonstrates mastery of concepts and their accompanying terminology. There's a lot of truth to the saying that you really learn something when you have to teach it to others. Writing is perhaps the next-best test. If it's challenging to understand a lecture sprinkled with new words and ideas, it's doubly hard—but extremely valuable—to use the new material on your own, applying it yourself in a fresh situation. The reward is high: once you can write in an academic discipline, you can join its scholarly activity rather than merely observe it.

Figure 1.1 is a simple but instructive drawing about vocabulary. It emphasizes that there are many more words in English than you or anyone else knows. Similarly, all of us understand far more words than we actually use in writing. The fact that you write using a small subset of English words does not make you stupid; there are thousands of words that are virtually useless in all but the most specialized communications. Focus instead on what the drawing suggests about how you can *learn.* There are two areas of possible growth: you can expand the borders of the medium-sized box, familiarizing yourself with words now unknown to you, *and* you can expand the borders of the little box, pushing more of the words you already know into your active writing vocabulary. It's helpful to think consciously about learning in both these areas.

There are several easy ways to do this. First, simply make a note of any unfamiliar words you encounter in readings, lectures, or discussions. Look these up daily. Unless you begin to see a new word repeatedly, you need not necessarily memorize it—just be sure you understand what it means in the context of your reading or listening. The words you most need to know will recur, and you'll learn them.

A more ambitious step is to try using some of the new terms in your own writing, perhaps at first in a journal or study log, then

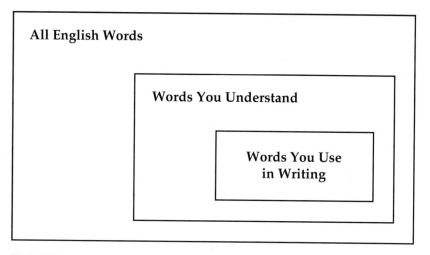

FIGURE 1.1

when revising a more formal assignment. Don't go overboard, but be willing to make some errors with new words. Also make a conscious effort when revising to use a wider range of the words well known to you. Beware the thesaurus, however: it can remind you of words you know, but if you use it to "translate" your natural voice into elevated language, you are likely to make many mistakes.

Defining

I saw that the best thing I could do was get hold of a dictionary—
to study, to learn some words.—Malcolm X

The most obvious kind of naming, and perhaps the most common and most important for writing in college, is defining. You will see a few kinds of definition in a moment, but there are many others; as you read, pay careful attention to how experienced writers and speakers define words and ideas in various academic contexts such as books, articles, lectures, footnotes, and glossaries. Remember that definitions can range from single words (*autonomous* means "independent") to lengthy discussions (for example, a definition of *capitalism* might take up a full lecture in an economics class).

Dictionary Definitions

If you and your dictionary are "strangers of long standing" (to borrow a phrase from E. B. White), now's the time to introduce yourself. You don't have to imitate Malcolm X, who jump-started his self-education by copying an entire dictionary by hand, but do put this essential reference tool to use systematically. In addition to looking up unfamiliar words in your reading assignments routinely, you may occasionally want to check the meanings of words you use in your own writing. (If you never need to do this, either you're not being ambitious enough or you're not being careful enough.) Expert writers consult dictionaries all the time, though novices seldom picture experts doing so.

Remember that consulting a dictionary does not oblige you to insert the dictionary definition into your paper! Quoting dictionaries is an overused strategy, especially in the opening paragraphs of student essays, and is rarely necessary. Instead, simply use the dictionary to make sure you are using a word correctly.

"The question is," said Alice, "whether you can *make words mean so many different things."*

"The question is," said Humpty Dumpty, "which is to be master— that's all."—Lewis Carroll

Describing and Naming

How can you define something without citing a dictionary, encyclopedia, textbook, or other authoritative source? One simple but immensely useful way is to describe something (whether an idea, an event, a person, or anything else) and connect your description to a particular word or phrase. It's a bit like writing your own dictionary entry, but you can be casual, elegant, or humorous as you see fit. Below are two examples demonstrating somewhat different approaches. Observe how, in the first passage, Stephanie Coontz, who is defining an unfamiliar concept (*hanai* adoptions), strives to be very straightforward, very clear:

> There are certainly historical precedents demonstrating that people are capable of seeing children as a valued social good, not simply as the private luxury or burden of their own parents. Among traditional Hawaiians, for example, it was common to offer a child to a relative or friend in a *hanai* arrangement. The word comes from a verb meaning "to feed." Hanai adoptions did not normally come about because of parental disinterest or abandonment, nor did they cut the child off from the biological family of origin. They were ways of expanding the circle of close ties between adults and children. Instead of assuming that the love between hanai children and their adoptive parents would be less intense than a close blood tie, Hawaiians were sometimes said to favor hanai children over natural ones, and the ideal hanai relationship was seen as a model that biological relatives might strive to emulate.

In contrast, the second passage shows how Henry A. Giroux (re)defines a familiar concept, youth. Like Coontz, Giroux no doubt wants to be clear, but because we all have some notion of what *youth* means, he can move directly to a very sophisticated, abstract definition:

> As a concept, youth represents an inescapable intersection of the personal, social, political, and pedagogical. Beneath the abstract

codifying of youth around the discourses of law, medicine, psychology, employment, education, and marketing statistics, there is the lived experience of being young. For me, youth invokes a repository of memories fueled by my own journey through an adult world that was in the way, a world held together by a web of regulations and restrictions that were more oppressive than liberating.... I grew up amid the motion and force of mostly working-class male bodies—bodies asserting their physical strength as one of the few resources we had control over.

Ideally, the definitions you use in your papers, whether you write them yourself or quote them, will similarly take into account how much your readers already know and how much you need to tell them. After all, the definitions should appear for no other reason than to aid your readers.

Multicultural Definitions

If you are lucky enough to be bilingual, bicultural, or bidialectal (fluent in two dialects of English), you may occasionally have the opportunity to educate the rest of us concerning important words or concepts that don't translate easily into English. In its simplest form, this would mean introducing words or phrases from another language or dialect, as in "my sister's *quince,* or 'sweet fifteen' celebration." Even a single word such as *quince* can add a bit of spice to an essay, and when unfamiliar terms appear frequently, they can exert a powerful influence on the tone or atmosphere of the prose. Listen to award-winning novelist Michael Ondaatje name the names of winds in *The English Patient:*

> There is a whirlwind in southern Morocco, the *aajej,* against which the fellahin defend themselves with knives. There is the *africo,* which has at times reached into the city of Rome. The *alm,* a fall wind out of Yugoslavia. The *arifi,* also christened *aref* or *rifi,* which scorches with numerous tongues. These are permanent winds that live in the present tense.
>
> There are other, less constant winds that change direction, that can knock down horse and rider and realign themselves anticlockwise. The *bist roz* leaps into Afghanistan for 170 days—burying villages. There is the hot, dry *ghibli* from Tunis, which rolls and rolls and produces a nervous condition. The

haboob—a Sudan dust storm that dresses in bright yellow walls a thousand metres high and is followed by rain....

You'll rarely need to use so many exotic words so close together as Ondaatje does here, but don't be afraid to use terms such as *machismo* or *feng shui* or *roman fleuve* if you know and understand them. Provide a definition when appropriate, but let your special knowledge add to the richness of your voice.

Misdefinitions

When people are careless with definitions, things can go wrong in a hurry. For example, a student of mine recently reported that his school district had removed *Huckleberry Finn* from the required high school reading list because of its offensive language. So far so good, but then he wrote that he was opposed to such *censorship*. His statement is an example of misnaming, because *censorship* ordinarily implies steps much more aggressive than removing a book from a privileged position on a short list of required books; deleting passages, removing the book from the school library, banning its presence on campus, burning the novel—these constitute censorship.

A slip like this can easily be remedied, but note that bad definitions from powerful organizations like corporations, courts, and legislatures can have far-reaching social consequences. For example, look at this definition of *persons under guardianship* from a 1924 Arizona Supreme Court ruling:

> Broadly speaking, persons under guardianship may be defined as those who, because of some peculiarity of status, defect of age, understanding or self-control, are considered incapable of managing their own affairs, and who therefore have some other person lawfully invested with the power and charged with the duty of taking care of their persons or managing their property, or both.

This language may seem harmless enough until you learn that it was categorically applied to the tribal peoples of Arizona and helped deprive them of the right to vote until 1948. Similarly, shared cultural misdefinitions—for example, the original perception of AIDS as a gay man's disease—can prove not only misguided but outright dangerous.

Names and Political Correctness

All of the American categories of male and female, straight or not,
black or white, were shattered, thank heaven, very early in my life.
Not without anguish, certainly; but once you have discerned the
meaning of a label, it may seem to define you for others, but it does
not have the power to define you to yourself.—James Baldwin

In the situation comedy *Mad About You*, Hank Azaria plays the role
of Nat the dog-walker; Nat refers to himself, however, as a "canine
leisure engineer." This is a pretty good joke: It satirizes a modern
trend by poking fun at the way most people try to glorify their jobs.
On the other hand, joking about the names groups and individuals
give themselves can be a way of attacking them or trying to trivialize their concerns. There *are* differences between the phrase "victim of
rape" and the phrase "rape survivor," between "Negro" and "black"
and "African American," between "disabled" and "challenged."

A good rule of thumb is that the right to choose a name belongs
to the people it describes. If a Chicana sculptor does not want the
label "Hispanic" attached to her or her work, the rest of us should
respect that. Similarly, if my university asks newspapers to retain
the accent in San José State University, they ought to listen, even if
it's inconvenient. When in doubt, err on the side of respecting other
people's wishes, especially when the others are not well known or
highly sympathetic to you. You may open yourself to the charge of
being politically correct, in its meaning of "pandering to every silly
whim of every supposedly victimized group," but if you ignore this
advice, you may write things that are perceived as sexist, racist, or
simply ignorant.

Admittedly, the choices you face as a student writer can be confusing. How many people do you think really know when to use
"Hispanic," "Latino," "Latina," "Mexican American," "mestiza," or
"Chicana/o"? In college writing, distinctions between related words
like these will be very important. You will likely need to be more
precise and subtle in your word choice than ever before. It's a big
challenge, but the difficulties are not insurmountable. A current dictionary will help immensely; you should also listen carefully to
people you respect, and pay close attention as you read. Get used to
the fact that politically correct usage will change with the culture,

and begin training yourself to notice shifting terminologies. Being persuaded that it matters is half the battle.

> *How little is communicated about who we are when we are labeled:* Black/white, queer/straight, male/female.—*Ann Filemyr*

To illustrate how important using politically correct names can be, I'd like to give three brief examples. The first concerns the pair of words "transsexual" and "transgender." These two words may seem to point to the same thing: behavior that crosses traditional borderlines between male and female—for example, a biological male wearing clothing a particular culture considers female. But it's not quite that simple. In her review of *Transgender Warriors* by Leslie Feinberg, Jeanne Bergman defines *transsexual* and explains an important problem with it:

> [Transsexual] refers to people whose sense of themselves as female or male contradicts their anatomy and physiology. Paradoxically, transsexuality reasserts the restrictive oppositional duality of gender even as it recognizes that individuals may cross over the boundary that separates men from women.

For example, transvestites cross a male/female boundary by dressing counter to mainstream expectations, but they leave the line between male and female intact. The newer concept *transgender,* Bergman explains, is a more subversive, even revolutionary idea. It attempts to break down the clear distinction between male and female, envisioning "a more fluid gender identity" and accommodating not only those who "cross the gender divide," but also those like Feinberg and RuPaul, who "occasionally or always situate themselves on the razor separating male from female, and who, by gathering there, dull its edge." Importantly, "transgender" is a word that has emerged within diverse "trans" communities, unlike "transsexual," which was imposed by outside researchers. In addition, the newer term "transgender" reflects a substantial change in how gender boundaries are perceived; it is emphatically not a merely arbitrary switch in labels. In fact, one could argue that the appearance of "transgender" in discussions of human sexuality significantly changes the meaning of "transsexual."

The source of the politically correct term is again important with the words "Chicano" and "Chicana," my second example. I'll summarize here a few of the key points made by Norma Alarcón in her essay "Chicana Feminism: In the Tracks of 'the' Native Woman." Alarcón notes that "Chicano" (the masculine form) and "Chicana" emerged from a working-class, oral culture. In the very act of naming themselves, the political class that adopted these terms challenged mainstream concepts and labels like "Mexican American" and "Hispanic." For example, the term "Mexican American" identifies people in terms of two nations. "Chicano/a" tosses out the geographical map—intentionally ignores the issues of nationality—and redraws identity in terms of culture, class, and power; it asserts the commonality of people on both sides of the Rio Grande and simultaneously does away with the "hyphenated-citizen" name that can imply second-class citizenship. Use of the term "Hispanic," Alarcón asserts, is a conservative attempt "assisted by the U.S. Census Bureau . . . and the mass media to homogenize all people of Latin American descent"—something like carelessly lumping together Navaho, Crow, Apache, and Seminole peoples as Indians. And, once you look past a simple definition of *Hispanic* as "Latin American" and see that its root word is "Spain"—namely a country that colonized Latin America—the word seems doubly troublesome. As for "Chicana" and "Chicano," use of both the masculine and feminine forms, though sometimes cumbersome, is important not only to underline the contributions of feminists to the Chicana/o movement, but also to recognize the sexual dynamics within it.

Más hiere mala palabra que espada afilada.
A harsh word cuts deeper than a sharp sword.

My third example also concerns people straddling a border, namely, people of "mixed blood." I refer here to people of mixed Native American and "white" ancestry, but you may want to consider parallels to other "biracial" or "mixed race" groups. I'm relying primarily on an article by Patricia Riley called "The Mixed Blood Writer as Interpreter and Mythmaker." As her title indicates, Riley uses the term "mixed blood" as a politically correct term. She is careful to note that her Webster's dictionary does not have an entry for *mixed blood*, but does define *half-breed* as follows: "n. someone of mixed breeding, esp. of mixed white and American Indian parentage." The offensiveness of "half-breed" is perhaps immediately apparent, but think for a moment about what it might imply—for example, that only the white half of such a person's ancestry has any value. In the nineteenth century, indeed, some white writers saw half-breeds as distinctly better than purely native Indians: the bizarre racial arithmetic of the time suggested that half-breeds helped bridge the gap between "savages" and cultured Americans.

Riley quotes several mixed-blood writers, including Gogisgi/ Carroll Arnett, Rayna Green, and Paula Gunn Allen, who use the

---

⊠ WRITING BREAK
Language and Meaning

Below are several questions about language and meaning posed by Douglas R. Hofstadter in his marvelous book on translation, *Le Ton beau de Marot: In Praise of the Music of Language*. After reading the list carefully, try to answer one or more of the questions as precisely as you can; provide whatever reasoning or evidence you can to support your ideas. Your response may take the form of a group discussion, a journal entry, or an essay. If you are working on one of this chapter's Featured Paper Topics (pp. 4–5), try applying questions like Hofstadter's to your topic. In what ways is *context* important?

- Does a sentence written in American English mean what it means in British English? (Does the word "monarchy" mean the same thing in both places? How about "Yankee"? How about "jolly"? How about "you"?)

- Does a sentence written in British English mean what it means in Indian English? (Does "cow" mean the same thing in both of them? How about "beef"? How about "Crown"? How about "nose"?)...

- Does a San Franciscan speak the same language as a New Yorker? (Does "Chinatown" mean the same thing to both of them? How about "China"? How about "Broadway"? How about "earthquake"? How about "steep"?)

- Does a Manhattanite speak the same language as a Brooklynite? (Does "New York" mean the same thing to both of them? How about "D train"?)

---

noun "breed." My own dictionaries define "breed" as a mostly Western variation or abridgment of "half-breed" but don't help much with the term's connotations; in terms of connotation, "breed" as a mixed-blood response to "half-breed" seems to be a verbal subversion of the original insult. Riley also reminds us that there exist tribal words for people of mixed blood. Needless to say, while these words refer to the same group of people (that is, their denotation is the same), they may differ significantly in meaning and connotation. The Lakota word *iyeska*, for example, goes beyond describing a person of mixed blood to "[embody] the concept of one who not only interprets between the red and white worlds, but between the world of spirits and of human beings as well." Far, far in meaning from the pejorative "half-breed," *iyeska* confers on mixed bloods a special status. Finally, because the issue of mixed blood has entered both the oral and the written literature of many (if not all) tribes, a complete understanding of the various names given to "breeds" would demand familiarity with a broad array of Native American stories—Laguna, Lakota, Pueblo, and others.

This chapter won't take you any further down that road. The point is that the names matter and that their connotations can be at once subtle and important. You may never need to write sensitively about people of mixed blood, but you will surely have to write tactfully and accurately about topics of equal complexity.

DESCRIPTIVE AND EVALUATIVE LANGUAGE

I am sitting with a philosopher in the garden; he says again and again "I know that's a tree," pointing to a tree near us. Someone else arrives and hears this, and I tell them: "This fellow isn't insane. We are only doing philosophy."—Ludwig Wittgenstein

The Elusive Goal of Clarity

As long as people have been thinking about how language works, some folks have wished that it could be entirely clear and neutral. They have lamented ambiguities in language, the shifting meanings of words, and the difficulty and inefficiency of human communication. It's hard enough to observe the world clearly and reason about it accurately, they recognized, without having to sort out various kinds of verbal tangles, too. Some countries, most famously France, have tried to fix their languages in a particular stage—to forbid changes in meaning, the "immigration" of foreign words, and other such natural events in languages' histories.[1] Some academic disciplines, too, particularly the sciences, have tried to restrict their own speech and writing to what is "objective" and well defined. But for better or worse, languages have proved formidable opponents, defying all attempts to tame them. They seem to be as fluid and unpredictable as the histories of the people who speak them.

> *Words are chameleons, which reflect the color of their environment.*
> —*Learned Hand*

Although the quest for completely clear language is apparently doomed, it's worth examining some of the causes of ambiguity. Making a distinction between "descriptive" and "evaluative" language will help you become a shrewder reader and a more precise, controlled writer. Purely descriptive language, if there is such a thing, states facts. The best examples are probably sentences that closely resemble mathematical equations, definitions, or theorems, statements like Euclid's "Given any straight line segment, a circle can be drawn having the segment as radius and one end point as center." Purely descriptive language aims to be clear, to communicate ideas without making value judgments, to avoid "rhetoric" in favor of facts.

I can perhaps clarify the notion with a slightly more elaborate example. A "neutral," "scientific" description of a potato—one found in an encyclopedia, for example—might mention that it's an edible tuber, might provide its Latin name (*Solanum tuberosum*), might mention its typical size and weight, its geographic distribution, its importance as a food source, and so on. This is a far cry from Amy Tan asking her readers to imagine "a deformed potato that had the profile of Jimmy Durante," for in Tan's description,

---

1. Iceland has apparently been successful at minimizing language change and resisting foreign vocabulary, but not without problems; Microsoft's refusal to produce an Icelandic translation of Windows 95 was viewed as a serious affront, even though virtually all Icelanders also speak English.

there's clearly an element of evaluation at work—a comic leap that compares the entertainer to the spud. Because human judgment and imagination come into play when we see faces in potatoes, we can easily imagine someone saying, "To me, that potato looks more like the artist formerly known as Prince." On the other hand, it's hard to imagine a sane person saying, "I think that's actually a watermelon, not a potato." My point is not that Tan's writing is better than the encyclopedia's; she and the encyclopedist have different aims which call for different types of language.

It may seem like not much is at stake when we think about language, ambiguity, and potatoes that look like Jimmy Durante, but think about how troublesome ambiguity in language can become when we look at culturally central texts such as the Constitution or a legislative ban on bilingual education. The opening of the Gospel of John, for example, is a revered and famous passage, but just in my home office I can find these two very different versions:

> In the beginning was the Word, and the Word was with God; and the word was God.

> When all things began, the Word already was. The Word dwelt with God, and what God was, the Word was.

Of course, these are translations, and the translations are not necessarily contradictory, but that doesn't erase the problem. Indeed, the notorious difficulty of translating complex texts points precisely to the unavoidable deep ambiguity in language.

For the sake of accuracy, but also for fun, I'd also like to point out that even language that takes the form of the simplest declarations ("I know that's a tree," as the philosopher said) can be made ambiguous, perplexing, or paradoxical, as in these examples compiled by Douglas Hofstadter:

> When you are not looking at it, this sentence is in Spanish.

> I had to translate this sentence into English because I could not read the original Sanskrit.

Of greater importance to most college students than such highly artificial sentences is the ease with which writers and readers slip across the line between descriptive and evaluative language. For one thing, context is tremendously important. The sentence "This tree is an elm" seems at first glance to be an extremely simple, purely descriptive statement, but put into different contexts, it could express such complex human feelings as amazement or disdain:

> "They have never been observed in Venezuela before, but this tree is an elm!"

> "How ignorant you are! This tree is an elm, not a spruce."

Similarly, in different settings, words such as "conservative" and "liberal" can serve as relatively neutral descriptions, or can become compliments or insults.

Even language that seems very straightforward, then, can actually communicate lots of value judgments. Consider the events that followed the acquittal of the Los Angeles police officers in the Rodney King incident. Was it a riot? A rebellion? A civil disturbance? An insurrection? A protest? A violent protest? An uprising? When a TV news anchor describes what happened in the riot, her manner may be entirely neutral, detached, objective, and impartial, but the word "riot" is unavoidably evaluative, judgmental, rhetorical. Note that *there is no neutral name* for these events. Every choice says something about the speaker's or writer's interpretation of what happened. Even a lengthy phrase like my "events that followed the acquittal of the Los Angeles police officers" probably communicates a complex idea, namely, "I'm aware that the name I give these events will define my perspective toward them, and I'm bending over backwards to avoid doing that at the moment."

Note also that people need not be focusing carefully on a word choice in order for it to matter. A high school history teacher, for example, might ask his students to memorize the date of the "riot" or the names of the officers involved, but the unintended, unconscious political message—that this was indeed a riot—may be what students remember five years later.

Denotation and Connotation

The terms "denotation" and "connotation" are often used to designate the descriptive versus the evaluative aspects of language, especially at the level of individual words. *Denotation* refers to the literal meaning of a word. A rose is a prickly-stemmed, showy-flowered shrub of the genus *Rosa*. *Connotation* refers to associated, secondary meanings; roses connote romance, love, poetry. This simple distinction between two different ways words mean things to us—a distinction perhaps long familiar to you—is an unending source of both delight and dispute throughout our culture. For better or worse, we're stuck with the fact that words almost never just point to things. Whether it's a Harley, a rat, a snowflake, or a slipper, the name of a thing carries with it a set of related ideas. To our delight, good writing uses connotations to trigger deep and moving reactions to the written word; to our occasional despair, we seem never to be able to fix the meanings of words and guarantee clear communication.

In a culture as diverse as ours, it's only natural that the connotations of many words and phrases will vary substantially among different regions, ethnic groups, social classes, religions, and age groups. Pick any social issue—homelessness, welfare, same-sex marriages, gun control, you name it—and it's easy to imagine different groups having vastly different ideas of what words really mean. To some,

---

⊠ WRITING BREAK

Connotation

Discuss with friends or classmates the denotations and connotations of some of the terms below. For example, which do you find offensive or problematic, and why?

handicap parking	the Lady Buffaloes
freshman	the Lady Gamecocks
retarded	disability
co-ed, coeducational	welfare mother
illegitimate child	overachiever, underachiever
basic writer	ESL students
illegal alien	provocative clothing
deaf	female athlete

If you are working on the Featured Paper Topic about the meanings of one or two important words or phrases, be sure to talk to some other people about the denotation and connotation of your chosen word(s).

---

welfare "reform" means progress; to others, it's a violent act of one social class against another. To some, recognition of same-sex marriages means establishing civil rights; to others, it illustrates moral decay.

WORDS AS WEAPONS

I will speak daggers to her, but use none.—Hamlet

Libel Law as a Guide for Writers

You may know the saying "sticks and stones may break my bones, but words can never hurt me." It's a good response to playground taunts, but don't take it to court. The idea that words can be weapons—that they can seriously hurt people—is not just a metaphor, it's a legal principle long recognized and enforced in United States law. *Libel* is a printed defamatory statement, that is, a statement that hurts another's reputation or brings shame upon her or him. (*Slander* refers to oral rather than printed defamation.) The odds of your being sued for libel based on writing you do as a student are low—in part because so few students have enough money to make it worth suing them—but I'd like you to think about a few basics of libel for a more practical reason: the law helps define what kinds of writing are and are not acceptable in our democracy. This section, then, will serve as a "heads up" against reckless writing. (Students interested in journalism or other areas of publishing will want to learn more soon.) To look at libel in a positive light, consider that avoiding defamatory language not only protects you from legal action, but also may in fact prevent you from unjustly injuring someone else, something you presumably don't want to do.

We can begin with a broad definition of a defamatory statement from Neil J. Rosini's *The Practical Guide to Libel Law:*

1. It is a statement of fact.
2. It has a tendency to injure reputation or diminish the esteem, respect, good will, or confidence in which the subject is held by at least a substantial and respectable minority.
3. It is made about a living person, corporate entity, or other business unit, without its subject's consent.

4. It is "of and concerning" someone—that is, the subject must be identifiable to a legally significant group even if not explicitly named.

This is very general language, and the main point I'd like you to think about is that lots and lots of specific cases can fall within the broad boundaries defined by the four principles above. Suppose you write a letter to the editor of the student paper that implies that a faculty committee has made decisions based on racist or sexist assumptions. Or a tiny detail in the background of a cartoon you draw suggests that your roommate's boyfriend has a venereal disease. Or you reprint on your Web page a story alleging that a local politician has ties to organized crime. Could you be successfully sued? I'm not a lawyer, but I believe so. Again, the point is not so much to avoid legal nightmares as to see that "freedom of speech" has its limits. Overstepping the limits can be serious, and it often involves a kind of unjustified labeling: Professor Smith is a racist; the mayor is a crook.

The first key strategy is to think first and publish second. You can't unwrite something once it has appeared. Recognize that libel laws, plus their interpretations by courts and juries, are designed to protect important civic rights, and circumventing the law is not as easy as naive writers might think. Note, for example, that you don't have to *intend* to hurt someone to be guilty of libel; you could just be careless or misinformed. Also, changing someone's name to "mask" the libel is no defense for you if the person is identifiable. Similarly, you cannot necessarily escape liability by merely implying something defamatory while being careful not to claim it explicitly. Libel can even occur in fiction.

> La mala llaga sana; la mala fama mata.
> *A bad wound heals; a bad reputation kills.*

The second strategy is to tell the truth and nothing but the truth. If you can prove what you've published, that will be a good defense. But remember how hard it is to prove things, and remember how much easier it is to delete a questionable sentence from an editorial than to defend yourself against a suit or even a flurry of angry letters.

In the book cited above, Rosini identifies eight "specially sensitive categories of defamation," which I've abbreviated for you here:

1. a loathsome disease
2. sexual misconduct
3. dishonesty
4. criminal acts
5. bigotry
6. poor financial health
7. association with criminals
8. incompetence in business, trade, etc.

If you are about to allege these or similar failings, even in an indirect way, seek experienced guidance and proceed cautiously.

Free Speech/Hate Speech

One central idea of the twentieth century is that contradictions, ambiguities, and paradoxes are absolutely unavoidable in complex systems. We've seen above how this works with language, how no one can freeze language at a given point or eliminate perplexing layers and shades of meaning. Even in physics and mathematics, certain things cannot be measured and certain propositions cannot be determined to be true or false. It should come as no surprise, then, that systems of human law and behavior are not always crystal clear. Many writers treat free speech versus hate speech as a particularly murky issue, a paradoxical area in which deeply held values clash (or at least seem to).

On the one hand, the United States gives its citizens extraordinarily broad license to speak freely, as guaranteed by the First Amendment to the Constitution. The Bill of Rights puts this principle at the core of U.S. law and culture. On the other hand, many people believe that because words can be such powerful weapons, the use (or abuse) of free speech can inflict real harm on others by substantially interfering with their civil rights as guaranteed by the Fourteenth Amendment—another sacred tenet of U.S. law.

In part because they are such diverse environments, college campuses have been important arenas for testing the limits of these principles, for determining when the principle of free speech no longer protects hostile speech or writing. Before you go further, I would like to alert you to the types of circumstances that can arise and ask you to think about what limits, if any, should be placed on campus expression. Consider the following scenarios and try to decide what you think would be the best response (if any) from students, faculty members, the college administration, or the legal system:

> A student gives her peer response group a draft of a paper that contains one or more racial slurs.
>
> Several fraternity members attend a private costume party dressed as Klansmen.
>
> A male student hands his female instructor a journal entry in which he graphically describes a fantasized sexual encounter with her.
>
> Throughout an essay, a student replaces the letter x with a swastika.
>
> A group of students formally complains to the university that their instructor is racist because he seems to them subtly to favor students of his own ethnicity.
>
> In a private meeting, an instructor politely and gently informs a blind student that her physical challenge plus shortcomings in her previous education make her unlikely to graduate; she is therefore wasting her time in college, the instructor says.
>
> When a class discussion deteriorates into an angry shouting match, a white student calls a black student a nigger.
>
> Before a student body election, one of two candidates in a debate calls the other a fascist.

The opinions of experts vary considerably on such issues. Near one end of the spectrum, the American Civil Liberties Union supports free speech, however noxious, at almost any price. Hostile speech, they say, can be countered with education, demonstrations, and intelligent enforcement of laws forbidding trespass, battery, vandalism, and so on. Other legal theorists dismiss the ACLU position as simplistic and historically misinformed but argue against restrictions on speech for different reasons; for example, they cite the fact that members of minority groups are more often charged with hate speech than defended from it. Some colleges have taken a much different approach and attempted to define and enforce speech or behavior codes to protect students and faculty from hate speech and other forms of obnoxious "expression."

If anyone can settle the issues, it will be the Supreme Court, not me. What I hope to accomplish is not to untangle the complexities but to show you enough of them that you won't be swayed by simplistic arguments. Thinking carefully about the scenarios outlined above is a beginning. Consider also these possible lines of argument, (recognizing that they represent several diverse points of view):

- Some speech acts that racists and sexists would like to characterize as "expression" are in fact simply attacks on groups or individuals that are nothing more than attempts to hurt. Saying you don't like Irish dancing expresses your opinion; calling me a Mick is purely a personal insult and an invitation to fight.
- Certain speech must be restricted because it can do serious and lasting harm to an individual, harm that in some cases outweighs the speaker's right to speak her mind.
- Speech must sometimes be restricted not to suppress any particular idea but because a pattern or repetition of hate speech can create a hostile, biased environment, on campus or in the workplace, for example. It thus interferes with the mission of the college or business and unjustly makes the environment intolerable for some group or individual.
- Guarantees of free speech granted by the First Amendment have never been considered absolute. Read literally, the amendment applies only to acts of Congress, not to states, cities, colleges, etc.
- Certain speech must be restricted not because it harms individuals, as libel does, but because it supports systematic oppression; protecting racist and sexist verbal assaults perpetuates racism and sexism.
- Whatever its intentions, restricting speech cannot substantially alter systems of oppression. Time spent policing hate speech would be better spent working against more tangible social inequalities such as poverty or housing discrimination.
- Even the Supreme Court makes mistakes. Interpretations may be narrowed or broadened by later Supreme Courts, for example; also, some rulings turn out to be of little value in deciding future cases.

This chapter has emphasized how language is crucially important in areas of cultural debate or even conflict—in gender or ethnic stereotypes, for example, or in hate speech. These are, or at least should be, matters of universal concern. But a heightened awareness of language, of words and meanings, of connotation, of nuance, will serve you well in any setting. The readings for this chapter and the writing assignments that follow them provide an opportunity for you to exercise and develop such verbal and cognitive skills.

　　　⊠　　⊠　　⊠

The three readings for this chapter deal with names, labels, and humor. "What's in a Spanish Name?" by José Antonio Burciaga is an instructive but often humorous look at the fate of several Spanish words that have entered English. "Enter Laughing," by Roger L. Welsch, argues that the offensiveness of names and stereotypes depends on who's speaking—whether he's in or out of the group in question. In contrast, Patricia J. Williams's "Town Hall Television" asserts that well-meaning humor may constitute dangerous, harmful labeling—even when no one objects. After the readings, you will find discussion questions on these three pieces and on Chapter 1 as a whole.

WHAT'S IN A SPANISH NAME?

José Antonio Burciaga

The first time I ever ran across a Spanish word in Anglo-American literature was in grade school when we were assigned to read Mark Twain's "The Celebrated Jumping Frog of Calaveras County." It was a fun-filled, humorous story. Despite my home-honed fluency in *Español,* I did not recognize the Spanish word in the title and story.

　　　I knew what a *calavera* was. It was a skull. For *el Día de los Muertos* in México, they were made into little skulls out of sugar and eaten like candy. In the Mexican game *Lotéria,*

La Calavera was illustrated with the crossed bones under the skull.

But within the context of an Anglo-American English class, in a school where Spanish was strictly forbidden and punishable by paddling, ridicule, and writing "I shall not speak Spanish in school" a hundred times, *calaveras* was pronounced anglo-phonetically *"kel-awe-ver-rahs."* The Spanish word Ca-la-ve-ras was hidden, disguised, nothing more than the name of a county. It was the mysterious name of an unknown person, place or thing. Innocently or naively, I took the word to be just another eccentric English word pronounced with a suave Anglo-American accent.

It took me a few years to discover that Calaveras County in California had been named for *Río Calaveras,* where a great number of skulls and skeletons had been discovered by early Spanish explorers.

Like Calaveras, hundreds of Spanish words remained in this country, changed, unchanged and disguised due to loss of meaning, evolution of misspellings, and mispronunciations. After 1848, when the U.S. took over the Southwest, Spanish had to survive on its own.

There's a town in Texas named Buda. With a Texas accent it is pronounced Bew-da. On the highway from Austin (pronounced Awe-stn or *Ostin* in Spanish) to San Marcos, pronounced Sanmar-cuss, there's a sign announcing Buda. That shouldn't have been odd but being from Texas it just didn't seem right. I could have understood Buddha or even Buttocks, Texas, but Buda?

It didn't take much ask'n before learning that the name was originally *Viuda,* which is Spanish for widow. Some monolingual Texan just didn't know any better and wrote it down just the way he heard it. That's how we got lariat from *la rieta,* hoosegow from *juzgado,* and buckaroo from *vaquero.*

What's Polamas? That's a street in San José, California. It's actually supposed to be Palomas, pigeons, but the person doing the lettering on street signs just didn't know better.

The Bank of America put out some cute little refrigerator magnets the size of a business card for its Spanish speaking clients where they could write important telephone "Numberos." Numberos? That's neither English, Spanish or Caló. The biggest bank in the U.S. of A. meant *números*. Even though it may have been an innocent bilingual typo, would you trust them with your *dinero*?

The one that has always troubled me is the English "tamale" pronounced tamalee. The Spanish singular for this food item is *tamal,* plural tamales. Don't go to the English language experts because Meriam-Webster's New Collegiate Dictionary also misspells tamale and its etymological rationale is that it comes from the Aztec Nahuatl *tamalli.*

Sarape is another such word. Webster says it's *serape,* but in the Spanish speaking world everyone pronounces it and spells it as sarape. Look it up in an English-Spanish dictionary or a Spanish-English dictionary and it's "sarape" in Spanish and "serape" in English. Why?

Throughout the last century and a half Spanish has had free rein, running wild, with complete freedom to produce some mighty interesting words and sounds, not only from Gringos but from Mexicans themselves. Murrieta is now spelled Murieta, Monterrey is now spelled Monterey and Arrastradero is now spelled arastradero. Why anyone decided to take away the rolling "r" from so many of the Spanish words is beyond *moi.* Did someone find the extra "r" unnecessary, were they in short supply of r's, or was it just too difficult to roll their r's in Spanish?

In addition, words from 16th-century Spanish still roam throughout the Southwest, along with Caló, the Chicano dialect. These words have flourished and even emigrated back to Mexico where they have become part of the popular vernacular of the masses. The opposite also happens in Mexico and France and the rest of the world for that matter.

Though there may be many innocent reasons for this evolution of language, the isolation and syncretism, fusion of two cultures in language is fascinating.

I ran across a word in Mexico that is related to this argument but couldn't find in any dictionary, much less a synonym. It was *resemanticización*—resemanticization, also absent from any English dictionary.

Resemanticization was not defined but it was derived from the word "semantics"—the historical and psychological study and classification of changes in the meaning of words or objects. In politics and cross cultural situations, words, ideas and objects constantly assimilate, "transculturate," or adapt for the sake of survival.

Thus the anglicization or hispanization of words in this country. The word "Chicano" was a resemanticized term that was once pejorative. Alurista, an early Chicano poet, resemanticized many words such as Aztlán, the ancient place of origin for the Aztecs was and is the Southwest. Amerindio came to describe not only an "American" Indian but all Indigenous peoples across the continent.

Chicano film, art and literature constantly redefines, resemanticizes, an experience that is part Anglo, part Español, part Mexicano. Resemanticization is also the exploitation of connotation and ambiguity in propaganda. Resemanticization deals not only with words but with ideas and symbols, that cross borders and languages to take different meanings.

We become chameleons, we are chameleon. As we move from one world to the other we exchange colors, ideas, symbols and words in order to fit, to relate and to survive. The result is a prismatic iridescence when the difference of colors play on each other, like a rainbow after a rainstorm in the desert. We are chameleons.

ENTER LAUGHING BUT BEWARE THE ES-EX FACTOR

Roger L. Welsch

In February's "Science Lite" column, entitled "Send in the Clown," I discussed the Omaha clown dancer as an example of cultural observation, a Native American perception of the ever-bumbling white man. Two readers wrote to scold me for indulging in stereotyping. In self-defense, I would point out that I was only reporting an interesting stereotyping by a subculture, not inventing one on my own. I think mainstream white America can handle being stereotyped. And a stereotype may contain some nugget of truth. But one letter writer did pose a very interesting question: "Would you," she wrote, "write something as offensive as 'Send in the drunken Indians?'"

The answer is yes. And no. If I were kidding around with a bunch of Omaha relatives or friends, in all likelihood there would be a lot of joking about drunken Indians, but only if there were no non-Indians present. I would never do the same thing in a circle of white relatives or friends. The idea that some things are appropriate for insiders to say, but inappropriate for outsiders, is a common cultural distinction. Folklorist William Hugh Jansen examined the phenomenon in careful detail in his 1959 article "The Esoteric-Exoteric Factor in Folklore" (*Fabula: Journal of Folktale Studies*). Based on the title of Jansen's article, scientific folklorists have termed it "the es-ex factor."

The es-ex factor is one of those marvelous cultural processes that we see and practice all the time but have a hard time coming to grips with. Saying things one way within one context and another way within another may seem inconsistent, hypocritical, even dishonest. Yet we know perfectly well that it is one thing for a guy named McCoy or Gomez to tell a Polish joke, quite another for a guy named Wroblewski. Wroblewski, on the other hand, is constrained from telling bean-eater or Mick jokes.

The es-ex rules are clear and absolute, and breaches are frowned upon. And yet the process remains invisible, sometimes even going unrecognized. Many non-African Americans were puzzled, even indignant, when Mark Fuhrman (the detective of Simpson trial fame) was so thoroughly castigated for using the "N-word," while African Americans seem free to use the word blithely—on the athletic field, the performance stage, even the streets. "How come they can use it and we can't?" was the question. The es-ex factor, that's how come. African Americans are in the group, the

Mark Fuhrmans of the world are out of the group. It's as simple as that.

Among those who are the ostensible butts of ethnic or racial slur jokes, such joking is a matter of self-confidence, of respect, of the tacit understanding that the humorous assertions are not true. Telling Polish jokes is acceptable to a Polish American as long as the teller has in-group credentials and the joke is clearly meant to be funny and not genuinely insulting. But let an outsider try to get in on the action, and he or she will be called to account ("Smile when you say that!").

Even in esoteric contexts, that is, within the group, there are strict rules. American male humor is based in large part on mutual insults. A group of men can sit around and tell jokes about unfaithful wives, even suggesting that the jibes are about each other's wives or about themselves. ("We kept having kids until I figured out where they were coming from, so I moved the mailbox from the house to the highway"—this told with the rural mailman in attendance.) But such humor disappears when a presumed or acknowledged cuckold joins the circle of jokers. In those circumstances, it is not even permissible to self-deprecatingly allude to possible indiscretions by one's own spouse. The esoteric context is gone, the subject is taboo. Talk then turns to gas-guzzling pickups, maybe, or useless hunting dogs.

We often know we have successfully entered a social circle when we begin to hear the es-ex factor kick in with ingroup language. I came from a German Lutheran family and married into a Czech Catholic family. I knew I was becoming accepted by my in-laws the first time I heard the term Bohunk—usually a pejorative for Czech Americans on the Plains—used in front of me by members of the family. They could laugh at themselves without worrying that I might take it seriously. The next step was when I heard the family making fun of my German Protestantism to me. Now, they could laugh at me. And finally I knew I was safely at home when I made an ingroup Bohunk remark myself...and got a laugh. My love for them had become

---

clear enough that I could joke about "our" group in a way that would not be tolerated from an outsider.

Perhaps the most vivid example of inclusionary es-ex material is when standard insults against one group are, in a humorous way, turned back toward a member of the usually offending group. I have been patted on the back by a militant Native American and laughingly told I am "a credit to my race." What this friend was doing was essentially honoring me by insulting me just as so many of his kinsmen have been insulted. He knew that I understood the remark said seriously by a white man was a foolish insult. And he knew that I would like nothing more than to be included in the insulted group—his. (By the way, this friend is a Winnebago—the only tribe, he says, that's named after a recreational vehicle.)

I have worked for many years alongside the Pawnee, a group for which I have great respect. I have seen Pawnee friends refused service in restaurants, insulted by government officials, treated with contempt by arrogant bureaucrats, so my hope to "fit in" was made all the more difficult because I could see why a Pawnee might have every reason to distrust me along with the rest of "my" people. The moment I gained acceptance was anything but subtle.

Three Pawnee leaders were our house guests, and we were just finishing up supper. My wife, Linda, who had prepared the meal, joked, "Where I come from, whoever does the cooking doesn't have to wash the dishes."

I quickly added my standard response to her standard hint: "Where I come from, we put the dishes on the floor and let the dogs wash them."

Without a moment's hesitation one of the Pawnee elders laughed, "Where I come from, we ate the dogs and didn't have any dishes."

It was an in-group joke based on a time-honored—or maybe dishonored—stereotype about Native Americans. He was saying, in effect, "This is an old joke about Indians, but what the heck, there's no one here but us Indians."

We didn't get around to telling any drunken Indian jokes that night, but we might have. We might have.

TOWN HALL TELEVISION

Patricia J. Williams

*Perhaps 6 April 1989 will go down in history as the first "designer drug raid." As heavily armed and flak-jacketed SWAT commandoes stormed the alleged "rock house" near 51st and Main Street in Southcentral L.A., Nancy Reagan and Los Angeles Police Chief Darryl Gates sat across the street nibbling fruit salad in a luxury motor home emblazoned "*THE ES-TABLISHMENT.*" According to the Times, the former first lady "could be seen freshening her makeup" while the SWATs roughly frisked and cuffed the fourteen "narco-terrorists" captured inside the small stucco bunga-low. As hundreds of incredulous neighbors ("Hey, Nancy Reagan. She's over here in the ghetto!") gathered behind the police barriers, the great Nay-sayer, accompanied by Chief Gates and a small army of nervous Se-cret Service agents, toured the enemy fortress with its occupants still bound on the floor in flabbergasted submission. After frowning at the tawdry wallpaper and drug-bust debris, Nancy, who looked fetching in her LAPD windbreaker, managed to delve instantly into the dark hearts at her feet and declare: "These people in here are beyond the point of teaching and rehabilitating."*

—*Mike Davis*, City of Quartz

If the pen is mightier than the sword and a picture is worth a thousand words, then a little simple multiplication is all it takes to figure out the enormous propagandistic power that television has to create truth and shape opinion. Within the world of TV land, into which American life has been re-duced as well as reproduced, the phenomenon of the talk show has emerged as a genre located somewhere on the spectrum between coffee klatch and town meeting, or per-haps between the psychiatrist's couch and the crowd scene at a bad accident.

Talk-show sets usually resemble the interiors of homes, if not my home; they employ as backdrops what appear to be living rooms or home libraries or other womblike spaces. There are usually some nice comfortable armchairs or a sofa or a round (not square) kitcheny table. Coffee mugs are of-ten strewn about, maybe an artsy bunch of jonquils in a nice vase. Yet these womb-rooms are always sawed in half somehow; they offer 180 degrees of pure schmoozey ambiance and then, at the 181st degree exactly, they open up to an amphitheater of perfect strangers, all of whom always look like my sunny neighbors when I lived in Wisconsin, and none of whom ever look like my lock-jawed neighbors in New York (with the possible exception of the audiences on the old *Morton Downey Show*).

To be a good talk-show host requires a personality that has been similarly sawed in half. "How does it feel," they ask their guests with the soft seduction of a mother cat licking her young, "to know you are feared and loathed by millions of our viewers all over America?" they finish, with the poisonous flick of an impatient rattlesnake. Talk-show hosts act like good parents with an unruly set of teenagers-who-also-happen-to-be-serial-killers: Life's a living hell these days...All his friends seem to be going through this phase...What's a society to do? Phil as Father-Knows-Best; Oprah as not Mom, because that's too close to Mammy, so Ur-Girlfriend instead.

All of this creates, I think, a very powerful illusion of intimate openness...yet...objectivity—*sincere* objectivity. It creates an illusion of care mixed with an illusion of rigorous inquiry—a species, I guess, of Tough Love. It creates an imagined world in which there is no permission for anyone's feelings ever to be hurt, even when they ought to be; in which good intentions and great attitude rule the day.

This results in a forum that is very persuasive by virtue of its form alone: an atmosphere of overdetermined consensus, much like the scene of that bad accident, in which everyone rushes forth with a blaze of inconsistent opinions and viewpoints, but everyone goes away agreeing or believing they agree that they saw the same thing. A Rorschach test of response in which a catharsis of agreement emerges—such as, sleeping with your girlfriend's boyfriend is right! or it's wrong!—even though the reasons underlying the consensus of rightness or wrongness are extremely varied or vastly contradictory.

Talk shows are sometimes touted as new-age town halls or minicourtrooms. I suppose this comparison reveals a certain longing for community that has arisen as the common turf of political and judicial space has become less and less accessible to all citizens as an arena for debate and resolution. But talk-show politics is hardly that summoned up by the image of the soapbox orator holding forth on the Boston Common or the village green: increasingly plugged into the bottom line of market ratings, the shows' ethics have less and less to do with the democratic constraints of fairness, due process, public accountability, or equality of access. If, again, the general expectation is that talk shows function as a way of airing all points of view or resolving disputes in the manner of a public trial, then we must take stock of the fact that the "talk" is managed with more reference to the rules of football than to any principles of justice; we must begin to wonder if the energy for public debate is not being siphoned off into a market for public spectacle. We must begin to unravel the political function of this jumble of stage-direction-qua-civics. Mangled metaphors of level playing fields tussling with invocations of zero-sum games in which the winner takes all. Bashing the stuffing out of each other but at the end, being good sports and shaking hands and agreeing to disagree and nothing is so important we can't go off and have lunch together. "Can you forgive your father for molesting you?" asks Sally Jesse Raphael. *"No,"* sobs the truly bad sport.

Talk shows as town meetings leave one with the impression of having had a full airing of all viewpoints, no matter how weird, and of having reached a nobler plane, a higher level of illumination, of having wrestled with something till we've exhausted it. And maybe that's true for programs that deal with women who drink their own blood or the joys of body piercing. But I am very concerned that when it comes to some of our most pressing social issues such as anti-Semitism and racism, TV talk shows perform an actual disservice, by (1) creating a sense both of false consensus and of false division, and (2) condoning and perpetuating racism, anti-Semitism, and gender stereotypes, even as they supposedly challenge them.

Let me give an example of a Phil Donahue show I saw some time ago. It was a program that purported to be

deeply concerned about the rise of anti-Semitism on campuses in general, and the proliferation of Jewish American
Princess jokes in particular. "How would *you* feel…?" Phil
kept asking by way of challenge to the studio audience.

The program opened with an extraordinarily long volley of Jewish American Princess jokes, not merely recited,
but written in large block letters across the screen—for the
hearing impaired presumably, although there was no other
part of the program so emphatically emblazoned. The jokes
played on mean-spirited, vulgar stereotypes; they were just
plain offensive, even though they were positioned as merely
"models" of the subject to be discussed. Although styled as a
repudiation, they reenacted the whole problem—over and
over and over again. The audience tittered and giggled its
way through this opening volley. It was significant, I think,
this tittering—after each joke, the cameras focused as in-
tently as a dentist's drill upon the stunned-rabbit faces of
the audience, people caught in a not-quite-sure-how-to-
respond mode that implicated them as they struggled to be
good sports while being broadcast live to millions of people. It was a marvelously assimilative moment; they were
like children trying to decide how to be seen at their best.
Smile? Frown? Which is the posture of belonging? So they
tittered. Nervously.

I think there is a real risk of destructive impact in jokes
that make fun of the supposed characteristics of historically
oppressed or shunned people. Of course all humor depends
on context, but, if it is possible to speak generally, I think
that such jokes too frequently are the enactment of a kind of
marking process, in which communities are described, kin-
ship delimited, the enemy imagined. An anecdote will illustrate what I mean by marking, how I think the bright
innocence of social divisiveness works:

Some months ago I was riding on a train. In between
napping and reading the newspaper, I languidly listened to
the conversation of a very well-dressed, well-educated family seated across the aisle from me. Here was a family with
traditional values *and* Ralph Lauren looks—mother, father,
bright little girl, and a big bearded friend of the family who
looked like that seafaring guy on the clam chowder label. It

was a fascinatingly upper-class conversation, about invest-
ments, photography, and Japanese wood-joinery. It was also
a soothingly pleasant conversation, full of affection, humor,
and great politeness. I enjoyed listening to them, and allowed myself the pleasure of my secret participation in their
companionability. Then they started telling redneck jokes.

There was no shift in their voices to warn me of it; they
spoke in the same soft, smiling voices as before, with those
deliciously crisp *t*'s and delicately rounded *r*'s.

The little girl, who was probably around seven or eight
years old, asked, "What's a redneck?" No longer napping, I
leaned closer, intrigued by what this moment of sharp but
innocent intervention promised in terms of drawing these
otherwise thoughtful adults up short in glorious contrition
and a renewed sense of social awareness.

"Drinks beer, drives a pickup, low-class, talks bad,"
came the unselfconscious reply. Then the three adults told
more jokes to illustrate. Being very bright, the little girl
dumped innocence by the wayside and promptly responded by telling a bunch of blond jokes and then one in-
volving "black"—but I couldn't hear if she was talking
about hair or skin.

The father told another joke—what's got ten teeth and
something I couldn't hear? The answer was the front row of
a Willie Nelson concert.

They were so pleasant and happy. Their conversation
was random, wandering. They showed each other pictures
of their kids, they played word games, they shared hot
dogs. And yet they were transporting a virus.

This process of marking. No wonder it is so hard to get
out of our race and class binds. It occurred to me, as I
watched this family in all its remarkable typicality, that that
little girl will have to leave the warmth of the embracing,
completely relaxed circle of those happy people before she
can ever appreciate the humanity of someone who drives a
pickup, who can't afford a dentist. "Rednecks" were lov-
ingly situated, by that long afternoon of gentle joking, in the
terrible vise of the comic, defined by the butt of a joke.

How *givingly* social divisions are transmitted was
brought home to me in an essay written by one of my

former students. She described her father as a loving family man, who worked six and a half days a week to provide for his wife and children. He always took Sunday afternoons off; that was sacred time, reserved for a "family drive." Yet the family's favorite pastime, as they meandered in Norman Rockwell contentment, was, according to this student, "trying to pick the homosexuals out of the crowd." ("Bill Clinton would have *homosexuals* in his administration!" railed Pat Robertson in his speech to the 1992 Republican National Convention, during which convention homophobic violence reportedly rose by 8 percent in the city of Houston.)

Hate learned in a context of love is a complicated phenomenon. Love learned in a context of hate endangers all our family.

But back to our show. The rest of the *Phil Donahue Show* on Jewish American Princesses was a panoply of squirmy ways of dealing with being marked. Phil's guests included not only a Real Live Jewish Princess, but a Black American Princess, an Italian-American Princess, and a WASP Princess as well. While they were all willing to be called *princesses* of X, Y, or Z flavor, they all denied that they were the *bad* kind of princess. They negotiated this good princess/evil princess dichotomy by at least four different maneuvers:

First of all, there was the "role model" response—yeah, well, I'm proud to be pushy, and I've made it into a positive attribute, look at how creative I am with the lemons life has handed me. Doesn't bother me a bit (even though an unfortunate cost of this survival mechanism would seem to be a rather defensive, cynical edge).

Second, there was the "But I really am a princess!" response—the attempt to remove the sarcasm from it and be taken as literal, real. The Real WASP Princess proclaimed herself as the inheritor of society's privilege and all the other ethnic princesses as mere wannabe imitations of herself; the black princess claimed to have been the real princess of a considerably smaller if warmer realm, in having been the apple of her protective family's eye; and the Italian-American princess claimed that her real name *was* Princess, at least that's what Daddy always said.

Third, there was the move to concede that while some women may be like that awful thing at the butt of all those jokes, "all Jewish women are not JAPs." There was, in other words, a concession of the category as validly descriptive, and then the attempt to exceptionalize oneself from it. This is, I think, a powerfully defeatist move because it concedes the category as given, it allows the stereotype legitimacy. The response to racist labeling is thus locked into the logic of merely defining oneself in or out of the label, rather than focused on challenging the prejudice and judgmentalism of the marking process at all. I think this resort to a "them-us" dichotomy or an "I'm different" strategy is perhaps the most prevalent individual response to bigotry, as well as the most destructive.

Fourth, there is the opposite move—and perhaps the most prevalent institutional response to bigotry—the tendency to generalize rather than to exceptionalize, to make shrill self-absorption a general feature of all women, who are arrayed so as to possess a panoply of generally negative qualities. Women of *all* ethnicities are bitchy, stupid, fluffy, greedy, sacrificial, ran the logic of a narrative that played sexism against anti-Semitism, that played general stereotype against its sub-components. Thus "equal opportunity bimboism" is proffered as an odd model of the way in which tolerating intolerance emerges as the new norm for tolerance itself.

Perhaps the best example of the new tolerance of the same old intolerance is the intriguing fact that Howard Stern's sidekick, Robin Quivers, is a black woman who sounds exactly like the quintessential, self-abasing, totally concessionary but not dumb stereotype of a white woman. A *blond* white woman stereotype at that. A shrewdly submissive "bimbo" in blackface. "Oh, *How*ard," she sighs. This weird component is so manifest that Garry Trudeau parodies it in his *Doonesbury* cartoon, in which a movie is supposedly being made of Stern's book *Private Parts*. Boopsie, Trudeau's blonde update of Betty Boop, is sought to play the part of Robin Quivers. "But Quivers is black," says Boopsie. "Don't worry, it's radio," comes the reply. It is a cartoon that echoes the pre-*really*-weird weirdness of Michael Jackson's Unbearable Lightness of Being—specifically, when he attempted to cast a little white boy to play himself as a child in a Japanese-produced video of his life.

Trudeau's cartoon is a complex commentary on the strange post-civil rights era configuration of what integration seems to have become: to the extent that it exists, it does not merge black and white people as much as it hybridizes troublesome stereotypes of women and minorities. Barbie now has cornrows and six little gold earrings. Ken has two-tone hair, one earring, and for a brief moment in doll-making history sported a necklace with a cock ring hanging from it. (Mattel executives claimed they had no *idea…*) If black women are still having trouble breaking into the world of high fashion modeling, the same cannot be said of RuPaul, whose glittering, towering, snap-queen transvestism has made him the toast of the MTV crowd. Mammy dolls have gone Hispanic. The most racially and philosophically conservative justice on the Supreme Court in at least fifty years is a black man. The Victorian image of the "fallen woman gotten with child" has merged with that of the black Jezebel and produced the always-rollicking "welfare queen."

It's an interesting development beyond the time-honored use of blackface makeup to mock black people: just use a black *person*. It's a move that was captured in the casting of the movie version of *The Bonfire of the Vanities;* the role of a judge who spews racist claptrap to black defendants was recast from that of white man in the novel to black man in the movie. Let the black judge deliver the racist rebuke because then it's not racist, seems to be the logic of the day. So confined are black bodies by the rigors of puppeted rebuke and suffocating buffoonery that there is a certain sociopathic logic in Michael Jackson's repeated surgical attempts to escape the stereotype of the societally scourged "black male" body.

The powerful weight of stereotypes about blacks as not seriously human was painfully visible in the (how shall I put this gently) incomprehensibly miscalculated spoof undertaken by the actor Ted Danson of his then-girlfriend

Whoopi Goldberg, in which Danson donned blackface, ate watermelon, joked about their sex life and her genitalia, and used the word "nigger" repeatedly. Supposedly mystified by the storm of public reaction, Danson made much of the claim that Whoopi had approved of the material, even helped write it, and that therefore it couldn't be racist.

Only weeks after that fiasco, Goldberg's recipe for "Jewish American Princess Fried Chicken" was published in a book entitled *Cooking in Litchfield Hills.* The recipe "instructs you to 'Send a chauffeur to your favorite butcher shop for the chicken,' 'Watch your nails' when you shake the chicken in a brown paper bag, and 'Have Cook prepare rest of meal while you touch up your makeup.'" Again there was a big debate about whether it was funny or whether it was anti-Semitic (as though these are necessarily oppositional). Again the handwringing about subject position, although I'm sure that's not what people imagined they were doing. "'This is in worse taste (than the Friars Club debacle) because she could get away with that because she is black,' said one Litchfield resident." Let's sidestep for just a moment the complicating detail that Goldberg didn't "get away with" much of anything precisely because she employed the body of Danson as the time-honored comedic vehicle of racial minstrelsy—a white man in blackface mouthing too-familiar-to-be-ironic stereotypes, albeit supposedly written by a black woman to parody herself. Rather, I would like to examine the retort by Goldberg's publicist: "Maybe (the critics) are not aware that Whoopi is Jewish, so she is certainly not anti-Semitic." It's a familiar litany: I heard a Jewish person tell this joke so it's not anti-Semitic. And of course, a Jewish person wrote this joke for me, so I couldn't possibly be anti-Semitic just because I'm trying to lighten things up with a little Holocaust humor. In fact, goes the next line of the argument, *you're* intolerant for claiming intolerance. And a bad sport besides. (It is by a reversed but mirror-image logic, perhaps, that two Oakhurst, California, high school youths who dressed up in the white robes and hoods of the Ku Klux Klan and reenacted a lynching of another student for a Halloween party—and who were rewarded with a prize in the costume competition—

sought to justify the event by saying that *no* blacks were at the party so it was okay.)

What does this humor mask? At what point does black-face minstrelsy converge with white-hooded threats? Look at *this* and fear for your life; look at *that* and laugh, just laugh and laugh. "My boot came from the area of lower California and connected with the suspect's scrotum around lower Missouri," wrote the Los Angeles police sergeant Stacey Koon of the arrest of a Latino suspect that occurred before his beating of Rodney King. "My boot stopped around Ohio, but the suspect's testicles continued into upper Maine. The suspect was literally lifted off the ground. The suspect tried to speak, but it appeared he had something in his throat, probably his balls." Where are the borders of this cartooned life and that imprisoned one? Is it all just one long joke without end, amen? And when will someone let up on the laugh-track button and just let me breathe?

The *Washington Post* ran an article after the Whoopi and Ted incident that asked all the wrong questions: Was it funny, why not? Was it offensive and why? Yet I wonder if it is not possible to cross well into the realm of the offensive *and* be "funny." I wonder how line-crossing from not-funny to funny seems to redeem any degree of threat or insult. The *Post* article ends with a quote from Tim Conaway, *Hustler* magazine's humor editor, whose last word is "If you're hurt by a cartoon in a magazine…I think you ought to look at the real root of that pain." But in bigotry's insistent blindness, humor is precisely the device by which discussion of the roots of pain is most consistently deflected.

DISCUSSION QUESTIONS AND WRITING ASSIGNMENTS

On the Readings by Burciaga, Welsch, and Williams

1. Burciaga begins "What's in a Spanish Name?" by telling a story, not by explicitly stating a thesis. Can you point to a thesis elsewhere in this reading? What are Burciaga's main points, and to what extent do you agree or disagree with them?

2. Use Burciaga's reflections on Spanish names to inspire your own consideration of some of the names around you, whether from Spanish or any other culture or language whose influence you see. Research selected words and names as Burciaga did, and pool your findings with those of classmates. If appropriate, write a paper based on what you have learned.

3. In "Enter Laughing," Welsch writes that "mainstream white America can handle being stereotyped. And a stereotype may contain some nugget of truth." Explain to what extent you agree or disagree with these two statements.

4. How would you define the "es-ex factor"? What examples of the es-ex factor have you observed around you? Does it help explain any of your own speech or behavior? Do you agree with Welsch that the issue is a simple one of group membership— that is, that "it's as simple as that"?

5. Compare and contrast Welsch's and Williams's attitudes toward offensive humor, supporting your observations with specific references to the readings. Do you see any conflict between the idea of an es-ex factor and the idea of "marking" that Williams describes? Whose approach do you find more useful or insightful?

6. Williams seems more serious about offensive humor than Welsch does. Do you think Welsch underestimates the seriousness of jokes based on slurs, insults, or stereotypes? Do you think Williams would see him as "transporting a virus"?

7. Watch a talk show hosted by Oprah Winfrey, Montel Williams, Ricki Lake, Maury Povich, Phil Donahue, or another celebrity. How accurately do Williams's claims fit the sample you view? (You might want to look at the show's set and the "illusion of care mixed with the illusion of rigorous inquiry" as well as at groups, humor, and the use of labels.) Write up your findings in a journal entry or short paper.

On Chapter 1

8. Write a journal entry or short paper in response to one or two of the quotations included in this chapter. Possible approaches include the following:

- Explain the meaning of the quotation. For example, what might it mean to "speak daggers" to someone?
- Use the quotation as a starting point for your own reflections or experience relating to the topic. For example, recount an incident in which someone used language as a weapon.
- Amplify upon the quotation: develop it, provide examples.
- Explain why you agree or disagree with the quotation.
- Compare and contrast two or more quotations.

9. In 1997, I sent the letter below to the Washington Redskins. Having received no response, I sent another copy a year later with a cover letter explaining this was a second attempt to communicate. Again, no response.

   Read the letter and answer these questions: Why do you think I received no reply? Does the lack of response mean that the letters were complete failures? Do you think that any letter from an ordinary citizen could have an impact? If personal letters are ineffectual, what other strategies could be employed by those of us outraged by the Redskins name and mascot?

   Dear Mr ___: [the Director of Public Relations]

   When I attended Stanford University, I was embarrassed that our collegiate athletic teams had formerly been named the Indians but proud that the university had recently changed the name to the Cardinal. That was in the early 1970s; I'm astounded that as the end of the century approaches there can be a professional team still using the name Redskins (not to mention the mascot).

   This can hardly be a new issue for you, but please don't brush me off with a form letter. My basic complaint is very simple: *Redskins* is a derogatory racial epithet that offends many Native Americans and is disconcerting, to use a mild term, to all of us who oppose stereotyping and derision based on ethnicity. I'm hard-pressed to imagine how you can counter this claim. Does the organization believe Redskins is not an offensive name? Does it put tradition ahead of civil rights? I'm baffled.

   I have two more questions: Who decides whether the name will change, and when will the issue next be reviewed?

Thank you for listening, and thanks in advance for your response.

Sincerely,

Robert Cullen

P. S. I discover that *Redskins* is not in my spell checker. Hmmm.

10. Working from memory, write descriptions (short or extended) of five words or ideas you've recently learned in another class. Then compare and contrast your definitions with the versions you find in your textbook, lecture notes, or reference books. How accurate and precise were your definitions?

11. Choose a front-page story from today's newspaper. Examine it closely to determine how much of the language is descriptive and how much could be considered evaluative in some way.

12. Research speech and conduct codes at your college or university. Are any in force currently? When were they written, and why? Have they been revised? What sorts of speech or other forms of expression are forbidden? How clear or hazy are the guidelines? Have they been tested by specific cases, and with what results?

REFERENCES

Alarcón, Norma. "Chicana Feminism: In the Tracks of 'the' Native Woman." *Cultural Studies* 4 (1990) 248–56.

Bergman, Jeanne. "A Gender of One's Own" [Review of *Transgender Warriors: Making History from Joan of Arc to RuPaul* by Leslie Feinberg]. *The Nation* 263:5 (Aug. 12/19, 1996) 32–34.

Bosmajian, Haig A. "Defining the 'American Indian': A Case Study in the Language of Suppression." In Gary Layne Hatch, *Arguing in Communities*. Mountain View, California: Mayfield, 1996.

Burciaga, José Antonio. *En Pocas Palabras = In Few Words: A Compendium of Latino Folk Wit and Wisdom: A Bilingual Collection.* San Francisco: Mercury House, 1997.

Coontz, Stephanie. *The Way We Really Are: Coming to Terms with America's Changing Families.* New York: Basic Books, 1997.

Dingwaney, Anuradha and Carol Maier, eds. *Between Languages and Cultures: Translation and Cross-Cultural Texts.* Pittsburgh: University of Pittsburgh Press, 1995.

Gates, Henry Louis, Jr. "War of Words: Critical Race Theory and the First Amendment." In Gates et al., *Speaking of Race, Speaking of Sex: Hate Speech, Civil Rights, and Civil Liberties.* New York: NYU Press, 1994.

Giroux, Henry A. *Fugitive Cultures: Race, Violence, and Youth.* New York: Routledge, 1996.

Hofstadter, Douglas R. *Le Ton beau de Marot: In Praise of the Music of Language.* New York: Basic Books, 1997.

———. *Metamagical Themas: Questing for the Essence of Mind and Pattern.* New York: Basic Books, 1985.

Macaulay, Ronald. *The Social Art: Language and Its Uses.* New York: Oxford University Press, 1994.

Riley, Patricia. "The Mixed Blood Writer as Interpreter and Mythmaker." In Joseph Trimmer and Tilly Warnock, eds., *Cultural and Cross-Cultural Studies and the Teaching of Literature.* Urbana, IL: NCTE, 1992.

Rosini, Neil J. *The Practical Guide to Libel Law.* New York: Praeger, 1991.

Tan, Amy. *The Hundred Secret Senses.* New York: Ivy Books, 1995.

2

Bedrock Strategies: Invention and Organization

*Writing is an exploration. You start
from nothing and learn as you go.*
—E. L. DOCTOROW

The advice in this chapter and the next is organized according to the simplest useful view of the writing process—inventing or discovering ideas, organizing them, writing them out in draft form, and revising the draft into a finished product. You will find strategies for creating a good environment for writing, for unlocking your creativity, and for invigorating your style. Some of the suggestions are modern, others ancient. Some will no doubt work better for you than others. Rather than attempting to impose one single way of writing, these chapters share strategies that many, many writers have found helpful. You will have to experiment to find out what works best for you, but please be flexible enough to do so; you have habits as a writer, no doubt, but as you mature as a person, and take on more ambitious assignments as a student, expect some of these habits to change. As you work through Chapters 2 and 3, try the approaches that are new to you and add the ones you like to your repertoire.

The first section of Chapter 2 explains and illustrates various ways writers generate ideas, ranging from simple brainstorming sessions to the more elaborate creative device called Burke's Pentad. The second main section covers organization, a key to successful writing in college. The chapter's readings discuss creativity and creation. The first, an excerpt from Roger von Oech's bestselling *A Whack on the Side of the Head: How You Can Be More Creative,* offers tips you can use to think creatively about any topic in any setting. The second, focusing more specifically on writing, is Juanita Johnson-Bailey's interview with poet Sonia Sanchez. The chapter concludes with discussion questions and writing assignments.

⊠ FEATURED PAPER TOPICS

There are two suggested paper topics for Chapter 2. The first calls for a personal essay; the second will accommodate a variety of approaches.

Write an essay about a change, transition, or discovery in your life. This could involve a triumph, a failure, or simply a new understanding of something, a new perspective. You may choose to write about a matter of momentous importance (e.g., religious conversion or coping with a divorce) or about something more subtle (e.g., a better understanding of a sibling or an adjustment to a new environment). In either case, try to give your audience a glimpse into some facet of your life and especially into how you think about it.

Throughout our lives, the culture all around us teaches us how to behave according to accepted gender roles. We learn, often unconsciously, how to talk, dress, and behave in "feminine" or "masculine" ways. Pick one age group (e.g., infants, sixteen-year-olds, thirty-somethings) and write an essay comparing and contrasting the culturally dominant gender expectations for girls and boys (or women and men). You may be able to write a short speculative paper based on personal experience and observation; you could also observe cultural sites (malls, advertising, children's books, movies, TV) where gender roles are demonstrated and learned; you could also do more formal academic research in your library or on the Internet. Consult with your instructor to determine an appropriate focus and scope for your paper. Approaches to organizing this paper appear on pages 83 to 85.

AIDS TO INVENTION

> *Until I read Baldwin I never knew that one could write about being Black and poor and get published. I assumed that the only way you could write or be a novelist was to write about well-off white people.* —Barbara Smith

This section covers a number of methods writers have found useful in coming up with ideas to write about. Some of them may be familiar to you, but you'll probably find at least something new here as well. Remember that people think and work and create in very different ways: what works wonders for a classmate may prove of limited use to you, and vice versa. Experiment with all of the techniques in order to find those that suit you best. Give them an honest try; you may be surprised at the results. For example, I've sometimes found that writing with the monitor on my computer turned off—a notion that once struck me as ludicrous—sometimes helps me through a problem area because I share with many of my students the habit of tinkering too much with what I've just written rather than forging ahead with a draft. You may also find that certain techniques work better in some situations than others: a loose and free session of brainstorming may really open up the possibilities for a personal narrative but accomplish less in a tightly constrained analytical assignment.

Brainstorming

> *Well begun is half done.* —Horace

There are many different ways to brainstorm, but most share the common goal of getting some of the sparks in your brain down onto paper. You should have plenty of paper—the bigger the sheets the better—and a starting point of some kind (whether a teacher's assignment, a word, an image, an essay by another writer, a claim, an object, a sound, whatever). Then you just need to let yourself go, which is easier said than done but which gets easier with practice. Write down *everything* that comes to mind, using as few words as possible so as not to slow down the flow of ideas. Drawing pictures, abbreviating, and generally making a mess are all allowed. Nothing is out of bounds, nothing is too silly, nothing is irrelevant, nothing should be discarded as a dead end. *Don't* worry about organizing things; many writers think the key to brainstorming is to silence temporarily the parts of our minds that order and critique so that imagination, association, emotion, and memory can come alive.

It's hard to print excellent examples of this process in a book, but Figures 2.1 to 2.5 should give you the idea.

Figures 2.1 and 2.2 focus on a topic that could be the subject of a serious academic paper, namely, interracial adoption (that is, adoption of a child by parents of a different ethnicity); Figures 2.3–2.5 illustrate one approach to writing a personal essay. Each sample was originally created in ten minutes or less.

Figure 2.1 is a first rough pass at generating some ideas for an essay on interracial adoption. I don't know much about this topic, but that's actually one reason I chose it. Because asking questions during brainstorming is as important as recording knowledge, a lack of information did not prevent me from creating some potentially useful notes.

It's OK if brainstorming notes confuse everyone else as long as they make sense to the writer. Here the dollar sign, for example, stands for the economic side of the issue. The arrow symbol is shorthand for "This way madness lies" and will be explained further in Figure 2.2.

Overall, the brainstorming session identified a number of directions one could pursue in research and writing. One cluster of ideas is a reminder to define the essence of the controversy, the "heart of the issue." What's difficult, as I understand it, is balancing a child's right to her cultural heritage against her perhaps limited opportunities to enjoy a more-or-less normal family life instead of a childhood spent in institutions. The ideal adoption scenario, I think most people would say, is for a child to be adopted by parents of the same ethnic background. But is it better to forego adoption altogether than to match an African American child with European American parents? Who can judge such things?

Another group of ideas concerns legal issues. What is the law, if any, in this area? Are adoptions covered by federal law, state law, or both? Does the law address race in any way, and how has the law evolved in response to changing ideas about race in America? Who sets policy where the law ends?

It's immediately clear that I would need a much tighter focus to write a coherent paper on this topic. Figure 2.2 is a step in that

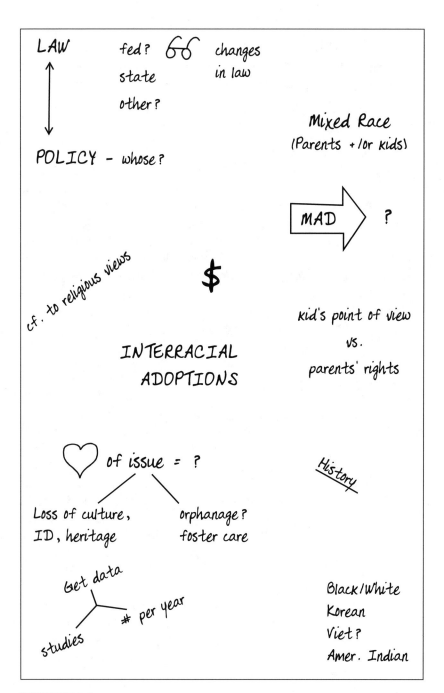

FIGURE 2.1

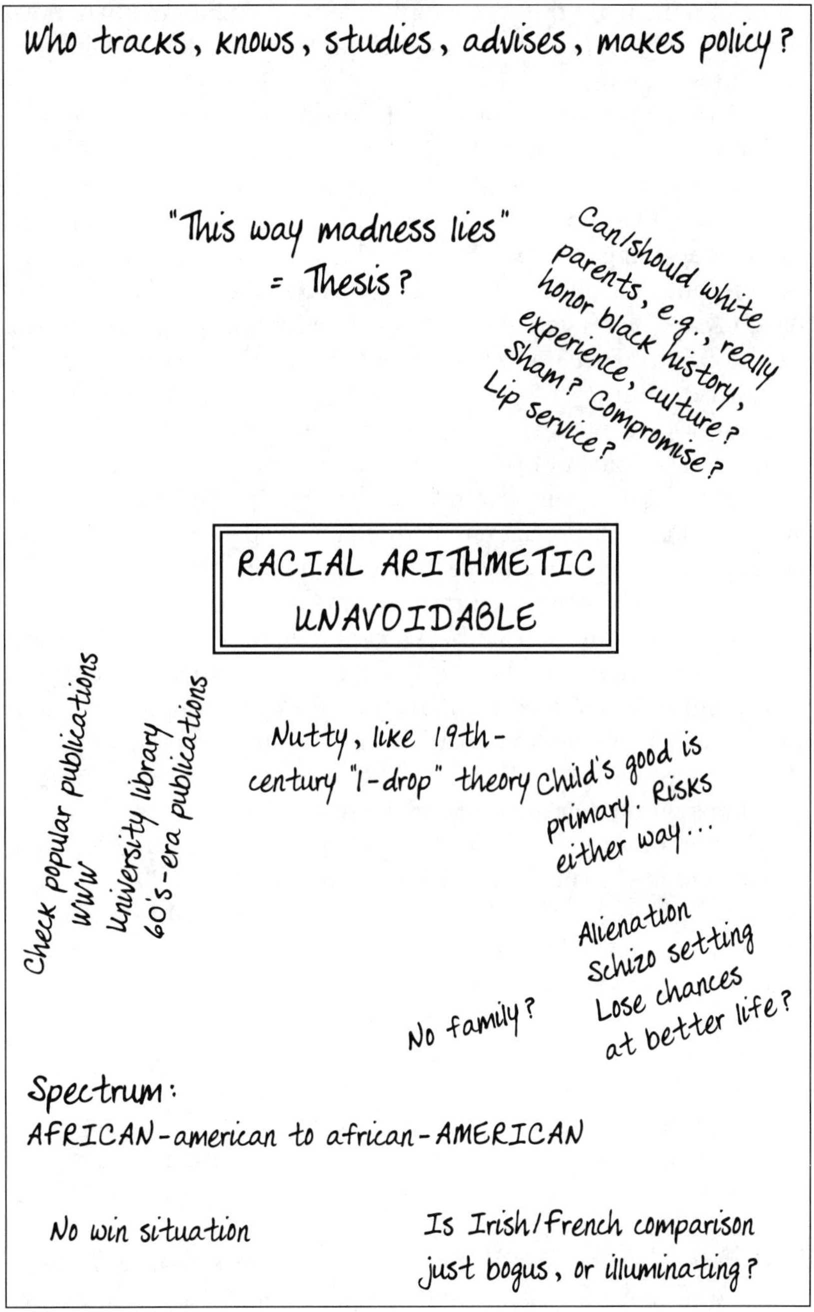

Who tracks, knows, studies, advises, makes policy?

"This way madness lies"
= Thesis?

Can/should white parents, e.g., really honor black history, experience, culture? Sham? Compromise? Lip service?

RACIAL ARITHMETIC
UNAVOIDABLE

Check popular publications
WWW
University library
60's-era publications

Nutty, like 19th-century "1-drop" theory

Child's good is primary. Risks either way...

Alienation
Schizo setting
Lose chances at better life?

No family?

Spectrum:
AFRICAN-american to african-AMERICAN

No win situation

Is Irish/French comparison just bogus, or illuminating?

FIGURE 2.2

direction. The main thing accomplished in this first jumble of notes is that I've gotten past the fearsome blank page—I have words and ideas to work with.

Figure 2.2 is a somewhat more focused set of ideas on interracial adoptions. The key here is that I've taken one idea from my first set of notes and used a second brainstorming session to explore it in more detail. (Naturally, this process can be repeated as often as you like.) Everything remains very tentative—note all the question marks—but I'm following the ideas further, spelling them out less sketchily, trying on various strategies like comparing a Korean/Anglo adoption to an Irish/French one. This strikes me as a bogus comparison, but I don't want to throw out the idea or fail to record it before I have a chance to consider it carefully. (It might even be productive at some point to show *why* the comparison is invalid.)

Again, I will not explain my every notation, but linking most of the ideas here is a suspicion that when race and ethnicity play a role in adoption policy, unsolvable dilemmas become unavoidable. "Racial Arithmetic" is one such troublesome dilemma. If the goal is to place Hispanic children with Hispanic parents, are two Hispanic parents better than one? Is an Anglo adoptive mother less desirable than a highly assimilated woman who is half or one-quarter or one-sixty-fourth Mexican American? Even if a hundred other considerations come into play, it seems difficult to let race play a role in adoptions without getting into sticky questions like these.

On the other hand, should white parents, for example, make special attempts to honor black history and culture if they adopt an African American child? (Beyond what we all should do, that is!) Or are such efforts doomed to become some kind of play-acting, a kind of insult to the complexity of ethnic experience in the United States?

Producing Figures 2.1 and 2.2 leaves me far from a finished paper, but in twenty minutes I've garnered enough ideas to plan some library research or begin some preliminary writing. "Beginnings are always hard," says the German proverb ("Aller Anfang ist schwer"), but brainstorming is a relatively painless way to start your work.

Figure 2.3 is the first of three clusters of ideas about my cousin Pat, one of my best friends and one whose willingness to be discussed in public I knew I could count on. Figure 2.3 is a super-quick

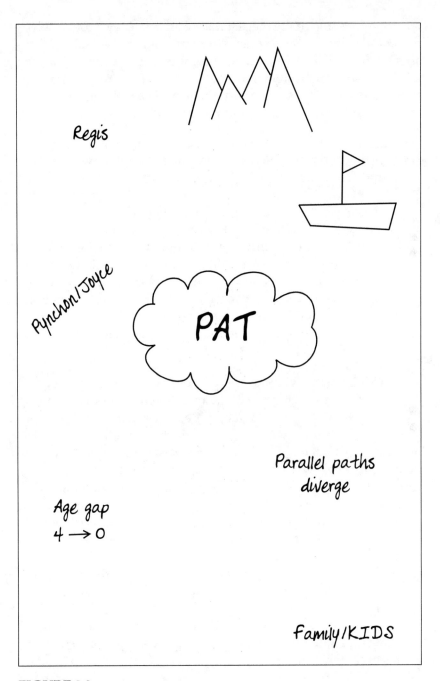

FIGURE 2.3

recording of some of the biggest ideas I associate with him. I recognized right away that I could write any number of short essays about Pat, and I moved on to the more detailed brainstorming shown in subsequent illustrations. The notes here are like hot buttons I know I can push to generate memories, feelings, and ideas; here's what they refer to:

- Regis was our high school.
- Pynchon and Joyce are two favorite authors to whose novels Pat introduced me.
- "Age gap 4 → 0" is a sloppy way of recording the idea that the four years between us once seemed huge (he went to college when I went to high school) but now seem miniscule.
- "Parallel paths diverging" points to how we started out in very similar directions (e.g., we both did graduate work in English literature) but diverged; one big difference was his having children.
- The pictures represent two shared hobbies (mountaineering and bicycling) and an unshared job (Pat is a ship's pilot in Puget Sound). The mountain memories are developed further in Figures 2.4 and 2.5.

Figure 2.4 starts with the idea of mountains from Figure 2.3 and begins to make explicit some of the memories and stories featuring Pat in a mountain setting. Again, these are essentially private triggers or catalysts for my later writing which I wouldn't expect anyone else to understand clearly. "Snow-shoeing with Lady by moonlight" might sound romantic, but it refers to learning to snowshoe in almost total darkness with a St. Bernard dog stepping on the snowshoes. "Camp S/M!!—cf. *Lolita*" refers not to a retreat for sadomasochists, but to Camp St. Malo—yet there might be a joke in there somewhere, or a connection to Nabokov's Camp Q. in his novel *Lolita*. These are likely dead ends, but the point is to withhold that judgment until later. Similarly, *in retrospect* I see the whole cluster around "Michael the climber" is a digression, but I want to nourish the habit of writing down everything I can.

Just as these notes grew from a single idea in my original brainstorming on Pat, Figure 2.5 takes one story from this collection and begins to flesh it out.

Figure 2.5 starts with one idea from Figure 2.4, gathers some of the raw materials needed for an essay, and takes me to the stage that

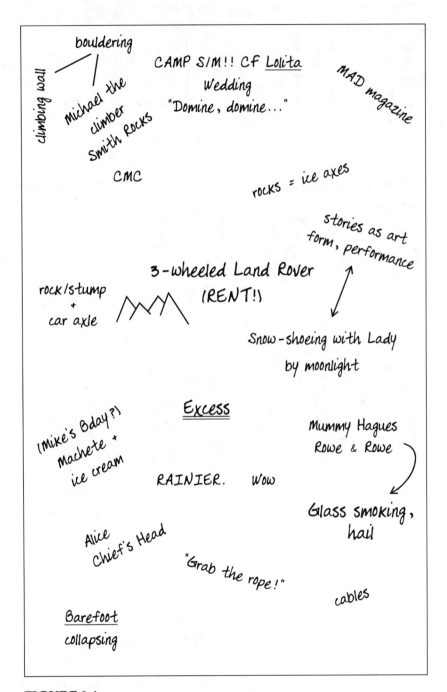

FIGURE 2.4

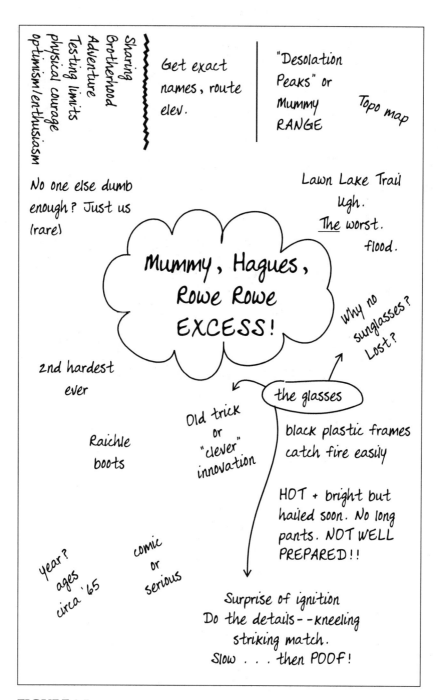

FIGURE 2.5

I could tentatively organize or outline an essay. My narrative would be about a challenging and eventful hike during which we climbed four peaks in one day, got hailed on, and lit Pat's prescription glasses on fire in an effort to smoke up their lenses and make them sunglasses. Ah, youth!

Note that I'm working on several levels at once here as I begin to think not only about what happened but about how I'm going to write about it and create some meaning for my narrative. I'm recording physical details (e.g., the black plastic frames of the glasses, the brand of boots I wore) but also setting myself tasks as a writer (e.g., get the exact names of the peaks). Most importantly, I identify two possible directions for my essay. One would stress the comic element—two kids climbing with inadequate gear and lighting it on fire. The other would stress the more serious things that I also savor about the hike—the shared excitement, Pat's unquenchable enthusiasm (which usually conquered my doubts), and meeting a difficult physical challenge.

The key things to remember are that it's OK to be disorderly, that you can repeat the process as often as you want (perhaps trying out a peripheral idea from one brainstorming session as a generating idea for the next), and that you can eliminate and organize ideas to your heart's content, *later*. That's all you need to know for now. Try your hand with the following Writing Break.

⊠ WRITING BREAK

Brainstorming

1. To warm up, brainstorm all the uses you can imagine for a paper clip or everything you can possibly imagine happening to the Statue of Liberty in the future. Don't be limited by what is likely or reasonable! Imagining that the statue will be stolen by art collectors from another galaxy is a perfectly good idea. If possible, share your results with others or try these or similar activities in a small group.
2. To get started on the first Featured Paper Topic for Chapter 2, brainstorm at least ten or twenty changes, transitions, or discoveries in your life. Record them all; *then* consider which might develop into good essays.
3. For the Featured Paper Topic on gender socialization, list all the ways you can imagine that people learn "appropriate" gender roles.

Exploratory Writing

One of the best ways to get ready to write is actually to write. There are a host of ways to do this, and, as always, you should try different approaches and find what works best for you. The main things to keep in mind with any of the exploratory methods described below are:

- You can't do it wrong.
- This writing belongs entirely to you, and you don't have to show it to anyone if you don't want to.
- You can be disorganized, wordy, redundant, and ungrammatical without penalty.
- This is a warm-up exercise, not an attempt to produce an essay, and it's perfectly all right if 100 percent of what you produce ends up in the recycling bin.

One of writers' most popular tools is the journal, and one excellent use of the journal is for exploratory writing. There are of course many kinds of journals, with aims ranging from constructing personal memoirs to healing one's psychic wounds, and many writing classes invite students to keep journals (or require that they do so). If you've already settled into a journal habit that pleases you, stick with it. If that hasn't happened yet, remember you can't do it wrong, and try some experiments. There's no need to be consistent in form or content: you can record personal feelings one day and explore an academic topic the next; include drawings, write poems, draft angry letters to the editor as the mood strikes you. Somewhere in this mix of activities there may be room for trying out ideas that could turn into a formal essay.

A more unusual form of exploratory writing is to type with the computer screen turned off so that you can't see what you've written. I sometimes use this strategy because I revise and edit more willingly than I write in the first place; typing "blind" helps me move forward. Naturally I end up with some ugly, ugly writing— huge paragraphs or piddling little ones, schizophrenic transitions, abundant typos, garbled syntax, even clauses that no verb. Sometimes, though, I find a groove, and produce more useful material in fifteen minutes than I ordinarily would in an hour.

If you don't have a computer, or if you type slowly, work long-hand and simply force yourself to keep moving ahead, covering up what you've already written with a second sheet of paper. Once this routine seems only mildly strange, you can challenge yourself further by never stopping. If your mind is a blank, write "my mind is a blank" until something else comes into your head. As with brainstorming, the goal is to remain open to unexpected ideas that may come out of nowhere and to get them down on paper before you can prematurely reject or critique them. This approach is hard work, and ten- to fifteen-minute sessions may be plenty long enough.

> *I have decided to keep a full journal, in the hope that my life will perhaps seem more interesting when it is written down.*
> —Sue Townsend

More leisurely approaches also help many writers. Try setting aside half an hour or so to write a no-pressure exploratory piece, in your journal if you like, or just as a separate chunk of writing. Don't worry about coherence, transitions, the accuracy of your facts, or any other such technicalities. Just see if you have anything to say, any directions to pursue. You may want to use a very informal, conversational tone; it may help to imagine yourself talking to yourself or to a friend rather than to a teacher; you may want to ask lots of questions for which you don't yet have any answers. It's possible that you'll write something that will be "salvageable" for a draft of your paper, but don't set that goal. What you're really doing is practicing thinking about the topic, much as you would be doing if you were talking casually about it with a friend. Which brings us to our next topic…

Conversation

Conversation is a very natural rehearsal for writing, one so obvious that it is almost embarrassing to mention, yet many students don't take advantage of it. It does take time, but otherwise it's a fairly painless enterprise. You can determine when to talk to whom about what assignments, but do get in the habit of thinking of classmates, roommates, friends, and family members—and, of course, tutors and instructors—as people who might be willing to chat with you for a while about your work. Such conversations don't always need an "agenda"—you need not articulate a goal or purpose—but think for a moment about what you may gain:

- You will be practicing talking about a given subject—warming up, as it were.
- You may get a stronger sense of what you understand well or are interested in versus what you understand only superficially or care little about.
- You may get a better fix on your audience, sensing which of your ideas are easily understood and which will have to be carefully explained. Likewise, you may learn what ideas are controversial and what some opposing points of view might be.
- You may pick up suggestions about what to read, who else to talk to, or what example(s) to use.
- You may see entirely new directions and possibilities or may get early warnings that you're headed for trouble (e.g., that you have misunderstood the assignment).

I remember a first-year student who had spent hours in the UCLA library searching in vain for materials on incest, an immensely broad topic which she was researching for another class. After a good deal of frustrating and unproductive work, she reached the erroneous conclusion that UCLA libraries contained no information on her topic, whereas in fact, the libraries held more information about incest than she could ever have digested in one semester. Obviously, the young woman lacked adequate research skills, but a moment's conversation with a librarian, teacher, or almost any other student would have spared her much fruitless labor. If you are in your first year or two of college, you are surrounded by a few clueless folks but also by people who know more than you—people who have written more papers, studied subjects more deeply, searched more databases, made more silly mistakes. Talk to them!

Here's a final tip for bold and gregarious students: talk to your instructors about work you are doing in your other classes. That is, talk to your history professor about your *Macbeth* paper, to your psychology professor about your Watergate paper, to your English professor about your research on madness. Most teachers like students and are flattered to be used as sounding boards. What's more, we often know just enough about other fields to ask good questions or point to an interesting resource. I haven't studied math since 1969, but mention fractals to me and I can point you to a contemporary play, *Arcadia*, that discusses them in very elegant ways.

The Classical Topoi *and* Loci—*and Beyond*

Forgive my using the foreign terms here, but they've been hanging around for thousands of years and are useful in discussions of writing. They refer to methods of inventing or discovering ideas. The Greek *topoi* is often translated as "topics," and sometimes as "regions," which stresses that these are places to look for ideas. (The Latin equivalent, *loci*, similarly points to *loc*ations where ideas hang out.) The terms may be odd, but the inventive process they refer to is easy to understand. By the time you entered high school, you were no doubt familiar with most of the methods I'm about to discuss; what may be new is using them in an organized way to produce ideas for your writing.

The easiest way to understand the function of these methods is with an example. Suppose you have been asked to write about Spike Lee's 1996 film, *Get on the Bus*. The topic called comparison suggests that one way to develop material to write about is to compare this film to something else. "Well, duh," you might say. It really is just about that simple; the topics help writers because they remind us of natural, logical, and time-tested ways of thinking about things. With the example of *Get on the Bus*, comparison could lead in several useful directions:

- How does this film resemble Lee's earlier works, such as *Do the Right Thing* and *She's Gotta Have It*? How does it differ (e.g., in style, sophistication, budget, political message, ideas about race and gender)? Is it essentially an extension of Lee's earlier work, or does it signal a brand-new direction?
- In what ways does this film resemble or differ from the work of other directors in the mid-nineties? In particular, how does the film compare to others that deal with issues of ethnicity or gender in America, such as *The Joy Luck Club* or *Grand Avenue*?
- How does the film compare to other accounts of the Million Man March, which is its subject? For example, what similarities and differences may be observed if you compare the film to mainstream news stories about the event?

If you were to turn next to the topic called definition, you might generate some potentially useful ideas in different areas:

- Should this film be considered a documentary? A docudrama? A historical film? A piece of propaganda? That is, what family or genre or subdivision of film best describes *Get on the Bus*? (A natural extension of this kind of question is to speculate about why Lee chose to produce a scripted film with actors rather than a documentary. How does this choice affect your understanding of the Million Man March?)

Of course, you could use the topoi to ask questions about parts of the film as well as about the film as a whole. Depending on your goals and your audience, you might want to focus on the performance of actor Ossie Davis, for example, or on key scenes, or on the sound track, and so on.

The topics don't guarantee intellectual brilliance, of course, but they point you in likely directions. If I may be permitted one fishing analogy in tribute to my cousin Barry, an accomplished angler, you could think of ideas as trout you're trying to catch. The topics are a sort of map of the river. They tell you where the fish are likely to be, but you still have to catch them. The smarter you are, the more creative, the more patient, the better read, the more experienced, the more likely you are to come up with good questions and answers, good ideas to write about. The truly massive trout may elude you for a while, but you might as well be fishing in gold-medal waters and not in barren streams.

Below is a list of questions, loosely based on the classical topoi, which you may use to generate ideas for writing. They are necessarily rather general questions, because they are meant to address any idea that anyone might want to write about, from invertebrate anatomy to quasars. Study them now, but recognize that they can only reveal their power when you apply them to a particular subject. Once you have a main idea, or even a tentative starting point, these probing questions should help spark ideas.

> *Defining Things, Ideas, and Words.* What precisely am I talking about? What group, class, family, etc. does it belong to? What distinguishes it from objects or ideas that it superficially resem-

bles? How can it be recognized? What is its essence? What are its key attributes, characteristics, signs, or symptoms? Is it a natural or a human product? How does it work? In precisely what sense am I using a word or phrase? How have others defined it in texts or in dictionaries? Has the meaning changed over time? What words and ideas can I trust my audience to understand as I wish them to, and which should I define specifically?

Comparing. What are the similarities between this thing or idea and others to which it might logically be compared? What are the differences? Are the similarities or the differences more important? Are the differences essential, fundamental differences, or are they differences in amount or degree? Which is better, preferable (and why)? Which is the lesser evil? Are there enough similarities to warrant conclusions, hypotheses, or analogies based on the similarities? Might I help explain a thing or idea by differentiating it from what it is not?

Cause and Effect. What are the causal relationships in the subject at hand? Given an observed condition, result, or outcome, what are its possible causes? Which are the most likely causes, and why? Which causes might be working together, and which are mutually exclusive? Given an action or a proposed action, what results can be observed or hypothesized? Is the result inevitable or merely probable? If probable, how likely is it? How do we know observed results are not the result of some unknown, unrecognized cause? Are the claims about cause and effect based on direct observation, on logical reasoning, on experimentation, on the authority of experts, or on mere association in time or place? How confident are you about the sequence and logic of the cause–effect relationships in question? Can the cause–effect relationship be directly tested, the result replicated? Is the cause–effect relationship consistent with what current theory would predict? Are there any anomolies or inconsistencies that deserve explanation or further study? (Note that Kenneth Burke's Pentad, described later in this chapter, is particularly helpful in posing questions concerning cause and effect.)

Authority and Evidence. How do you "know" what you know? On what are your claims based? Is your evidence statistical, anecdotal, theoretical, autobiographical, empirical? How much research, and what type of research, is appropriate for this work?

Are you relying on an expert text? An eye witness? How reliable are these? Are you arguing from law, from religious belief, from personal experience, from common knowledge, from historical example? What assumptions do you share with the authority you are using? Does your audience share these assumptions?

To the foregoing questions I would like to add a supplemental list that emphasizes contemporary concerns for writers. These are my questions, not part of the classical topoi, so they have not stood the test of time. They do, however, provide more direct access to certain ideas than the extremely general, all-purpose topoi:

- How do other cultures or subcultures view the object or idea in question? Do you know, or should you learn, anything about how foreign cultures view the issue? What about earlier American culture(s), women's culture, ethnic cultures within the United States, or gay culture? Why do different cultures have different viewpoints? On what issues, if any, is there universal or nearly universal agreement?
- What roles do ethnicity, gender, and class play? How might your own views, or those of others, be influenced by these factors? Would your claims stand up to scrutiny by a broad cross-section of readers, including women and men, gay men and lesbians, rich and poor, rural and urban, and so on?
- What do artists, poets, and musicians have to "say" about the issue? How about lawyers, elected officials, and judges? How about observers from outside the United States?
- What do the experts say? Do their opinions support or contradict popular opinion?
- What relevant ideas are being promoted by TV, movies, popular music, or other media? What messages are advertisers, promoters, and marketers sending? How strong are these messages, and what is their appeal? How much do you trust them?
- What ideas are being promoted by our educational system?

Incubation

This is everyone's favorite creative strategy because it takes virtually no effort. Incubation simply refers to letting ideas sit a while in your head, maturing, developing, taking shape. Apparently, your brain thinks about things without your conscious effort; you might even be writing essays while you sleep! The one thing that *is* required—and this can be difficult in college—is to begin the task early enough that there is time for the incubation to occur. Very soon after you receive an assignment, do enough work on it to engage your mind. You don't need to forge a thesis or outline your paper, but do try some brainstorming, or skim a couple of relevant articles, or talk to classmates about the topic. The idea is to plant a seed, as it were, in the back of your mind. This gives your mind a chance to play with relevant ideas and to notice things in daily life, reading, lectures, films, and so on that might contribute to your writing. Naturally, the results of incubating will vary from topic to topic and from writer to writer, but putting in a half hour's work early is a very low-cost investment that can pay big dividends. Also, doing this little bit of work should erase from your mind one of the worst negative thoughts about any assignment—"I've haven't even started it!" As little bits of inspiration make their way into your conscious mind, be sure to write them down.

A MULTICULTURAL PENTAD

Hollywood doesn't believe that in 1998 you can make a movie about Indians that doesn't rely on loincloths and romanticism. But we have stories like everybody else.—Chris Eyre

The pentad is a well-known intellectual tool fashioned by philosopher and literary critic Kenneth Burke about fifty years ago. This section explains how to use Burke's approach to help generate ideas, gives simple and extended examples of the pentad at work, and concludes with strategies for maximizing the pentad's usefulness in multicultural thinking and writing.

Burke's Pentad

Burke's pentad consists of five analytical prompts. These five terms echo the well-known reporter's questions—Who? What? Where? When? Why?—but Burke's terminology stresses how his method treats events as drama. Here are the five terms of the pentad:

Act: something that occurred—a deed or even a thought
Scene: the act's background, situation, circumstance, setting
Agent: the person who performed the act
Agency: the means or tools she used
Purpose: the motivation of the act

Listed in this simple way, the pentad may not seem spectacularly new, inventive, or surprising. Part of its power, though, actually comes from its simplicity and familiarity; like the classical topoi, the pentad will help you think clearly about the fundamental aspects of a wide range of issues.

It is possible to write a specifically "Burkean" essay—that is, to analyze a political situation or a poem or a scientific breakthrough from a Burkean perspective, using his terminology and methods quite explicitly. This would be akin to writing a specifically Freudian analysis of some neurosis or a specifically Marxist analysis of a revolution. To accomplish this, you would need to know more than this chapter will tell you, and for most audiences, you would have to explain Burke's methods. Rather than follow that path, this brief introduction to Burke's thinking will treat the pentad as a means of invention, as a way of developing interesting ideas to write about, as a means of thinking about issues in ways that are likely to be productive.

Let's start with a very simple example: Bicyclist A is at the side of the road with a flat tire. Bicyclist B stops and repairs the flat, enabling Bicyclist A to ride again. This event may seem dull compared to *Macbeth,* but to get in a Burkean frame of mind, picture this happening on a stage. As a member of the audience, you might pose and answer the questions suggested by the pentad as follows:

What is the Act?

One cyclist completes a simple repair job for another.

What is the Scene?

Let's assume a sunny day, probably Saturday or Sunday, a quiet road.

Who or what is the Agent?

Bicyclist B, who proves handy with tools.

What Agency does the actor employ?

Tire irons, patch kit, pump, hands.

What is the agent's Purpose?

To help a fellow cyclist, be a good Samaritan.

So far, so good, but this would make for a pretty dull play. Imagine for a moment, though, that cyclist A, with the flat tire, is female and cyclist B is male. Now notice the kinds of questions you could ask: Is the nice guy also figuring it can't hurt to meet an active, athletic woman? Would he have stopped to help another man? Is he showing off? Does he go through life assuming women need his help? And what's with this woman I've put on stage before you? What's she doing? Why isn't she an *agent* here? Does she lack the equipment to make her own repair, or the knowledge? Why? Does she at least help with the repairs? If the playwright wants you to understand the action in a certain way, she could provide clues such as dialogue or significant gestures/emotions projected by the actors (annoyance, frustration, desperation, gratitude, etc.).

To push the example to an absurd extreme, let's imagine another explanation for the same action. This time, B is a technology whiz at a cutting-edge company. Cyclist A is a corporate spy, who, having observed B's routine for weeks, fakes a flat along B's predictable route, in hopes of triggering an "accidental" meeting and beginning an acquaintance. The action on the stage might look exactly the same, but the pentad could be charted quite differently:

Act: Corporate spy pulls off "cute meet" of unsuspecting target.

Scene: Suddenly, it matters that the road is in Silicon Valley.

Agent: Bicyclist A—not B, as originally. B is only an agent at a superficial level.

Agency: Observation, patience, guile, and a nail to create the flat.

Purpose: (Eventually) to steal technological secrets in order to engineer hi-tech sabotage.

I suggest these alternative explanations of a single scene because the pentad is not designed to reveal some obvious and noncontroversial truth about an issue or event. Rather, it leads us to ask questions about what we observe. It helps us think about "what's really going on here?"

There are a couple of other things you should know about Burke's approach before you try putting it to work for yourself. One is that he saw his five terms as connected and changeable; they are not rigid categories, and they can sometimes blend into one another. Burke's own metaphor for this was that the five terms are like the five fingers of the hand—each distinct but deeply unified nevertheless and able to work in concert. Another key point is that Burke recognized the power of thinking about the *relationships* of one finger to the others—the ways in which, for example, a particular scene could exert an influence on an agent (e.g., how being put in a jury box might put someone in a serious, contemplative mood).

An Extended Example

This section provides a more extended, detailed, and realistic application of Burkean thinking, specifically an analysis of a story by David Guterson (reprinted below) called "Wood Grouse on a High Promontory Overlooking Canada." Guterson is the author of *Snow Falling on Cedars,* an award-winning novel that will probably have been made into a film by the time you read this. Despite its sizeable title, "Wood Grouse" is a very short story, conveniently divided, for my purposes, into three sections. I've used Burke's pentad to organize some thoughts on the first two sections, and I'll invite you to analyze the third section on your own. The story is not difficult, but please do read it carefully so that my subsequent comments make sense.

WOOD GROUSE ON A HIGH PROMONTORY OVERLOOKING CANADA

David Guterson

I went up there with my brother, Gary—up on the side of Goat Peak: a high promontory overlooking Canada.

That day we caught no fish at Wall Lake. They were there, watching what we did, but the weather was all wrong, too sultry, and the fish stayed down in the deep water.

That day Gary wouldn't talk about the war he'd only just come back from. "You don't want to know," he said to me. "Take my word for it, Bud." So after a while I didn't ask anymore. But I could see Gary had seen things I hadn't.

I don't know. I was fifteen. I spent a lot of time throwing rocks, I know that. Building stacks of rocks, backing off thirty yards, then throwing for as long as it took to knock the stacks of rocks apart.

We saw a flock of sheep, a sheepdog and a shepherd, up on the Wind Pass trail. "Aren't they beautiful?" said Gary. The shepherd was a silent Mexican on a horse, his dog a ragged mutt; the sheep flowed away from us in a slow white wave as we waded through them in the cloudless sunlight.

There were no trout for lunch but some cheese I'd kept in the streambed and a can of sardines and some dried pears. Then—later—we smeared ourselves with jungle juice, put our sunglasses on and took the compass and the Geological Survey map up on the side of Goat Peak.

Up there Gary spread the map out on a slab of rock, and laid the compass down and watched while it settled. "There's Canada," he said. "That's Eldorado Peak way over there and that's the Chilliwack Valley."

I looked up into a world of blue spruce that rolled on endlessly to a land I dreamed about. I didn't say a thing about this dream to my brother, though—about the mountains or about living off the land. It seemed the wrong dream to tell him about, now that he was back in America.

"This is the border," Gary said. "We're in Canada, Bud." Driven into the scree up there we found the mounted iron border marker—number fifty-five, it read. We sat by it: a place to rest and watch the sun go down.

"Draft-dodger heaven," said Gary.

We kept crossing from country to country, back and forth, reveling in the freedom of not answering to anyone about it.

Eventually to the northwest there was no light other than a crescent of orange wavering on the horizon. The sky over our heads lit up, while the earth we sat on went cold in the last sweet twilight.

It was in this last light that we saw them—*hooters,* that was the name our father used—a covey of wood grouse dodging through a broken tumble of sharp gray talus rock.

"Look," Gary said. "There."

I picked up a stone about the size of a baseball and watched them—imagining myself a hunter of wild animals.

"They're beautiful," Gary said. "Just look at them."

I let fly hard and in the gray light the covey scattered, a drilling of buzzing wings, birds tossing themselves down the Mountainside, but one seemed to leap up so that for a moment it was painted like a shadow against the sky, the tips of its wings wide, a sound like *whoot whoot whoot whoot whoot to-whoot* aimed at the heavens, it did a half-roll in midflight and plummeted, describing an arc, headlong into the darkening scree.

"Jesus," Gary said. "What did you do that for?"

I had no good answer. I said, "I didn't think I was going to hit one, Gary."

We went down and stood by her where she was dying among the rocks. She was a large female—soot-colored tail feathers, some white hind shafts, a narrow, bluish band where her flanks narrowed. My stone had caught her flush in the breast. One wing had been crushed in her fall to earth.

"Jesus," Gary said. "Look what you did."

I didn't speak, though. What could I say? We stood there, the two of us, watching her.

"Jesus," Gary said again.

There was nothing left for her. The other birds were long gone. The one good wing only twitched along the rock. Her life flowed out of her, into the scree, back into the earth it had come from.

"I'm going to finish this pain," Gary said. "God forgive me."

There were tears in his eyes I hadn't figured on.

He put his boot on the dying bird's head—the sole over one alert, clear eye—and ground it suddenly into the rock while the wings gave a last frenzied shudder. They fluttered out to their full span spasmodically in the moment just before she died.

"That's it," Gary said, not ashamed of his crying—just crying now while he spoke to me. "That's all it is. That's all there is to it, Bud."

We went down the mountain and around the canyon head to Wall Lake. No trout were feeding there; not a sound except the croaking of the marsh frogs.

After we had eaten the pinto beans with chili powder and white rice for supper we sat by the propane stove for a while.

"How has it been?" Gary asked. "What have you been up to?"

I told him about not making the basketball team, the fight I'd had with Mike Kizinski, other things that didn't really matter.

"I like hearing all this," Gary said. "Tell me some more, Bud."

But I didn't. I was young and didn't know any better. So instead I asked him about the thing on my mind: "Did you kill anyone in Vietnam?" I said.

"Did I kill anyone in Vietnam?" said Gary.

"Did you?"

"Did I kill anyone in Vietnam," said Gary. "Did I kill anyone in Vietnam."

And again he began to cry silently, in a way I hadn't figured on at all.

"I'm sorry," I said. "Really."

But he went on crying. He cried with no shame. He cried in a way I didn't think was possible. He didn't rub his eyes or try to stop it. He just cried.

Later we took down our sleeping bags from where they'd been airing over the branch of an arctic pine, and laid them out on the flat ground we'd cleared the night before. The two of us lay buried in our bags, only our faces showing, the drawstrings pulled around our heads so that the spilling of the snowmelt over the pebbles in the streambed was like a muted roar, a streaming music beginning and ending in our ears. We lay there side by side staring up at the stars, and talked about how unfathomable was the phrase *light years*, the possibility of life on Saturn's seventh moon, the years that would have to pass before NASA put a man on Mars. We talked about a theory Gary read about in a book—

that time and space didn't really exist, that everything was in reality something else we didn't know about.

After a while we gave up on the useless things and watched for the points of light that were satellites among the forever-fixed stars. We watched them hurtling slowly to the horizon, gravity tugging them always toward the earth so that they moved in a relentless straight line out of vision. Gary said that, if need be, a satellite could take a close-up photograph of us in our sleeping bags, as soon as the sky became light enough.

"But it doesn't matter," he said. "It's beautiful up here. I'm glad we came. I'm glad we're here."

I heard him, minutes later, moving toward sleep, and I began to feel alone among all those mountains. And then I couldn't fall asleep that night; I felt ashamed of myself. But later on I found that Gary was awake too, and then we passed the dark hours talking.

"Two insomniacs," he said after a while. "Crazy, Bud. Insane."

"At least we've got someone to talk to," I said.

"At least we've got that," said Gary.

Figure 2.6 charts the scene, act, agent, agency, and purpose for the first two sections, leaving the third section for you to work on. Please note that at this point, I am only generating ideas about the story, trying to understand it. To write an actual essay on the story I might eventually narrow my focus to a single issue, like the theme of (mis)communication or the importance of setting.

The *scene* of the first section is a region near the Canadian border—overlooking Canada, as the title indicates, overlooking "draft-dodger heaven," as Gary says. Surely this borderland setting is no accident. One can get to Canada from a bar in New Orleans, but one can't imagine this story's conversations taking place in a juke joint. The setting makes the option of dodging the draft real, and perhaps rather attractive for an outdoorsy young man. We know that for whatever reason, Gary went to Vietnam, not Canada; we don't know if it was the right choice, but the scene invites us to wonder about it. Again and again, Gary and Bud step into Canada and back. Should Gary have crossed that border once before…and stayed?

FIGURE 2.6   Notes on "Wood Grouse on a High Promontory Overlooking Canada"

	Section One	Section Two
Scene	Overlooking *Canada*. Sultry. Post-Vietnam for Gary. Pastoral, explicitly: sheep, shepherd. "Draft-dodger heaven." At the border.	Evening of same day. Again, contrast of this setting vs. Vietnam. Major crying.
Act	Fishing, hiking, lunching, sunset, <u>wood grouse</u>. Bud injures grouse, Gary kills it & cries.	Gary on small talk: "I like this." Bud's failure: "Did you kill anyone in Vietnam?" Probe about Vietnam. |
Agent	Gary teaches lesson about fragility of life? Also cries, shows emotion, though he doesn't talk much about emotions.	Bud |
Agency	Mercy-killing of grouse.	Asks a too-blunt question. |
Purpose	Act as brother/mentor?	Curiosity? Know his brother?

Other details of scene lend a hand, like the sultry, cloudless day or the trouts' refusal to bite, but the second key to the scene, I think, is that it is a peaceful, pastoral setting. *Pastoral* has come to mean "simple" and "serene," but at root it means "having to do with sheep"[1]—and Guterson indeed provides a sea of sheep. The more I think about this the better I like it; it's an unobtrusive detail, but it winks meaningfully at the alert reader. Why the shepherd is Mexican I have no idea, but at least Burke provoked me to think about it.

In terms of *acts*, the first section provides several (fishing, hiking, eating lunch, watching the sunset), but apparently the most important is the killing of the grouse. As an *agent*, the narrator

---

1. Note the words *pasture* and *pastor* (the religious leader who is a metaphorical shepherd to his flock).

foolishly injures a grouse. He precipitates an event—and spoils an enjoyable moment—but that's about as far as his agency goes. Once the grouse is wounded, Gary takes over, mercifully killing it and, not incidentally, crying as he does so. There's a strong suggestion that Gary is trying to teach Bud something about the fragility of life, as he repeats phrases like, "That's all it is." Looking forward for a moment to the second section and Bud's question about killing, I would suggest that Gary at this moment is reminded of other killing he has done.

Burke's terms are flexible; applying them to something is not like labeling it in indelible ink. In the case at hand, we can trace different paths of action and motive. At a superficial level, Bud (agent) injures a bird (act) with a rock (agency) to fulfill a macho boyhood fantasy about being a "hunter of wild animals" (purpose). More interestingly, Gary (agent) educates his brother (act) by killing the grouse, showing his emotions, and commenting on the events (agency), perhaps with the purpose of acting as a mentor or big brother.

Note just one other interesting idea that the pentad revealed early in the story. In the third paragraph, Bud asks his brother about Vietnam, repeatedly, perhaps in an attempt to know him better or simply out of curiosity. These questions don't have their intended effect, though. Gary won't talk about the war, and there's an obvious failure of communication. The *non*conversation in section one sets up section two, in which Bud again asks about Vietnam.

The *scene* of the second section is basically the same—it's now evening of the same day. Again, the implied contrast of the beautiful setting with the horror of combat adds tension to the story. It's interesting that the important, even crucial scene of the Vietnam war is not directly portrayed; we are invited to imagine Gary's experience, but it is never described directly; we only know that he doesn't want to talk about it, and that his memories make him cry. The key *act* in the second section is another mistake by Bud, echoing his poor judgment of throwing the rock in the first section. Ignoring Gary's statement that he enjoys the small talk—"I like hearing all this" he says, "Tell me some more"—Bud bluntly asks Gary if he killed anyone in Vietnam. Again the brothers fail to communicate well, though it's likely that they share the common *purpose* of trying to bond, of acting as brothers. Gary can only cry, and Bud can only be surprised. Though he is apparently wiser by the time he narrates the story, Bud comes across as impatient, overly direct, self-centered. As he says himself, "I was young and didn't know any better."

Now you do some of the thinking: take a close look at the third section of the story and use Burke's pentad to spark and organize your responses. Jot down a few notes, and if possible, compare your ideas to those of classmates. Remember that the test of the pentad is not whether or not you all come up with the same answers but whether you come up with some interesting ideas, some possibilities worth considering and exploring.

Guterson's story is about 1,500 words long. Obviously, you wouldn't want to work your way through the 600 pages of *The Mambo Kings Play Songs of Love* at quite this level of detail. One of the attractions, though, of Burke's pentad, is that it works with things as small as the fourteen lines of a sonnet and with ideas as big as "feudalism" or "commerce." In explaining his ideas, Burke himself applies them to such diverse topics as Christ's crucifixion, slavery, a play by Ibsen, *Gulliver's Travels*, the interning of Japanese Americans during World War II, Freud, and primitive magic.

Using the Pentad for Multicultural Thinking

Burke's approach can be used to explore virtually any idea in any context, and it's easy to incorporate multicultural thinking into Burkean brainstorming. Simply remember issues of diversity as you think about scene, act, actor, agency, and purpose. Race, social class, and gender, for example, deserve your consideration because they matter so much in our culture. Careful thinking about a Burkean actor will often involve consideration of his or her gender because gender plays a role in so many cultural settings. The same goes for race and class. Burke's pentad leads naturally enough in such directions; I'm not really extending his approach, just emphasizing one aspect of it.

Of course, there are many dimensions to American diversity beyond race, class, and gender. Think about regional differences, generational differences, religious differences, political differences, and educational differences. It boils down to some pretty simple advice: as you practice using the pentad, keep in mind the incredible spectrum

of American thought, belief, and experience, and let these complicate and enrich your brainstorming.

It's especially useful to look at actor and scene from a multicultural perspective. Here is a sampling of the kinds of questions you
can ask:

Actor

- If the actor is an individual (not an institution, etc.), how important are race, gender, and economic class?
- How important are the individual's religious or political beliefs?
- What are the key elements of the individual's personality, circumstances, or background—for example, being an immigrant,
being an orphan or a twin, suffering an addiction, etc.? What
makes this person tick?

Scene

- What is the historical setting of the act? In what ways is the era
of the act important?
- What is the cultural setting of the act—for example, mainstream
American culture, a foreign culture, or a subculture of some
kind (deaf culture, gay culture, an ethnic culture, etc.)?
- What are the most fundamental values within the cultural setting?
- Is the setting relatively homogeneous (people are mostly similar, their beliefs and values largely in accord) or heterogeneous
(diverse people, possibly with conflicting values or beliefs)?
- If there is conflict, what is its fundamental source? What is its
history?
- How familiar or unfamiliar are you as a writer with the historical and cultural setting? What kind of research could help your
understanding or analysis?

Let me return for a moment to Guterson's story to illustrate just
one of these principles in action. My earlier notes and comments on
the story did not address gender directly, but it turns out that the
story is quite interesting when viewed through a gender lens.
Women did not face being drafted to fight in Vietnam, for example,
though of course the draft had a huge impact on women's lives by
taking sons and lovers, husbands and brothers. And the story itself
is very "male" in that no women are present or even mentioned (al-

---

🔯 **WRITING BREAK**

Burke's Pentad

Use the pentad to generate ideas for one of this chapter's Featured Paper Topics or for any of your other writing assignments that is currently at the invention stage.

---

though the slaughtered wood grouse is distinctly and perhaps significantly described as female). One might also speculate that throwing a rock at a bird while imagining oneself an "ancient hunter" is a markedly masculine idea in American society. Thinking about gender—one way of being aware of cultural diversity while playing with the pentad—turns up ideas well worth pursuing. But I still don't know why the shepherd is Mexican. What do you think?

ORGANIZATION

Organization is one of the easiest aspects of writing to learn and one of the areas in which students make the most rapid progress. If you someday write a thesis or dissertation, you will most likely face some difficult organizational challenges, but most undergraduate work—papers under fifteen pages, say—can be managed effectively with the handful of easily understood techniques described below.

Organization and the Writing Process

Most students I've encountered in twenty years of teaching writing end up writing well-organized compositions, at least by semester's end, but the ways they arrive at this goal are varied and idiosyncratic. Perhaps some rigorous elementary school program could teach young children to go about organizing ideas all in the same way—I have my doubts—but there is usually considerable variety in a college class. Some people like to make detailed, carefully numbered, elaborate outlines before writing a single sentence; arranging their ideas carefully gives them confidence and direction as they proceed to the writing stage. Other people organize mostly after the fact—that is, they produce a lot of draft writing, concentrating on developing and exploring their ideas and knowing that these can be reordered later. Most of us, I think, work somewhere between these extremes, perhaps jotting down a rough outline or even a simple list of key ideas before writing but making organizational changes as we work.

What's important about all this is that you should expect considerable variation within any class and even in your own writing process. There is no single right way to approach organization, and perhaps the only truly wrong way is to ignore it altogether. Begin with a bit of self-evaluation: if your current approach produces good results with a reasonable amount of effort, stick with it; on the other hand, if you sweat bullets trying to order your ideas, or find yourself tearing up numerous failed outlines, or if you puzzle your readers, think about making big changes in how you work. This book may help; in addition, teachers, tutors, or classmates can talk you through a specific assignment the way no book can, so don't hesitate to ask for their help.

The second big tip is to remember that a successful writing process is almost always recursive, or cyclical. This book follows the natural progression from inventing to organizing to writing to revising, but this is only a rough guide. In practice, writers move back and forth freely between stages: the effort to organize the results of one's research, for example, may reveal a gap in that research; stylistic revision of an essay's ending might produce, by lucky accident, the perfect opening paragraph.

Creativity and Convention, Freedom and Restraint

As you take classes in different academic areas, you will encounter many different kinds of writing assignments, from personal narratives to lab reports. The organization you choose should reflect the purpose and the audience for the assignment. (If you are unsure about these, ask questions early!) It may help you to think of your various writing assignments as falling along some spectrum from creativity and freedom on one end to restraints and adherence to convention on the other. The personal essay offers you virtually complete freedom in terms of organization. Though you are ordinarily not required to get fancy, you may use any organizational device you can think of, such as inserting a flashback or keeping an important secret until late in the essay. Scientific writing, in contrast, will expect an orderly march from hypothesis to methods to results to conclusions. Surprising results may be welcome, but surprising organization is not. Argumentative or analytical writing in many fields—political science, history, women's studies, philosophy—will fall somewhere in the middle of the spectrum: readers will expect a clear thesis and tight organization, but you will not be guided by an organizational formula or recipe.

By the way, I'm not knocking the scientists here; I'm merely suggesting that you may have to be nimble-minded as you work on biology, drama, and anthropology papers on the same Thanksgiving weekend. Notice, too, that "restraints," or conventions of organization, actually help you by reducing the number of decisions you have to make.

Easy Large-Scale Strategies

By "large-scale strategies" I mean organizational techniques you can apply to the essay or paper as a whole. (Tips on organizing paragraphs and short groups of paragraphs appear in the next section.) Here are a few that have served writers well for centuries.

> *Thesis and Evidence.* Sometimes known as the KISS approach (Keep It Simple, Stupid), this general scheme is so indispensable and effective that it might prove the only strategy you truly need. The idea is to move quickly toward a very explicit statement of your main idea or argument (usually in the first paragraph and no later than the second) and then get right to business explaining, illustrating, or defending that idea. Frequent reminders of how everything supports the main ideas are generally appreciated. If you have a striking thesis, you might make it your very first sentence; I can still remember an essay from years back that began with words to the effect that "The most important thing about Shakespeare's *Othello* is that its hero is a black man." The advantage of the KISS approach is that it puts ideas, arguments, and evidence distinctly in the foreground—hence its high value in academic writing.

Chronological Order. An obvious strategy for storytelling, simple chronology works equally well for many other types of assignments. Imagine how natural it would be to discuss any of these diverse issues using a chronological organization: AIDS research, the 1916 Easter Rebellion in Dublin, the films of Spike Lee, foot-binding, mitosis, bridge construction. The beauty of straightforward chronology is that once you've chosen this approach, virtually everything falls into place. Remember that if you're working in an unrestrained area such as the personal narrative, you can toy with chronology.

> *The five-paragraph theme was also a charade. It not only paraded relentlessly to its conclusion; it began with its conclusion. It was all about its conclusion. Its structure permitted no change of direction, no reconsideration, no wrestling with ideas.*
> —Cynthia Ozick

No "Five-Paragraph Essays"

The infamous five-paragraph essay consists of an introduction (main idea and three supporting ideas), three body paragraphs (one to develop each of the three supporting ideas), and a concluding paragraph that usually looks suspiciously like the opening paragraph—an indication that not much has happened between beginning and ending. This predictable, mechanical, rigid, mind-numbing, idea-squelching approach to organization has been and still is taught in many high schools and colleges. If you are one of its victims, get beyond it in your very next writing assignment. Your organization should help demonstrate your thinking, not conform to some formula.

Paragraph-Level Strategies

A paragraph is what you make it. Attempts to define what a paragraph is tend to be extremely vague, like "a series of sentences concerning a coherent idea" or "the unit of thought larger than the sentence." In professional writing, paragraphs can range in length from a single word to over a thousand words, though such extremes are of course rare; similarly, professionally written paragraphs often lack "topic sentences," though teachers urging clarity frequently stress these. To a large extent, paragraphing reflects not only the conventions of a particular kind of writing—novel versus textbook versus advertisement, and so on—but also strictly visual concerns: a large newspaper page, for example, dictates short paragraphs so that readers are not put off by dense masses of dark type. Double-spaced, typed student papers often average two or three paragraphs per page, but you can vary this substantially to develop a complex idea or to change the pace with a short paragraph. Give your ideas first priority and let the paragraph breaks fall accordingly.

Paragraphs versus Sections. In keeping with the above idea, recognize that having four important ideas in a paper does not limit you to four paragraphs. For example, a paper on the American family in 1800 might feature three paragraphs about the father's role, five about the mother's role, and two each on children and grandparents. The three paragraphs about fathers might well belong together as a kind of subsection within the paper but need not be subtitled or otherwise set off.

Topic Sentences. Although not all paragraphs have topic sentences, they can be extremely useful. A topic sentence is merely the explicit statement of a paragraph's main idea. It will often be the first, second, or final sentence of a paragraph. In argumentative or analytical writing, the topic sentence may take the form of a claim or opinion which the other sentences support or illustrate.

Transitional Sentences. Writers who focus exclusively on topic sentences and place one first in every paragraph sometimes produce confusing papers despite their attention to organization. This happens because each paragraph is carefully organized but the relationship or connection of paragraphs is unclear. Transitional sentences bridge the gaps between paragraphs and help keep readers on track. They can be as simple as "There's another reason frontier families tended to be large." (This conveys no concrete information, but it orients the reader by letting her know what kind of information is about to appear.)

An Extended Example: Comparison and Contrast

This section presents five different ways of organizing a comparison/contrast essay like this chapter's Featured Paper Topic on gender roles. Specifically, it will address the ways first-graders might learn gender roles. The most important thing to learn is that you do have options. If you can understand the outlines below, a little work will let you construct similarly sensible outlines for your own papers. Comparison/contrast papers are among the most challenging to organize; many of the strategies displayed here will also work with analytical, argumentative, or other essays.

For the next few essays you write, try to come up with at least two substantially different schemes of organization; choose the one that's clearer or more logical or that lets you begin and end with your best ideas.

Here are five outlines for a paper on first-graders and gender roles:

An unimaginative but useful approach

Introduction
Similarities
    Both learn gendered speech
    Both learn gendered play, toys, games
Differences
    Girls at this age have wider range of acceptable clothing
Discussion, conclusions, or recommendations

A second standard approach

Introduction
    Lessons girls learn about clothes
    Lessons boys learn about clothes (*Note:* Girls' clothing vs. boys' could be 1 paragraph total, 1 paragraph for each sex, or several paragraphs.)
    Lessons girls learn about speech
    Lessons boys learn about speech
    Lessons girls learn about games and play
    Lessons boys learn about games and play
Conclusion

A third scheme

Introduction
Where we've made progress
    Girls' clothing: wide range is OK
    Girls' activities: wide range again OK

Where we have problems
> Boys' clothes: rigid requirements
> Boys' activities: competition, violence

Conclusions, recommendations

And a fourth

Introduction
> Dramatic male/female differences: 1–2 paragraphs on clothing
> Less obvious differences: 2–3 paragraphs on games
> Very subtle biases: 4–5 paragraphs on speech, books, posture, gesture

Conclusion, recommendations

An option that usually works poorly. Why?

Introduction
Gender lessons for male first graders
> How to dress
> How to talk
> How to play

Gender lessons for female first graders
> How to dress
> How to talk
> How to play

Conclusion

Organization and Multiculturalism

Worldwide strategies of indirection—linguistic, rhetorical, poetic, psychological—create richness that to world majority students makes the spare, relentless logic of the western tradition seem meager in comparison.—Helen Fox

Good organization might seem like a matter of simple logic and common sense; you might expect strategies and conventions to be universal, regardless of culture. This seems to be not quite true, though *relatively* few students run into organizational problems because of cultural differences. The area where problems most frequently arise, in my experience anyway, is in the tension between American directness and some other cultures' tact and patience.

The KISS (Keep It Simple, Stupid) mindset mentioned above is strong in American colleges and universities. Given a choice between a paper that blurts out its thesis in its first breath and one that works its way slowly in that direction over the course of several pages, most American teachers favor the former. They would describe such an approach as "direct, straightforward, businesslike, efficient." To some cultures, however, this approach might seem "jarring, blunt, simplistic, crude, abrupt." Such readers and writers may expect to see background information before the thesis—they may want to appreciate the historical dimension of the problem or see the writer's knowledge of previously published materials.

In my experience, cultural disagreements about how to organize writing have surfaced more often in advanced work like a master's thesis than in introductory courses, where the options are more limited and the assignments more specific. Other teachers, however, report observing such cases at all levels. An Islamic student, for example, might begin with lengthier discussion or quotation of the Koran than most teachers would expect; the student's gesture of respect and deference to a holy text could be misunderstood as an attempt to pad a paper. If you are advanced enough to have absorbed the rhetorical preferences of another culture, be aware that American colleges and universities may have different preferences even in such matters as organization. Don't hesitate to talk to instructors if you have questions or concerns. If you're *not* rhetorically sophisticated in another language, the main things you might want to remember are that "the American way" is not the only way and that pieces you read in translation may occasionally seem excessively leisurely or unfocused not because they are poorly written, but because they are written to a different standard.

⊠   ⊠   ⊠

The two readings for this chapter have to do with creativity. The first, an excerpt from Roger von Oech's bestseller *A Whack on the Side of the Head: How You Can Be More Creative*, offers tips from an expert on how to see and think in fresh and productive ways. The second reading, an interview with poet Sonia Sanchez, moves to issues of writing in a (sometimes hostile) multicultural environment. Questions on both readings follow in Discussion Questions and Writing Assignments.

FROM *A WHACK ON THE SIDE OF THE HEAD: HOW YOU CAN BE MORE CREATIVE*

Roger von Oech

THE CREATIVE PROCESS

Where do you use soft and hard thinking? [Hard thinking is precisely logical. Soft thinking is playful, metaphorical.] To answer this question, we should turn to the creative process. There are two main phases in the development of new ideas: an *imaginative* phase and a *practical* one.

In the imaginative phase, you generate and play with ideas. In the practical phase, you evaluate and execute them. To use a biological metaphor, the imaginative phase sprouts the new ideas and the practical phase cultivates and harvests them.

In the imaginative phase, you ask questions such as: What if? Why not? What rules can we break? What assumptions can we drop? How about if we looked at this backwards? Can we borrow a metaphor from another discipline? The motto of the imaginative phase is: *Thinking something different.*

In the practical phase, you ask questions such as: Is this idea any good? Do we have the resources to implement it? Is the timing right? Who can help us? What's the deadline? What are the consequences of not reaching the objective? The motto of the practical phase is: *Getting something done.*

Both types of thinking play an important role in the creative process, but usually during different phases. Soft thinking is quite effective in the imaginative phase when you are searching for new ideas, thinking globally, and manipulating problems. Hard thinking, on the other hand, is best used in the practical phase when you are evaluating ideas, narrowing in on practical solutions, running risk-analyses, and preparing to carry the idea into action.

A good analogy for the need for both types of thinking in the creative process is a potter making a vase. If you've ever done any work with clay, you know that it's a lot easier to shape, mold, and throw the clay if it has some softness to it (brittle clay is hard to shape). By the same token, after the vase has been shaped, it has no practical value until it has been put into a oven and fired. Both the soft and the hard elements are required but at different times.

If soft and hard thinking have their respective strengths, they also have their weaknesses. Thus, it is important to know when each is *not* appropriate. Soft thinking in the practical phase can prevent the execution of an idea; here firmness and directness are preferable to ambiguity and dreams. Conversely, hard thinking in the imaginative phase can limit the creative process. Logic and analysis are important tools, but an over-reliance on them—especially early in the creative process—can prematurely narrow your thinking.

THAT'S NOT LOGICAL

The first and supreme principle of traditional logic is the law of non-contradiction. Logic can comprehend only those things that have a consistent and non-contradictory nature. This is fine except that most of life is ambiguous: inconsistency and contradiction are the hallmarks of human existence. As a result, the number of things that can be thought about in a logical manner is small, and an overemphasis on the logical method can inhibit your thinking.

Some people, however, have little use for soft thinking. Their feeling toward it is "that's not logical." When faced with a problem, they immediately bring in their hard thinking strategies. They say, "Let's get down to brass tacks." They never give themselves an opportunity to consider steel tacks, copper tacks, plastic tacks, sailing tacks, income tax, syntax, or contacts. If you use a little soft thinking early in the creative process, you may still end up going with the "brass tacks," but at least you will have considered alternatives.

Our educational system does a fairly good job of developing hard thinking skills, but there is not much to develop soft thinking. As a matter of fact, much of our education is geared toward eliminating soft thinking, or at best, teaching us to regard it as an inferior tool. Human intelligence is a complicated phenomenon, and yet many of our formal notions of intelligence are based on logic and analysis. Musical ability, decorating, painting, and cooking seem to have no place in many test-makers' conception of intelligence. As creativity educator Edward de Bono points out, if someone says he has learned to think, most of us assume that he means he has learned to think logically.

There is another reason for the "that's not logical" mental lock. As an historian of ideas, I've noticed that the models people use to understand mental processes reflect the technology of their time. For example, in the 17th century, people thought about the mind as though it were a mirror or a lens, and this "reflects" the advances made then in the fields of optics and lens-making. The Freudian model of mind, developed in the late 19th and early 20th centuries, seems based on the ubiquity of the steam engine locomotive. Ideas billow up from the subconscious to the conscious in the same way steam moves from boiler to compression chamber. In the early twentieth century, the mind was viewed by some as a vast telephone switching network with circuits and relays running through the brain.

For the past thirty years, we've had a new model of mind: the computer. This model does a good job of describing certain aspects of our thinking. For example, we have "input" and "output" and "information processing." There is also "feedback," "programming," and "storage."

This is fine as far as it goes, but some people take this model literally and think that the mind really *is* a computer. Indeed, they may not only dismiss the soft types of thinking for not being "logical," but even treat other people like machines. How many times have you heard someone say, "I interface with that person," or "I'm operating in panic mode," or "I need to make an information dump on you"? The best one I heard was from a person describing the different parts of a computer system: "There is hardware, software, firmware, and liveware." Liveware is the people-element of the system.

I believe that the mind is not only a computer that processes information, it's also a museum that stores experiences, a device that encodes holograms, a playground in which to play, a muscle to be strengthened, a workshop in which to construct thoughts, a debating opponent to be won over, a cat to be stroked, a funhouse to be explored, a compost pile to be turned, and forty-three others. There are a lot of right ways to model the mind all depending on what you think is important. One of the saddest consequences of the "that's not logical" mental lock is that its prisoner may not pay attention to one of the mind's softest and most valuable creations: the intuitive hunch. Your mind is constantly recording, connecting, and storing unrelated knowledge, experiences, and feelings. Later, it combines this disparate information into answers—hunches—to the problems you're facing, if you simply ask, trust, and listen. These hunches, for no apparent logical reason, might lead you to trying a different problem-solving approach, going out on a blind date, betting on the underdog in a sporting event, taking a spontaneous vacation, or ignoring a trusted friend's financial advice.

Exercise: What hunches have you had recently? Which ones did you listen to? How did things work out? What decision are you currently facing? What does your gut tell you to do?

MAKING THE STRANGE FAMILIAR

To combat the dangers of creative rigor mortis due to excessive hard thinking, I would like to introduce one of my favorite soft thinking tools. I'll introduce it with an exercise. As you do this exercise, think of yourself as a poet. This is a high compliment: our word poet comes from the classical

Greek word *poietes* which meant not only "poet" but also "creator."

Exercise: What do the following have in common?

A financial watchdog
An operational bottleneck
A communications network
The flow of time
The food chain
A leap of thought
Frame of reference
Moral bankruptcy

The metaphor is probably the most fertile power possessed by man.—Ortega y Gasset, Philosopher

In addition to everything else, they are all metaphors. They all connect two different universes of meaning through some similarity they share. In doing so, metaphors help us to understand one idea by means of another. For example, we understand the nature of a particular financial function by comparing it to a watchdog (they both protect), the passing of time to a river (flow), and the feeding interrelationship of the animal world to a chain (links).

The key to metaphorical thinking is similarity. In fact, this is how our thinking grows: we understand the unfamiliar by means of the similarities it has with what is familiar to us. For example, what were the first automobiles called? That's right, "horseless carriages." And the first locomotives were called "iron horses." We refer to resemblances between things all of the time. We say that hammers have "heads," tables have "legs," roads have "shoulders," cities have "hearts," and beds have "feet." It's all very soft, but it *is* how we think.

How about a metaphor for metaphors? Sure. Let's suppose that you fly to Salt Lake City, and that you've never been there before. You get off the airplane and rent a car. What's the first thing you should do? Probably get a map of the city to see how it's laid out, to find out where the freeways are, and to see where the sites are located. The map itself is not Salt Lake City, but it does give you a basic idea of the structure of the city. So, a metaphor is a mental map.

Metaphors are quite useful in helping you get a different slant on a problem. For example, in the early part of the twentieth century, Danish physicist Niels Bohr developed a new model of the atom by comparing it to the solar system. Within this framework, he figured that the sun represented the nucleus and the planets represented the electrons.

Another example: several years ago I had a client whose sales were flat even though there was a boom in the marketplace for the products they offered. We decided to make a metaphor for their company. We decided that their company was like a full service restaurant. Its menu (product line) was large, but there were many restrictions on what could be purchased—for example, a customer couldn't order chili with veal. Since the individual chefs (division managers) decided what was on the menu, there was no consistency in their offerings. This led to their having specialized waiters (salespeople). A typical result? A customer couldn't buy pasta from a steak waiter. We developed this metaphor further, but it quickly became clear to us that the large, restricted product line confused their customers, and was the main source of their flat sales.

Metaphors are also effective in making complex ideas easier to understand. Indeed, they can be good tools to explain ideas to people outside your specialty. Some examples:

Dolby Stereo. In the past decade the words "Dolby Stereo" have become familiar to music listeners and movie goers. I'm not an engineer, so I don't understand all of the bits and bytes of the Dolby process, but I once heard an engineer make the following metaphor for Dolby: "Dolby stereo is like a sonic laundry. It washes the dirt (or noise) out of the clothes (the signal) without disturbing the clothes (the signal)." I've asked other engineers about this, and they agree that Dolby is a "cleansing" process.

Personal Computers. Computer pioneer Steve Jobs once compared the personal computer to a bicycle in the following analogy:

> A few years ago, I read about the efficiency of locomotion for various species on the earth, including man. The study determined which species was the most efficient, in terms of getting from point A to point B with the least amount of energy exerted. The condor won. Man made a rather unimpressive showing about a third of the way down the list.
>
> But someone there had the insight to test a man riding a bicycle. Man was twice as efficient as the condor! This illustrated man's ability as a tool maker. When he created the bicycle, he created a tool that amplified an inherent ability. That's why I like to compare the personal computer to the bicycle. The personal computer is a 21st century bicycle if you will, because it's a tool that can amplify a certain part of our inherent intelligence....

In a strict logical sense, a personal computer is *not* a bicycle, and Dolby is *not* a laundry. But by using such analogies, we enable ourselves to gain a new perspective on both the unfamiliar and the quite familiar.

Exercise: Make a metaphor for a problem you're currently dealing with or a concept you're developing. To do it, simply compare your concept to something else and then see what similarities you can find between the two ideas. Basically, you're using one idea to highlight another. See how far you can extend the comparison.

I've found that some of the most fertile (and easiest to develop) metaphors are those in which there is some action taking place. You might try comparing your concept to several or more of these:

Running for political office	Going on a diet
Disciplining a ten year old	Performing a magic trick

Cooking a fancy meal	Colonizing a territory
Running a marathon	Building a house
Starting a revolution	Spreading propaganda
Riding a roller coaster	Negotiating a contract
Prospecting for gold	Going fishing
Courting a woman	Planting a garden
Putting out a fire	Having a baby
Fighting a disease	Getting a divorce
Running a day care center	Arranging flowers
Sailing a ship in rough seas	Pruning a tree
Doing standup comedy	Conducting an orchestra
Attending a church service	Learning a new language

How is developing a new math curriculum like producing a television program? How is motivating a sales force like feeding the animals at a zoo? How is developing a marketing plan for a new baby product like camping in a wilderness area?

Our language is quite metaphorical, so much so that we don't realize it. There are clusters of metaphors that reflect what we think about various activities. One example is the metaphor used by some teachers who view their work as though they were horticulturalists. They talk about their students' basic ability to learn as the "seed" and their role is to provide the right "soil" and "sunlight" for their "growth." A student who is curious is spreading out his "roots." Some students are "potbound," while others "flower" and reach "fruition." Some students need a "hothouse" to develop, while others could prosper in a "desert."

Another example is the "Game of Life" metaphor in which business people use sports terminology to describe what they do. Everyone is trying to be "#1"; there are "management teams," "kickoff" meetings, and salespeople with "proven track records." You may "spar" with your manager, deal with "heavyweights" and "lightweights," and give a "knockout" performance.

THE MEANING OF LIFE

As you may have guessed by now, metaphors are one of my passions, and so I hope you'll excuse me for one more metaphorical indulgence.

One question I have is, "What is the meaning of life?" To find the answer, I have asked my seminar participants to make a metaphor for life. Their ideas can be put into two groups: those that deal with food, and those that don't. Here is the meaning of life:

> Life is like a bagel. It's delicious when it's fresh and warm, but often it's just hard. The hole in the middle is its great mystery, and yet it wouldn't be a bagel without it.

> Life is like eating grapefruit. First you have to break through the skin; then it takes a couple of bites to get used to the taste, and just as you begin to enjoy it, it squirts you in the eye.

> Life is like a banana. You start out green and get soft and mushy with age. Some people want to be one of the bunch while others want to be top banana. You have to take care not to slip on externals. And, finally, you have to strip off the outer coating to get at the meat.

> Life is like cooking. It all depends on what you add and how you mix it. Sometimes you follow the recipe and at other times, you're creative.

> Life is like a jigsaw puzzle, but you don't have the picture on the front of the box to know what it's supposed to look like. Sometimes, you're not even sure if you have all the pieces.

> Life is like a maze in which you try to avoid the exit.

> Life is like riding an elevator. It has lots of ups and downs and someone is always pushing your buttons. Sometimes you get the shaft, but what really bothers you are the jerks.

> Life is like a poker game. You deal or are dealt to. It includes skill and luck. You bet, check, bluff, and raise.

You learn from those you play with. Sometimes, you win with a pair or lose with a full house. But whatever happens, it's best to keep on shuffling along.

Life is like a puppy dog always searching for a street full of fire hydrants.

Life is like a room full of open doors that close as you get older.

WHAT DO YOU THINK LIFE IS LIKE?

POET SONIA SANCHEZ
Telling What We Must Hear

Juanita Johnson-Bailey

INTRODUCTION

With the unblinking and critical poet's eye, Sonia Sanchez has been setting her readers straight, telling the "terrible beauty," and reflecting images in ways that simultaneously solicit tears and laughter. For over thirty years this revolutionary poet has been undeterred from a path that began in the sixties when Black militancy was the vogue. Still, she has not given up the struggle to let her poetry be what she refers to as a "call to arms" for her people. But her people have not always responded with reciprocal dignity and purity of heart. So her way has at times been solitary, weary, joyful, and painful.

She has won numerous awards, including the prestigious PEN Writing Award, a National Endowment for the Arts fellowship, the Lucretia Mott Award, an American Book Award, and an honorary doctorate in fine arts. Her latest book, Wounded in the House of a Friend *(1996), follows a long, consistent line of such outstanding works as* Under a Soprano Sky *(1987),* Homegirls and Handgrenades *(1984),* A Blues Book for Blue Black Magical Women *(1978),* We a BaddDDD People *(1970), and*

Homecoming (1969). Her work also includes plays, children's books, short stories, and essays.

In this conversation she moves between discussing her poems and artistry with a ready laugh and a fast staccato speech. Her words are audible in personal moments of active resistance, her mettle is evident in the stance of contemporary courageous Black women writers, and her truth ever echoes in her work—always militant, always radical, always challenging.

THE POETIC BEGINNINGS

I really think my first exposure to poetry was from my grandmother, who spoke in what we call Black dialect. My earliest remembrance is when I was around fourish. She would say things in a certain way, and I would repeat it. And she'd look up at me. I would kind of do it again, smile, go off in a corner someplace, and go on saying it. Some people felt that I was mocking her. I was not. It was just that something in my ear told me it was a brilliant way of saying it. So I would repeat it. Grandmother knew books were important to me, and naturally we had a lot. I would always pick up a book, open it, and try to figure out what was being said. Either my grandmother or cousin Louise taught me how to read at four.

What I remember most is the love and respect my grandmother had for me. She knew that I was different. I already had figured out that I was odd; children figure that out at an early age. She said, "Just let the girl be. She be all right. She gonna stumble on her gentleness one of these days." Grandmother passed on the whole idea that I could do what I wanted to do. Women like her kept hopes and dreams alive in us. Once when I jumped out of a second-story window all she said to me is, "You okay?" And I said, "Yes." And she said, "Well, go on and play." She didn't grab me, even though I did have some bruises. She would shoo me out to do this world. And that's what I've been trying to do—this world.

My mother died giving birth to twins when I was one year old, and my grandmother died when I was six. The response to my grandmother's death made me tongue-tied, and after that I stuttered. This meant that people left me alone. So I started writing little things that everyone said were poems because they rhymed. I wrote because I stuttered and no one ever wanted to take the time to listen. I used to pass little notes; it was the way that I spoke.

One of the first little poems I did was to Walter, who was a terrible little boy, but I liked him and he liked me. I also wrote a poem about George Washington crossing the Delaware, which my sister found and read to the family. Everybody fell out laughing. After this I began keeping journals, which I couldn't hide in the bedroom that I shared with my sister. There is no privacy with a sister. Since it was my job to clean the bathroom every Saturday, it was no problem hiding my journals there. I stuck everything I was reading and writing underneath the tub, the kind with the raised legs. I would be sitting in there at three o'clock in the morning, writing.

I believe that I was born a poet. A lot of people are poetic but never really learn or nurture the craft. Therefore they'll write a poem once or twice a year. A college poetry teacher, Louise Bogan, told me two important things. First, she told me that a lot of people have talent, but they do nothing with it. The other thing she said is that you have to write on cue because if you wait for this muse to drop down on your shoulders, it might drop once a year. Therefore she made us write a poem a week. That's when I first got disciplined.

I ran across certain people growing up in New York City who helped me along the way. One of these people was Jean Blackwell Hutson, the curator at the Schomburg Library. I had finished school and needed a job. I read the ads in *The New York Times* for writers and sent samples. I got a telegram—that's what they used to do, send telegrams—that said, "You are hired." I jumped up and down and celebrated with some of my friends. Then I went to work. I had on my blue suit, my blue pumps, my blue bag, my white gloves, and my blue hat to let them [Whites] know that I knew how to go to work. In my purse I had money to eat lunch, money to get back home, and the telegram. They said report at nine o'clock. I got down there at eight-thirty. I handed the telegram to the woman secretary—and she said, in a soft voice, "All right, okay, have a seat." So I sat down with a magazine, and someone came and peeped around the corner, looked at me, and went back. Then another face came. Finally a man came and said, "We're sorry, but the job is taken." And I said, "I have a job here." And he said, "Well, the job is taken," like "Well, what's your damn problem?" I said, "But no one else has come in here except me. How could…?" I was amazed. It was just that fast. The secretary was sitting there with her eyes downcast. And I said to his retreating back, "I am going to report you to the Urban League!"

I left so angry that I got on the train and, instead of getting off where I was supposed to, I ended up at 135th Street and Lenox Avenue. And all of a sudden here's this place. I am hot. I am sweaty. It said "Library" and I said, "Let me go in, pick up some books, and read." A guard outside made me sign in. I asked, "What kind of library is this?" and he said, "The Schomburg." And I said, "The Schomburg. What's the Schomburg? Is it special?" He said, "Well, why don't you ask the lady inside." Inside to the right was this glass area where Jean Hutson, the curator at the time, sat. I went over, gestured to her, and she came out. I asked, "What kind of library is this?" And she said, "This library contains all books by and about Black folks." And I said in my sharp, acerbic fashion, "Must not be many books in here, then."

She told me to sit down and she'd bring me some books. As I inched myself into a long table with all men sitting around it, they looked up at me. I was the only female there. She brought me *Their Eyes Were Watching God, Souls of Black Folks,* and *Up from Slavery.* I picked *Their Eyes Were Watching God* and started reading. Softly I said, "Oh, my God. Oh, my God. Look at this." The language was so beautiful. I read maybe a third of it. I went to Ms. Hutson and said, "This is a beautiful book." She said, "Yes, dear. Go read now." When I finished the book I stood up again and said, "Oooh, what a beautiful book." One of the men said, "Miss Hutson, will you please tell this young woman to stay still or leave." For an entire week I hung out at the Schomburg when I was supposed to be looking for a job. And Ms. Hutson fed me books. She asked, "Is there anything you like to read?" When I said gently, "Poetry," she sent me all the poets she knew. On the last day I said to her, "I have to go and look for a job. But one day my books will be in here." Years later, when I was a professor at Amherst College and I brought classes to the Schomburg, she would tell that story much more beautifully than I do, with a very funny smile on her face.

THE SISTER CIRCLE

I used to have trouble sometimes when I read my poetry. I took a lot of abuse. The first time I read in New York City, people just sat and looked at me. Some people booed 'cause I said, "I'm a Black woman poet." I'll never forget it. I wrote poems that were obviously womanist before we even started talking about it. Men would get up and go on about their business because they said I was reading only for women. So one day I said out loud, "My poetry is just as important as your poetry." It was at a huge conference. And I was not invited back to a major conference for three years.

In my head my audience has always been Black folks, Black women. I am not a revisionist. I don't say that I have always understood sisterhood. Most women are socialized not to believe a whole lot of loving things about women. My generation began to forge a new way of looking at the world. We began to say to each other, "I don't take your husband. You don't take my husband." We began to work in women's groups. So now I greet all women as sister. Some Black women get upset about that because they say, "White women are not your sisters." And I'll say, "Yeah, and a lot of Black women are not my sisters, either." The point is to understand that until we organize women in this country the way we should be organized, we are in a lot of trouble.

The premise that we are sisters brought me full circle, back to the church where my grandmother and the women called each other sister. My grandmother was the head deaconess in the church. So on Saturdays her sisters came to do the cooking and the talking. I would come in and slide behind the couch that sat away from the wall so they would not put me to work. The women would be in there snapping beans, peeling potatoes, and fixing up the ham. In the midst of their work they would start talking about people—about somebody beating up somebody. And they would say, "Well, we don't let that happen." I knew Mama (my grandmother) wanted me to hear this because I would snicker and she would shoot her eyes behind the couch. Her eyes said "If you want to hear this, you keep quiet."

I used to hear her say, "Well, that ain't right of Sister Smith to do that." And someone would say, "You know, she really ain't nice." Although they called her sister, they knew some of those sisters weren't sisters. So I'm not inventing anything new. I'm just picking up on the ideology of my grandmother that says simply "Yes, I will call you sister, but you gotta make yourself sister."

The things we heard in the conversations among the women taught us something. I learned to curse by listening to Miss Dixon, a friend of my stepmother. When Miss Dixon came to our house, my father would leave. He couldn't stand her because she drank and cursed. But I loved when Miss Dixon came. I knew I would learn another curse word. She would come in loudly and say, "Sonia, bring me some beer." I would open the beer, taste the foam, bring it to her, and listen to her tell stories.

Miss Dixon was a huge woman, a big woman, who had been in show business. And she was the one who taught me how to watch people. She would say, "Girl, you cannot get along on this earth without knowing who people are. You gotta listen to people. Hear what's coming out of their mouths and hear what's coming out of their bodies, and know what odors they have."

The first poem that I wrote to Miss (Mama) Dixon was in *Under a Soprano Sky*. It was about being downtown at City Hall when this man pulled his car up on the sidewalk and pulled his penis out and said, "Do you want some of this?" I'd been talking to African women from all over the world, and this man could only see me as a whore on Market Street. I called on my old friend Miss Dixon, and she said, "What you gonna say to this man? You better tell him what needs to be said, Sonia." And I did. Afterward I wrote the poem "style no. 1," which mentions her by name.

When I finished cutting him up with my mouth he turned red and drove off real fast. I laughed out loud on Market Street. And Miss Dixon said, "I bet you he will think twice about coming up to somebody else."

EXTENDING THE CIRCLE

Teaching a course on the Black woman taught me what it was to say "sister" to people. It was a very hard time for me; I had separated from my husband, Ethridge Knight, a poet, who was on drugs. The female students were driving me insane, always coming in for conferences. They needed help being Black women on a White campus. Jokingly I said, "We need a course called 'The Black Woman.'" And they said, "Teach it!" So I designed this course. But I had not put into that syllabus what happened after we were in there maybe the third or fourth week. This young woman stood up and said, "I hate all Black men." And she started to talk about incest. I hugged her, and we all collectively caught our tears. I instinctively began to talk to her and that weekend read every damn thing I could find on incest. And it became part of what we talked about forever.

I tried to write to those young sisters about what it was to love themselves. I wrote *We a BaddDDD People* that year. Ethridge tore up the finished manuscript for this book because he was not writing. When I found myself on the floor, trying to piece together this book, I knew it was time to leave. At that moment I understood why those sisters gathered in my grandmother's house every Saturday. Ostensibly it was to cook the meals to sell on Sunday to raise money for the church. But it was really where they passed on information to each other, where they helped each other, and where they passed on information to some little terrible kid sitting behind the couch. They were telling me how you don't let someone hit you twice.

One night I got a frantic call that a former student was climbing the walls. Some of the sisters and I went to her house. She had taken something because this man that she had married had come home and she smelled his former lovemaking as she was making love to him. She flipped. We pumped her full of coffee and walked her back to sanity. It was for her I wrote,

> *he poured me on*
> *the bed and slid*
> *into me like glass.*
> *and there was*
> *the sound of splinters.*

You can't put splinters back together, but that's what we did as sisters. Sisterhood is very important. That hood is a covering. Sisters make everything possible on this earth.

CALLING UP THE ANCESTORS

Because of women like Miss Dixon and Mama (my grandmother) I've always been in touch with our female ancestors. In that sense my work is spiritual. And most of the work has a history to it. I am always researching and then creating from that research. I carry the mamas, I carry the sisters, the women who were on the block being sold. I carry those first Africans who came to this country and must have screamed out at the gods.

But in spite of our oppression we have maintained our humanity. We might be in danger of losing it with this younger generation, so our work is very important. We must work hard to make them understand the history/herstory that we have in the world—the humanity and the love that we have. I say to young people, I did not fight all these years to pull these sisters out of history, to put African women back on the world stage, to write about them and teach about them to have you get on stage and act like a fool or to become sex objects on MTV. It is a constant fight at the university and all over the earth to bring African women on center stage again, out of people's homes where they have relegated us—always somebody's mammy—public or private.

When I started to read literature I realized we'd been taken off the world stage. I say to young people, I didn't write "Improvisation," which is about the middle passage and those sisters screaming when they are being sold on these American planks, for you to get on MTV in a state of undress, rub your crotch, or make believe you are making love to the microphone. When you know your history, it means you don't allow someone to come up and record your derriere while you shake it back and forth. You don't go across the floor, lapping up toward a man.

It hurt me to see a woman on television announce that a young Black woman had performed a sexual act in the middle of a dance floor and that later the guy turned her over to his posse. I wrote a poem based on this incident and read it at the Bronx Community College to young African American and Latino women. They were returning students, and many of them had a child or two. I pulled out the proofs of *Wounded in the House of a Friend* and read the poem "Like." It begins:

Like

All i did was
go down on him
in the middle of
the dance floor
cuz he is a movie
star he is a blk/
man "live" rt off
the screen fulfilling
my wildest dreams.

They said, "That's just like Tenisha." Then somebody said, "Yeah." And someone said, "Ms. Sanchez, that's not right, is it?" And I said, "Sister, that has nothing to do with right. She went down on the young brother because she was ahistorical. When you have history, you don't ever embarrass yourself or your people on the planet Earth." I told them how at the turn of the century Black women started clubs because White women would not let them into their clubs. We were called whores and prostitutes because of our enslavement. We couldn't help it. It wasn't prostitution. They raped us. These Black women went to newspapers and said, "We're not whores, we're not prostitutes, we are church women, we are good women. You cannot denigrate us in the newspapers the way you have done." And now, I said, "You willingly denigrate yourself on TV." They cried and they said no one had ever told them that before.

MEMORIES THAT HEAL AND PRESERVE

One of the things I'm trying to pull on is our residual memory as women. Somebody has said something somewhere along the way to help us. We have just blocked it out. Education has blocked it out. You forget that you see. What I try to do with these young girls is to tell things we were told when they straightened our hair in the kitchen on Saturday nights.

We are in danger, great danger, of losing the memory that connects us, that keeps us alive. The thing that has sustained us as African people was that we had memories. The woman on the dance floor should have known what she was saying very distinctly, that "we [Black women] are immoral, promiscuous, and unreliable." But she was ahistorical.

Once, when I read that poem, a very middle-class woman said, "You know, I love your poetry, but you really shouldn't read a poem like that out loud. White people think we are all like that." And I said, "Yes, I should. They know we don't all take crack. But these incidents are reported in the news."

I took another idea from the newspaper—about a sister leaving her child at a crack house. I put it up on the bulletin board in my bedroom. Every morning I read it and cried. Later I wrote, "Memories. What happens with memories? Crack kills memories." And the second thing I wrote was, "Child. This will silence the child." Then I wrote, "Will silence the people also. That's why crack is here, to silence the people and to silence our memories."

Crack wounds. And that's what I said in *Wounded in the House of a Friend*. The title of that book is from Zachariah, and the whole section is about prophecy. "And what of these wounds, naked in our back?...For we have been wounded in the house of our friends." That's not just a personal house that we are wounded in. It is the house of America that has allowed this to happen. But as Africans we are also wounded in our private houses, our bodies. When you bring crack into Black neighborhoods, it makes you forget all memories of yourself. So in "Poem for Some Women," about the young woman selling her daughter for crack, she couldn't even remember her daughter's name or what she looked like. Crack will kill memories so you *can* sell a daughter, give her up as a virgin. People dealing crack might not take it, but they also lose their memories and their history.

The first line of "Poem for Some Women" is "Huh?" And I started off on that level because it had to be a question mark. There was nothing that was final there. The woman's voice had to be first. It was not going to be my voice.

In telling, I try to give Black people strength, power, and a sense of themselves—who they are—who they must be—and what they must do during the short period they're on this earth. I try to make my people laugh, at the same time to teach and inform, to make us know and feel our beauty.

And another goal of my writing has been to reconcile us with ourselves and to reclaim our history/herstory. We must understand that before we can move on. Although we think we do it without them, some ancestor is pushing us. The title *Wounded in the House of a Friend* came at three o'clock in the morning while I was asleep. I woke up and wrote down the title. You see, our ancestors will wake us up in the middle of the night if we are not on time.

Poetry has kept me connected to this long line of African people who stayed alive just to tell their stories. I understand why I keep doing this work. It is part of a long tradition. It is what I am supposed to do. Writing poetry has kept me alive. It kept me breathing. It kept me human. It kept me a woman. It kept me from killing people. It kept me from killing myself.

DISCUSSION QUESTIONS
AND WRITING ASSIGNMENTS

On the Readings by von Oech and Juanita Johnson-Bailey/Sonia Sanchez

1. The reading by von Oech contains its own exercises to practice creativity. If you skipped any of these, go back and try them now.

2. Von Oech shares several metaphors for the human mind (playground, muscle, etc.) and says that he could name forty-three others. Accept his challenge: individually or in a small group, see if you can come up with forty-three metaphors for the mind. Which are your favorites, and why?

3. What advice from von Oech do you think might prove most valuable to writers, and why? In what specific ways can you put this advice to work for you?

4. Von Oech says that the American educational system does a poor job of developing "soft thinking" skills. In a discussion, journal entry, or short paper, assess how well or how poorly your education has developed your ability to "think softly."

5. What were the key elements or influences in Sonia Sanchez's development as a poet? What aspects of her experience might speak to nonpoets as well—for example, to individual students, to schools, to teachers, or to families? What could nonpoets learn from her struggles and from her responses to challenges?

6. Find and read several poems by Sanchez. In what specific ways do they show the concern with race and gender that permeates her interview? If you were a poet or other kind of artist (sculptor, choreographer, composer, painter, playwright, etc.), what themes, ideas, and places would be most critical to you?

7. Read the explanation of "Signifyin(g)" in the Selected Tropes section of Chapter 3. What examples of Signifyin(g) can you find in the stories Sanchez tells in her interview?

On Chapter 2

8. Write a journal entry or short paper in response to one or two of the quotations included in this chapter. Possible approaches include the following:

- Explain the meaning of the quotation.
- Use the quotation as a starting point for your own reflections or experience relating to the topic.
- Amplify on the quotation: develop it, provide examples.
- Explain why you agree or disagree with the quotation.
- Compare and contrast two or more quotations.

9. If you write with a computer, try doing a journal entry with the screen dimmed, off, or hidden. If you write with pen and paper, try writing for ten minutes without stopping even for a moment.

10. Review the list of questions on pages 64 to 66, questions based on the classical topoi and designed to help you generate ideas to write about. Practice using these questions to generate ideas (not necessarily *facts*) about some of the following:

Puritanism	"fine print"
the Great Wall of China	monarchy
harmony	photosynthesis
the men's movement	Passover
Pop-Up Video	fairy tales
creationism	the Cold War
sleep deprivation	machine translation

11. Below is a list of ideas, circumstances, well-known people, and so on. Beginning with the items that are most familiar to you, try seeing a few of them from a Burkean point of view, that is, as elements in a human drama. How might the terms *scene, act, agent, agency,* and *purpose* help you think about them creatively? For example, with the first item, "the world's cathedrals, mosques, temples, synagogues, churches, etc.," you might consider these buildings as the *scene* of worship. These religious settings are as carefully designed as any movie set—moreso, in fact—and you could see important differences in religions reflected in their approaches to architecture (a grand European cathedral, for example, versus a plain Quaker hall). The pentad might spark interesting questions about *agency,* too: praying is an *act,* but does it have *agency*? Does it accomplish something, internally, externally, or both? How?

     It's better to think carefully about two or three of the ideas below than superficially about lots of them; push yourself toward complex ideas. Explain your ideas to classmates, jot them down in a journal entry, or work them up into an essay.

the world's cathedrals, mosques, temples, synagogues, churches, etc.	cameras in courtrooms
	Dennis Rodman
	Madonna
a psychoanalyst's couch	the Holy Land
the State of the Union address	oil
the AIDS quilt	bull fights
your favorite Website	high heels
the United Nations	national parks
the vice president of the United States	the Batmobile
	the Vietnam Memorial
Michelangelo's *David*	the college library
the headline story in today's newspaper	Thanksgiving

REFERENCES

Bizzell, Patricia and Bruce Herzberg. *The Rhetorical Tradition: Readings from Classical Times to the Present.* Boston: St. Martin's Press, 1990.

Burke, Kenneth. *A Grammar of Motives.* Berkeley: University of California Press, 1969. (Originally published in 1945.)

Guterson, David. "Wood Grouse on a High Promontory Overlooking Canada." In Guterson, *The Country Ahead of Us, the Country Behind.* New York: Random House, 1989.

3

Bedrock Strategies: Imitation, Writing, and Revision

A professional writer is an amateur who didn't quit.
—RICHARD BACH

Chapter 3 begins with a discussion of imitation as a way of learning to write, an essential strategy that all writers use unconsciously and intuitively, but one that can also be usefully studied. Next, the chapter offers guided practice in different types of imitation. It then addresses the final two stages of a bare-bones writing process, writing and revising, emphasizing practical advice for college writers. The readings for this chapter illustrate two very different styles. The first, a speech by the Reverend Jesse Jackson, is constructed for oral delivery to a large group on a momentous occasion. The second, a wonderful essay by Jamaica Kincaid, shares a concern with history but is much more private and personal. The readings are followed by discussion questions and writing assignments.

☒ **FEATURED PAPER TOPICS**

The first recommended topic lets you practice academic analytical skills with a multicultural emphasis. Write a short essay analyzing one or two magazine ads that you find particularly interesting in terms of some cultural issue such as gender, ethnicity, social class, generational differences, or physical challenge. Explain the strategies the ad uses to sell its product or service *and* discuss the ad's portrayal of gender, ethnicity, or other cultural issue. Examine both words and visual image(s) in the ad, and be sure to look for subtle messages or assumptions—things the advertisers might not expect you to scrutinize so closely.

If you choose two ads, make sure they are somehow related; for example, you might work with two ads for similar products but for different magazine audiences—for instance, male versus female readers or mainstream versus minority readers. Tips for organizing comparison/contrast papers appear on pages 83 to 85.

The second recommended assignment lets you practice revision. *With your instructor's permission,* thoroughly rewrite a paper you completed at least three months ago. This exercise can be extremely instructive, but only under certain conditions. Most important, you must have a previously written paper that's good enough or promising enough to merit a rewrite but that you can nevertheless improve dramatically. (This is not about cleaning up a few grammatical errors or typos!) If you have a promising but flawed paper, treat it now as a draft: amplify or develop ideas; expand or reorganize if appropriate; energize the style with stronger vocabulary and more varied syntax; edit meticulously. Hand in the old and new versions together, along with a note discussing the rationale for your most important revisions.

IMITATION

Imitation is how people learn. This is as true for writing as for any other human endeavor, and the history of writing instruction has consisted largely of devising myriad ways to entice (or force) students to imitate the masters. At times, such assignments have been extremely rigorous, demanding and tedious—for example, the rote memorization of long passages. The suggestions below, while challenging, come from the fun end of the spectrum.

Please keep in mind that imitation is not just for those of us who are not bright enough to be creative. *Au contraire!* By its very nature, writing will always require creativity: when writing, you can never attempt the absolute duplication that you might strive for in imitating a tennis pro's backhand volley, or a math teacher's bulletproof method for solving single equations with one unknown, or Herb Caen's perfect martini ("You pour the gin, I'll imagine the vermouth"). The closest you can get to exact duplication, I suppose, is to try what essayist Joan Didion says she has done to get her engine started: simply type pages of Hemingway verbatim. This sounds stunningly boring, but having typed my own dissertation and most of my wife's—to say nothing of hundreds of handouts for students— I can vouch that something very beneficial happens when you slow down your reading to the speed of your typing. You appreciate the complexity of the sentences, feel the weight of individual word choices, are surprised anew by a phrase such as F. Scott Fitzgerald's "yellow cocktail music." Copying longhand would probably be even better if you can stand it.

Imitation is the sincerest flattery.—Colton

The next-closest form of imitation I know is one devised by a student of mine, whom I misled into writing a fabulous essay. Her story speaks to the power of imitation but should serve at the same time as a warning against going over the edge with the advice later in this chapter. "Anisette" was a very intelligent, enthusiastic, and hard-working student in one of my advanced writing courses. It's probably worth mentioning that she had been educated primarily in France and that English was her second language. At my request, students had been imitating selected sentences and paragraphs by famous writers, as you will be encouraged to do below. We had also been talking about how students could use metaphor and alliteration and long sentences and dashes and so on just like professionals do.

Anisette put all of this together and drafted a personal essay that was a very, very close imitation of "Once More to the Lake," E. B. White's widely anthologized account of taking his son to a special spot that had been important to White's own childhood. Anisette did not copy a single word from White, but she took everything from him nonetheless. Her essay, too, concerned returning to a special location; it was France, not New England, and she went back with a husband, not a son, but Anisette had closely studied the types of observations White shared in his essay, and she made similar remarks about what had changed and what had not. She also imitated the way White constructed individual paragraphs, the way he balanced abstract speculations about time and family with vivid, concrete details. As White was by turns philosophical and comic, so was Anisette. Finally, in some instances, Anisette carried over a sentence-imitation exercise into her essay writing and created sentences that mirrored White's; the words were completely different, but the structure was quite similar.

Most writing instructors would agree that Anisette's method was unacceptable for college writing. It's hard to call what she did plagiarism, because she transformed things so radically as she appropriated them for her own use, but it wasn't exactly original composition either. Thanks to inadequate explanations from me, she had turned an *essay* into an imitation *exercise.* As you do the exercises later in the chapter, keep that distinction in mind.

Don't replicate Anisette's experiment, but notice two important points about it. First, if I hadn't immediately recognized her debt to "Once More to the Lake," I would have judged Anisette's essay as phenomenally successful. It was thoughtful, detailed, fresh, well organised—everything one could ask of a student and more. In that sense the imitation worked perfectly.

> *When you steal from one author, it's plagiarism; if you steal from many, it's research.*—Wilson Mizner

Second, it may be that the only difference between Anisette's excessive imitation and perfectly legitimate imitation is that she imitated a single source. Imagine that instead of imitating the subject matter, organization, and language of just one author, Anisette had begun with a dilemma from a Shakespearean tragedy, taken a radical feminist approach from bell hooks, relied on an organizational scheme worked out with her tutor, aimed for Oscar Wilde's honest self-revelation, and seasoned it all with a dollop of a second language in imitation of Gloria Anzaldúa. This would not just *disguise* the near-plagiarism but begin to erase it. And if Anisette owed tiny, tiny debts to thousands of authors instead of a big debt to one author, the near-plagiarism would not just be well hidden—it would vanish.

To a great extent, your writing will imitate—usually unconsciously—the speech of your friends and family as well as the reading you have done throughout your life. (If you have any doubt about this, read anything written a century or more ago, such as the passages by Stowe and Douglass on pages 191 to 194; this language may speak to you, but it will be distanced from your own dialect in a hundred ways because your own language is a product of your time and place.) Your writing will improve as you extend the range of your reading and listening, as you increase your awareness of how other writers work, and as you self-consciously imitate what appeals to you.

Imitation in a Multicultural Context

You could do worse than to imitate E. B. White—he was a marvelous essayist—but the world of American language, literature, and composition has expanded immensely in the half century since his prime. Today's acclaimed authors, like today's college students, are much more diverse than those of 1950—in ethnicity, gender, and politics and in the subject matter they write about. As you'll see in more detail in Part Two of this book, people have invented new ways of writing, not only by tackling subjects that were formerly taboo, but also by reimagining the forms or genres of writing, the range of acceptable styles, and the relationship of author to reader.

This wealth of innovation—as well as the demands of once-marginalized groups to be heard—means your choices of who and what to imitate are broader than ever before. Imitation need not be the deeply conservative strategy it was throughout previous centuries of writing instruction: rather than teaching the one acceptable way to write, imitation today means sampling an incredibly broad array of writing strategies and choosing the ones that work for you. Women and minority students, for example, don't have to imitate white male writers if they don't want to, and they don't have to feel like they are the first to try writing from their particular point of view.

The examples and exercises in this book hint at the diversity of contemporary writing, but can only hint at it. In your college work and your pleasure reading, seek your own models. Pay attention to how your favorite writers do their work, and begin to integrate their methods into your own compositions. The imitation strategies described in subsequent sections and the exercises at chapter's end will give you a place to begin. Many of these can be repeated indefinitely with whatever models you or your instructors choose.

Structural Imitations

This exercise in imitation asks you to duplicate the grammatical *structure* of a model sentence or passage while supplying new words and ideas. For example, in imitation of Kate Chopin's sentence, "She was flushed and felt intoxicated with the sound of her own voice and the unaccustomed taste of candor," you might write, "We were exhausted but felt proud of the progress of our rehearsals and the growing naturalness of our dialogue." Almost every word has changed, as has the idea of the sentence, but the structure remains the same. You may want to type or write out the model sentence, triple-spaced, and work from there, as in this example:

Imitation: Wide, powerful, sure to flood during heavy rains,
Original: Solid, rumbling, likely to erupt without prior notice,

the Platte makes everyone in its floodplain leary
Macon kept each member of his family awkward

of disaster.
with fear. (Toni Morrison, *Song of Solomon*)

The idea is to replace each noun with a noun, each adjective with an adjective, each verb with a verb, and so on. Beyond that, there are no rules, though you'll find it's usually easiest to make your sentence do the same kind of thing the original does; for example, both Chopin's sentence above and my imitation describe how people feel about something. Mirroring Morrison's description of a person with a description of a river is a bit more of a stretch. (In retrospect, I see that my approach was triggered by the fact that Morrison describes Macon as a kind of natural force, one that could "erupt."

Her metaphorical language here is the kind of thing you notice when you force yourself to slow down.)

The greatest reward of this game is that you can sometimes produce very interesting and sophisticated sentences that you might not generate on your own; too, attempting an imitation forces you to appreciate the construction of the original sentence and can stretch your grammatical as well as creative abilities. Some student writers find that when they have handled a rather complex imitation successfully, they grow more confident about aiming for greater variety and sophistication in their own prose. If you try the exercise with a favorite author, it may help you understand what you like about her style. Though you can do such imitations with any writing that happens to be at hand, question 10 in the Discussion Questions and Writing Assignment provides a handful of sentences and passages that have been "road-tested" by my students. If you prefer to choose your own passages to imitate, pick something that's challenging but not overwhelming.

Again, remember that this is a game, not a method for drafting college essays. Do an imitation once a week or so, maybe in place of a journal entry, but keep doing them over a long period of time so you have a chance to get better at it. Experiment with different writers whose styles vary widely.

Strategic Imitations

A second imitation game throws out the requirement for precise duplication of the professional writer's grammar, asking only that you do the same *kinds* of things observed in a model—that is, employ the same strategies. For example, where the original uses a metaphor, you should use one yourself; where it provides a detail, you should provide one; where it asks a hypothetical question, you should do the same. Don't agonize over the rules of the game: just pay close attention to how the model passage gets its work done and then try your hand at similar moves. As in the structural imitations, with a little luck you will produce a passage more accomplished than what you would have written entirely on your own. Ideally, you will increase your sensitivity to what you read and your repertoire of writing strategies.

Here is an example of a student imitating a passage by Annie Dillard:

First, the opening paragraph of Dillard's "Living Like Weasels":

A weasel is wild. Who knows what he thinks? He sleeps in his underground den, his tail draped over his nose. Sometimes he lives in his den for two days without leaving. Outside, he stalks rabbits, mice, muskrats, and birds, killing more bodies than he can eat warm, and often dragging the carcasses home. Obedient to instinct, he bites his prey at the neck, either splitting the jugular vein at the throat or crunching the brain at the base of the skull, and he does not let go. One naturalist refused to kill a weasel who was socketed into his hand deeply as a rattlesnake. The man could in no way pry the tiny weasel off, and he had to walk half a mile to water, the weasel dangling from his palm, and soak him off like a stubborn label.

Kelly Caufield's imitation (used with permission); for your information, an anole is an American chameleon:

An anole turns brown. Who knows why he changes? He sits on a pale rock, unmoving except for his independent eyes. Often he will not eat for days. When he does eat, he eats crickets mostly, and an occasional fly or beetle. Stalking the small creatures, clamping them between his jaws, he swallows them before their legs even fall still. Once the anole tried to eat a cricket that was far too big for him. He managed to get half of the insect's body down his throat, and stopped. He tried for many minutes to work the bug further down. Finally he gave up, having to release the victim, the bug backing out like a bee backing out of a flower.

Imitations of Larger Pieces

The two kinds of exercise above are admittedly quite artificial. Throughout most of your college writing, you will not focus so single-mindedly on imitation. Nevertheless, much of what you write in college and beyond will be loose imitations of models you have studied or read. In what is sometimes called "practical writing," for example, business letters, memos, and résumés will to a great extent have predetermined formats that you will be expected to duplicate. Scientific papers, lab reports, and grant proposals will similarly call for specified types of information, predictable schemes of organization, and styles deemed appropriate to each. The rules for these different kinds of writing, from sonnet to sermon, eventually become second nature to experienced writers. A scientist may labor long and hard to make the explanation of her methodology concise and clear, but she doesn't have to waste a millisecond deciding whether to include this information or where to put it—that much is determined by the accepted model she is imitating, by the writing conventions of the scientific paper.

When you don't read, you don't write.—Helen Barolini

Until you reach the point where such decisions become automatic, even unconscious, you would do well to read with your eyes open to how authors are working as well as to what they are saying. No one, after all, is born with any of this wired into her brain. You can't help but absorb some of it by osmosis, if I may switch metaphors, but you'll learn faster if you pay attention. You might even think of your reading as a kind of collecting—not only of information, but also of styles and strategies. Try to keep some of a writer's craft in your bag when you put down his article or story. You will soon be introduced to a handful of writer's devices, called schemes and tropes, which merit your attention, but the list of what you could usefully imitate is much longer. If you learn just one thing each week about writing from now until you graduate from college, you'll be a much better writer then.

⊠ WRITING BREAK
Imitation

To try an imitation exercise while the ideas are fresh in your head, do one of the structural imitations on pages 158 to 160, or pick any animal except a weasel or an anole and write a rough imitation of Dillard's paragraph on page 117. To begin work on the Featured Paper Topic on magazine advertisements, see the Writing Break on page 125.

AIDS TO WRITING

One day I handed in my writing assignment to my English teacher and told him I wanted to become a writer. He laughed in my face and told me Puerto Ricans don't become writers.
                                    —*novelist Abraham Rodriguez, Jr.*

Most overviews of the writing process anticipate that writers will plan, then write, then revise, and finally edit for details/proofread. That order of activities makes sense, of course, but you should recognize that the actual writing process, even for very successful writers, is frequently quite a bit messier. Especially with long or complex pieces, the actual writing of the paper may demonstrate a need for further research or a new scheme of organization. Don't be discouraged, then, if you don't feel in complete control as you work—you aren't supposed to. Your writing at this stage should be more purposive and goal-oriented than the exploratory writing described in Chapter 2, but a first draft is still an experiment. Try to remain open to new ideas, and remember that you can always revise.

Setting

Most writers are sensitive to their surroundings and cannot do their best work in unfamiliar or distracting environments. A first step toward writing effectively, then, is to exert some control over the time and place you write.

The first requirement for most people is that the setting be at least relatively quiet, if not tomblike. I recognize that there may be some serious generational differences in the ability to concentrate in busy or noisy environments—you might be able to think carefully in settings that would render me incoherent—but I can't help recommending that you at least try working in a quiet spot if you can manage to find one.

Appealing workplaces are to be avoided. One wants a room with no view, so imagination can dance with memory in the dark.
                                                —*Annie Dillard*

If possible (not all students will have this luxury) establish a single place where you do most of your writing. If possible, do nothing else in this location, or at least nothing nonacademic. Think of this setting as the place you write (or at least as a place where you study). Aside from being quiet, this place should have the tools you need to write—computer, perhaps, plus pens, pencils, lots of paper, and a dictionary. You might want to add a few favorite books, an inspirational poster, and a comforting object or picture. Keep things simple, though: this is a work place, not a shrine. In keeping with that idea, the setting should be comfortable but not luxuriant. If you lack the resources to construct an ideal place to write, at least think carefully about what options are open to you; the library, for example, may prove much more conducive to study than a dorm room.

Think about the setting of your writing in terms of time as well as place. Writing sessions, like research trips to the library, should be substantial blocks of time—at least an hour for most writers, with two to three hours at a stretch a reasonable goal to work toward as your concentration and the complexity of your writing assignments increase.

Putting Ideas into Words

> To write, for a lesbian, is to learn how to take down the patriarchal posters in her room.—Nicole Brossard

I've read many books and articles about writing, as you might expect, and one of the things I've noticed is that very little is said, ironically, about *the* central, crucial, defining moment of the whole process, namely creating phrases and sentences out of thin air. When texts do talk about this phenomenon, they usually stress how mysterious our abilities with language really are. I can't erase the mystery, but I'd like to help you think about it for a few minutes, and I can offer some practical suggestions that work, though I can't fully explain why.

It may be useful to compare the act of writing a sentence to a simple physical action, say that of turning your head to the left. Most of us can turn our heads whenever we want. Most of us don't know quite how we accomplish the movement, though, except in rather vague ideas like "stimulating the appropriate muscles." Specialists, on the other hand, do have a fairly detailed and sophisticated understanding of the muscles, nerves, and so on involved, plus their biochemistry. I'd wager that they could hook you up to a machine and make you turn your head at the flip of a switch.

> *Planning to write is not writing. Outlining...researching...talking to people about what you're doing, none of that is writing. Writing is writing.—E. L. Doctorow*

Anyone who can read this book can presumably write sentences, but as in the case of turning one's head, we don't quite know how we do it. Explaining something as rudimentary as how we can think of the word *pink* when we see the color turns out to be maddeningly difficult; try to imagine what went on in Edith Wharton's head to produce the following sentence:

> If he had probed to the bottom of his vanity (as he sometimes nearly did) he would have found there the wish that his wife should be as worldly-wise and as eager to please as the married lady whose charms had held his fancy through two mildly agitated years; without, of course, any hint of the frailty which had so nearly marred that unhappy being's life, and had disarranged his own plans for a whole winter.

How did these ideas take shape in precisely this form? Did some of the ideas exist "preverbally," even for a moment, before Wharton found words to express them? How did the novelist come up with "disarranged" instead of "interfered with" or "complicated" or some other option?

Writing differs from turning one's head in that not even the experts know how it works; I doubt Wharton herself could have fully answered my questions. Even writing much less elaborate and elegant than Wharton's sentence above calls on memory, imagination, emotion, reasoning, and whole sets of linguistic and grammatical rules which no one can observe, trace, measure, or predict with much accuracy. Once we can see or hear the language, we can analyze it and revise it, but its first coming-to-be as language happens at a level hidden not only from observers but from the speaker/writer herself. We can at least crudely manipulate our neck-turning system, anaesthetizing it, for example, or stimulating it, or massaging the muscles;

we can train it for flexibility or power or gracefulness. But we can't do anything so direct with our language. All the brain surgeons in the world could not implant the meaning of a single new word in your head. (Scientists have only recently realized, for example, that oral versus written verbal skills may operate in different hemispheres of the brain.)

Fortunately, though we don't know exactly how the brain is wired for language use, we know that it is, and we can develop writing skills by indirect but nonetheless effective methods. One key, again, is imitation, though most of it is unconscious imitation: you learn to speak and write by observing others speaking and writing around you. Your focus is on communication, but your brain is continually learning nuts-and-bolts things such as vocabulary and grammar as well as innumerable sociolinguistic distinctions such as what you can say in a classroom, what you can say at the dinner table, what you can say in a bar, and so on.

> *Somehow it seems more natural to try and recover the past with a pen in your hand than with your fingers poised over a keyboard. The pen is like a tool, a cutting or digging tool, slicing down through the roots, probing the rockbed of memory.*
> —*David Lodge*

The main thing you ought to do is immerse yourself in a sea of language. College students often become better writers as they mature even if they don't study writing, partly because they become more knowledgeable but also because they gain verbal facility through all the reading, listening, and talking they do in school. To speed up this process, read, then read some more. Many writing teachers never took a writing class: they tested out of all requirements, and they did so because they were avid readers. Read beyond what's required in classes. Read whatever will keep you reading. Read at least some works of substantial length, because then a writer's style has a chance to seep a little deeper into your head, perhaps leaving behind a useful residue. Whenever I teach *Their Eyes Were Watching God,* a novel by Zora Neale Hurston whose characters speak black English, I find echoes of the book's wonderful language in my head, and when I'm served a succulent, aromatic plate of shellfish paella risotto, I think of Hurston's phrase, "I reckon it'll kill hongry."[1] As an English professor, I can't often afford to sound like an uneducated agricultural worker of the 1930s, but the book tugs at one's verbal center of gravity, shifts it. The most traditional models in western culture are Shakespeare and the Bible, but there are thousands of authors worth your time. Try as many as you can; enjoy the variety; "wade," as Arthur Plotnick put it, "with some fervor in the Ganges of human expression."

Work from the Top Down, the Bottom Up, or the Inside Out...

> *Where the words of women are crying to be heard, we must each of us recognize our responsibilities to seek those words out, to read them and share them and examine them in their pertinence to our lives.—Audre Lorde*

One very easy trick that some students haven't yet learned when they begin college is that writers don't have to begin at the beginning. Working out of order is especially easy with computers, but writers have always done it; after all, the cut-and-paste functions of a word processor replace scissors-and-glue operations.

You may begin where you're most comfortable beginning. This might be at the beginning of your paper, but it can work just as well to draft a tentative conclusion first, to try to articulate where you want to end up, what you want a paper to achieve. Alternatively, you might want to begin with a key example, or an important issue, or with some section of the paper you're most confident you can handle (plot summary, review of literature, description of methodology, refutation of an opposing viewpoint—whatever it might be).

Obviously, you need to check carefully for cohesion, logic, and good transitions if you write piecemeal, but writing from first word to last doesn't guarantee these qualities anyway. So the key rule is that "anything goes" if you can make it work. Many writers draft their introductions last (or rewrite them very substantially), because plans so often change in the course of the writing itself.

---

1. Hurston herself, unlike many of the characters in her stories, was extremely well educated and could converse with equal ease with university professors and illiterate field hands.

A corollary to the rule that anything goes is that if you find yourself temporarily stumped, or "blocked," you might want to shift tasks for a while and work on a different section.[2]

Writing by Translating

Students who are more proficient in another language than in English are occasionally tempted to produce college papers by writing them in their first language and then translating them into English. The conventional wisdom—that this is a bad idea—holds true for most students. Aside from the fact that this strategy does not reinforce fluidity in English composition, many such writers routinely produce work in their first language which they lack the proficiency to translate gracefully.

For a relatively small number of students, however, working in another language may yield some benefits. Those who are highly proficient in two or more languages—students who can compose comfortably in English and don't *need* to translate—may learn a lot about language and a lot about their own thinking by completing the same writing task in more than one language or by doing even small chunks of translation, either into or out of English.

Another possibility is to draft papers in English but to incorporate another language into earlier portions of the writing process, such as brainstorming, journal writing, or free writing. Your precise combination of language skills and preferences is unique, so experiment to see what works for you. If you know another language as well as or better than you know English, think about how you can put this immense knowledge to work. English classes are naturally going to focus on working in English, but there's no English-only rule for thinking, planning, and personal writing. Think about your own priorities. Do you want to immerse yourself in English as fully as possible or to keep your two or three or four languages active and working?

---

2. Some quick advice on "writer's block": welcome the occasional mild case—if you have writer's block, it means you're a writer. Several of the strategies described in this book may help defeat a block, for example, conversation, exploratory writing, or even modifying your physical environment. If you experience persistent, agonizing, esteem-eroding blocking, talk to your instructor and learning resource center.

⊠ **WRITING BREAK**

Self-Analysis of Writing Skills

If you are writing the analysis of magazine advertising described on page 111, try getting some ideas down on paper now, working from the inside out: pick several small details in your ad or ads (for example, body language, facial expression, color scheme, headline, disclaimers or "fine print," background, clothing, jewelry), and write a sentence or two explaining the effect or possible significance of each.

Take ten minutes to write an informal self-analysis of your own writing. You could address several of the following ideas: what you like most/least about writing; your strengths/weaknesses as a writer; your goals; your typical writing process (e.g., do you outline? how much do you revise? where and when do you write?) You may wish to share this sketch with your instructor, tutor, or peer response group.

AIDS TO REVISION

Revising is the least natural and most neglected part of the student writing process, but it may be the most important. The temptation to skimp on revision is understandable. Late in the writing process, time is often running short; energy may be flagging as well, and after all, one does at least have *something* to turn in. Add to all this the fact that revising can be challenging, detail-oriented work, and it's no surprise that people turn from their revising to a computer game, a soap opera, a jog, or even the calculus. The tips below should make revising less difficult and more productive.

As noted earlier, it's a miracle that people can write at all. Revising, though, slows down the writing process. It lets you focus on one thing at a time, and you already have words and phrases to work with, not just a blank page. It lets you see your language tangibly, substantially on the page—and hear it, too. Given these advantages, it is possible for most writers to achieve levels of sophistication, accuracy, variety, coherence, and correctness that they cannot manage on a first draft. What's more, it's precisely the work on a second or third draft that lets you write a better first draft next time around. From doing the work in slow motion, as it were— that is, by revising meticulously—you train yourself to generate better work spontaneously later on.

> *Once you've got some words looking back at you, you can take two or three—or throw them away and look for others.*
> —Bernard Malamud

Perhaps revision is such a good teacher because it provides both feedback about what you have already done and practice in the form of writing new bits of prose. Imagine, for example, that in drafting an analysis of Michael Ondaatje's *The English Patient*, you used the word *amazing* five times in three pages. Well, it is an amazing novel, but you would do better to vary your vocabulary. This is the type of "infelicity," or minor problem, that is much more likely to be noticed in the revision process than during the rush of composition. The feedback (which might come from rereading your own work or from a teacher, tutor, or classmate) is that your vocabulary is repetitious. The solution in this case is quite simple, because there are many adjectives that might replace *amazing*, and the practice is your actually thinking of alternative words and choosing some to replace the repeated *amazing*s. The benefits are twofold: you have improved your paper, and you have made it somewhat less likely that you will repeat yourself in this way in the future.

Work from the Top Down

Let's assume for the moment that your writing—and thus your revising—can be broken down into these four components:

1. *Content.* Your ideas and arguments, your examples, the substance of what you have to say. This should include a sense of how your audience is likely to respond, what they need to know, and what will interest them.
2. *Organization.* The order in which you present ideas, the adequacy of development, the divisions into paragraphs or longer blocks, as well as transitions between ideas or repetitions of idea, theme, or image that hold your piece together.

3. *Style.* The particular language you use to express your ideas, the level of formality, the pace, the use (or lack) of humor, the tone or "voice" of your piece—any part of your craft that shapes the details of language to your message or audience.
4. *Mechanics.* The grammatical correctness of your writing, from the biggest issues (e.g., sentence construction) to the smallest (e.g., apostrophe use).

A moment's reflection will show that it's wiser to begin at the top of this list than at the bottom. There's not much sense in checking the spelling of *chiaroscuro,* undangling a modifier, and laboring long over lilting alliteration, only to decide that your now-beautiful sentence doesn't really belong in the essay in the first place. It's impossible to work with 100 percent efficiency, but keep in mind the general strategy of tackling the big issues first—what are my key ideas and how can I best organize them? Don't be surprised if you find your ideas and organization changing. It's usually a sign of growth, not sloth or stupidity, when a draft does not fully adhere to the plans you had when you began writing. You are, after all, supposed to learn from the writing itself. So expect to revise even the fundamental content and organization. Finally, note that when you are working on a draft with other people, whether teachers or classmates, some may tend to check mechanics and shy away from trickier but more important issues, like the persuasiveness of your evidence. Guide them, if you can, toward providing the type of feedback you need at whatever stage you're at.

Revise Recursively, with a Tight Focus

The section above makes an assumption that not all students share, namely, that a draft will be read numerous times during the process of revision. Until you're really, really good, this is a must. Instead of casually "looking over" a draft, examine the coherence, accuracy, and clarity of its ideas, ignoring everything else. Read it again—perhaps repeatedly—to check organization and transitions, again ignoring other areas. Then work for a long time on style (tips appear below), perhaps dividing this work into a few stages, such as work on sentence variety, work on vocabulary, work on sound and rhythm.

She and I have had heart-rending meetings by night, and her husband shall never find out about those dreams I've had of her.

Every other night I dream of her dresses and things on an endless clothesline of bliss, in a ceaseless wind of possession, and her husband shall never learn what I do to the silks and fleece of the dancing witch.—original and revised sentence by Vladimir Nabokov

The number of times you should read your paper to revise it will depend on the state of the paper, its importance, the time available, and your motivation. You are not going to reach perfection, but it's safe to say that most students quit working too soon. You might think of the revising portion of the writing process as deserving 30 to 50 percent of your total effort. If you can manage to set the paper aside for awhile and then return to it with fresh eyes, you give yourself the best chance to improve.

Make Revising a Social Activity

Composition teachers are fond of saying that writing is a social activity—not a task performed by isolated individuals, but rather communication about meaningful ideas within a cultural context. That's exactly right, at least when writing works as it should. Often, though, students do write in isolation, and their sole audience is an instructor. Revising, when it occurs at all, is sometimes entirely private.

You are bound to learn faster if you involve other people in your revision process, but this may take some work. I've had students report that they get a lot out of peer response sessions in their writing workshops but that they never get a classmate's opinion on writing for any other class. It's likely that your writing classes will at least introduce you to some varieties of peer response or peer editing (two different creatures, by the way) and that you will at least sometimes have the opportunity to share a draft with your instructor before turning in a final version of your work. To do your best, carry out similar activities with every important piece you write, for whatever class. People who might provide useful feedback include instructors, tutors, classmates, family, and friends.

Instructors, you may use the short student passages on page 163 to model (in)appropriate peer responses; a quick dry run with the writing of strangers may help true peer response sessions work more smoothly.

Tips on Style

Here are a handful of ideas my students have found helpful:

Imitation

Note that the long section on imitation at the beginning of this chapter and the imitation exercises at its end have lots to do with style. Learn the craft by observing those who are more proficient and imitating their techniques.

Sweat the Details

Working on style means being patient, trying things different ways, and being willing to toss out sentences or passages that don't work. One very helpful tip for dealing with a troublesome passage is to put it aside and write it entirely from scratch. Sometimes it can be both quicker and more effective to rewrite three full sentences than to patch up one troublesome phrase.

Less Is More

In general, the fewer words you use to express a given idea, the better. A "crisis situation" is simply a crisis, as an "end result" is simply a result. Be especially wary of sentence beginnings that serve little or no purpose, as in the sentence "Having taken into consideration all the pertinent factors that are currently available to us under these circumstances, we are of the collective opinion that the wisest course of action for us to adopt at this time is to close the store until the conclusion of the holiday season." Just get to the point: "The store will be closed until January 5."[3]

> *From p. 30 I began to like the novel but Ernest I can't tell you the sense of disappointment that beginning with its elaphantine facetiousness gave me.... Its 7500 words—you could reduce it to 5000.—F. Scott Fitzgerald, to Ernest Hemingway*

---

3. I highly recommend Richard Lanham's *Revising Prose* to combat wordiness and promote good verb use (see next paragraph). It's a short book featuring clear advice and many excellent examples. See also Chapter 6 of *Rhetoric for a Multicultural America*.

Focus on Verbs

When you use strong verbs, everything about your style improves. More good news: All verbs are strong verbs except for forms of *to be* (*is, are, was, were, been, being, am*). When revising, try to make improvements like these:

> Infelicitous sentence: There was smoke in the air.

> Revisions: Smoke hung in the air. Smoke polluted the air. Smoke pricked our eyes. Smoke darkened the sky. Smoke blackened the sky. Smoke streaked the sky. Smoke filled the room. Smoke clogged the room. Smoke bubbled from the fire. Smoke wafted through the forest.

Notice that you don't have to use fancy words. Just avoid overusing forms of *to be*. Generate a list of possible ways of saying something, then choose the best.

> *About this time I can hear you say "Jesus this guy thinks I'm lousy. + he can stick it up his ass for all I give a Gd Dm for his 'criticism'." But remember this is a new departure for you, and that I think your stuff is great. You were the first American I wanted to meet in Europe—and the last. (This latter clause is simply to balance the sentence. It doesn't seem to make sense tho I have pawed at it for several minutes...)—Fitzgerald, to Hemingway*

Strut Your Stuff

Whatever problems you may have as a writer, there are certainly things you do well, things you know how to do that impress readers. These could be as simple as using a semicolon correctly or backing up a statement with a vivid example. They could include new strategies or structures you learn from imitating other writers, or perhaps the schemes and tropes discussed later in this chapter. Whatever your strengths may be, find opportunities to demonstrate them. Your instructor is likely to see weaknesses and mistakes in your writing; make sure she sees the best you can do, too.

Read Aloud

When you give voice to your prose, you will often notice things you've missed in silent revising. Another extremely useful activity is to listen to someone else read your paper to you. Wherever the reader stumbles, misreads, or hesitates, look for trouble.

SCHEMES AND TROPES

Almost thirty centuries ago Homer used these simple tricks and I do not see why I should not.—Vladimir Nabokov

Schemes and tropes are as old as Western civilization. A trope is just the use of a word in a somewhat turned or twisted way, as in a metaphor, pun, or ironic statement; a scheme is a recognized pattern of sentence construction, for example, parallelism or intentional repetition. There are a barrelfull of schemes and tropes, many with ancient Greek names that torture American tongues; this chapter will introduce a handful of the most common and useful.

As you read this section, think about adding these "simple tricks" to your own bag of tricks, as Nabokov did. It may occasionally prove useful to be able to identify a scheme or trope—what teacher would not be impressed by your observation that Martin Luther King, Jr., relied heavily on anaphora in his speeches?—but the real point is to use these devices, or "figures of speech," yourself. It's OK to force yourself to use them for a while, to consciously construct a scheme or two in each essay you write, to say to yourself, "I'm going to get another metaphor in here somewhere if it kills me!" Some of your attempts may prove awkward, but many will work well, and eventually, your use of schemes and tropes will become more natural and fluid.

Selected Tropes

Signifyin(g)

Q: Who is buried in Grant's tomb?
A: Your mama.

Schemes and tropes are often considered stylistic embellishments, figures of speech used to add energy and variety to your prose. That's true enough, but I'd like to begin by discussing an especially important trope from African American culture, one that means a lot more than stylistic bells and whistles: Signifyin(g).

In 1988, social commentator and literary critic Henry Louis Gates, Jr., identified Signifyin(g) as the crucial trope of African American culture. Gates's unusual spelling of this word (a word spoken much more often than written) links it to the white English *signifying* and simultaneously distinguishes it from that term. If in standard English a word signifies a thing, in Signifyin(g) words point to things in indirect, veiled, reversed, playful, ironic, magical, or tricky ways, as when *bad* means "good." The confusing overlap of signifying and Signifyin(g) echoes the relationship of black and white language and rhetoric in the United States—largely identical and, paradoxically, immensely different at the same time. Gates's analysis of the rhetoric of Signifyin(g) shows how tropes can be much more than stylistic flourishes; he connects this rhetorical strategy to the cultural and historical circumstances of black Americans.

The easiest way to understand Signifyin(g) is perhaps by looking at some examples. Consider the following cases, the first from Gates's essay, the second reported to me by a colleague:

> Rochelle says to her sister Grace, "Girl, you sure do need to join the Metrecal for lunch bunch." This statement is not a suggestion to diet, as it appears to be; rather, it claims that Grace is pregnant (or perhaps it asks if she is). When Grace is noncommittal, Rochelle says, "Now look here, girl, we both standing here soaking wet and you still trying to tell me it ain't raining." The true substance of this conversation—pregnancy, sisterhood, communication—never appears explicitly, but emerges metaphorically through comments about dieting and weather. Notice that a superficial translation of the sisters' dialogue into some other language could easily miss the mark completely.

> Similarly, in at least some black communities, a seemingly casual statement like "There's a draft in here" or "It's a little drafty in this room" can alert others that there is a racist present. This amounts to a kind of code in which the truly significant communication is hidden behind a comment of little apparent consequence.

Signifyin(g), then, is an indirect method of communication. It is a "trope" (Greek for "turn") because the words are turned or twisted so that their superficial meaning is not the only or even the most important meaning.

Gates describes Signifyin(g) as a "master trope"—and, cunningly, as the slave's trope—a master trope that links other tropes with which you may or may not be familiar. Rapping, rhyming, and repetition, for example, are all forms of Signifyin(g). Another example, "playing the dozens," is a ritualized verbal contest in which speakers try to top one another with insults. The Grant's tomb joke, quoted above, similarly belongs to a recognizable group of jokes within black culture; the stock answer for these questions is "Your mama."

> *There was a moment, in time, and in this place, when my brother, or my mother, or my father, or my sister, had to convey to me...the danger in which I was standing from the white man standing just behind me, and to convey this with a speed, and in a language, that the white man could not possibly understand.—James Baldwin*

Although Signifiyin(g) is often comic, many instances feature a very serious point or contain some element of instruction or ethical guidance. Unlike many sermons, parables, and straightforward moral arguments, however, Signifyin(g) works indirectly. Ground-breaking researcher Geneva Smitherman cites these examples of what she calls "heavy siggin": black activist Stokely Carmichael's description of the University of California, Berkeley, as "the white intellectual ghetto of the West" and Malcolm X's critique of Martin Luther King, Jr.: "In a revolution, you swinging, not singing."

In some cases, it may take a while for the lesson to sink in, for the full meaning of a statement to become apparent. Here's such an example, cited by Smitherman:

> In Chester Himes's novel *Hot Day, Hot Night,* two black detectives are reporting to their white superior Anderson about a riot in Harlem. Himes writes this dialogue:
>
> "I take it you've discovered who started the riot," Anderson said.
>
> "We knew who he was all along," Grave Digger said.
>
> "It's just nothing we can do to him," Coffin Ed echoed.
>
> "Why not, for God's sake?"

"He's dead," Coffin Ed said.

"Who?"

"Lincoln," Grave Digger said.

"He hadn't ought to have freed us if he didn't want to make provisions to feed us," Coffin Ed said.

An important and complicated idea—real freedom versus freedom on paper—wears several rhetorical veils here: delay, surprise, misdirection, comedy, and rhyme. The detectives' meaning emerges fairly quickly in this example, but speakers also report cases in which the real message did not dawn on them for days.

Gates, Smitherman, and Baldwin sees Signifyin(g) as deeply woven into African American culture and experience. Even speakers who are unaware of the African and pre-Civil War roots of Signifyin(g)—Yoruba mythology and trickster stories featuring the Signifying Monkey—may know idioms, figures of speech, and other verbal patterns that broaden their verbal resources well beyond standard English. Naturally, Signifyin(g) is not taught in the schools; it's learned in the family, in the community, and on the streets. As H. Rap Brown wrote, "I learned to talk in the street, not from reading Dick and Jane going to the zoo and all that simple shit" (from his autobiography *Die Nigger Die!*, quoted in Gates).

> By transforming the oppressor's speech, making a culture of resistance, black people created an intimate speech that could say far more than was permissible within the boundaries of standard English.—bell hooks

Signifyin(g) is a fabulous example of the deep interdependence of rhetoric, culture, and history—a theme you'll encounter throughout this book. With its emphasis on misdirection, Signifyin(g) is also a good introduction to the more traditional tropes discussed next. For information on "Ebonics" or "black English," see Chapter 6, Dialects and Composition.

The Essential Trope: Metaphor

He was short-lived, beaten down beneath the spear of high-hearted Aias, who struck him as he first came forward beside the nipple of the right breast, and the bronze spearhead drove clean through the shoulder. He dropped then to the ground in the dust, like some black poplar.—The Iliad

Metaphor—the comparison of two unlike things (e.g., a falling soldier and a falling tree)—is perhaps the most useful of all the schemes and tropes. (Similes are just metaphors that use *like* or *as*— e.g., Salman Rushdie's description of "strange mobiles that looked like giant coathangers twirling in the breeze.") Practice in thinking metaphorically not only will improve your writing, but also can enrich your world. I don't know exactly what intelligence is, or how many kinds of intelligence there are, but I fervently believe that thinking metaphorically will make you more intelligent, not to mention more interesting. Of how many activities can you make that claim?

Sometimes, a single word can create a metaphor, as does the word *funnel* in this sentence by novelist Arundhati Roy: "A funnel of mosquitoes, like an inverted dunce cap, whined over her head." Did you notice in reading that sentence that imagining the mosquitoes as an inverted dunce cap is a second metaphor? Here are just three more examples from Roy's *The God of Small Things*, a book filled with vivid metaphorical images:

> The black hen left through the backdoor, and scratched abstractly in the yard, where woodshavings blew about like blond curls.

> Ridges of muscle on his stomach rose under his skin like divisions on a slab of chocolate.

> Insanity hovered close at hand, like an eager waiter at an expensive restaurant (lighting cigarettes, refilling glasses).

Don't be discouraged if at first your metaphors are clunkier than the best you read or hear. After all, Roy has won international acclaim for her graceful and imaginative style. The key is to take that first step into a metaphorical mode of thinking; after that, you can polish and refine, but without the thought, you're nowhere.

It's expected that poets, essayists, and novelists use metaphors and similes, but these tropes are more common in other types of writing than you might imagine. Writing about mathematical propositions, for example, Douglas Hofstadter says, "Like tea, the

Church-Turing Thesis can be given in a variety of different strengths." Indeed, his Pulitzer Prize–winning book *Gödel, Escher, Bach: An Eternal Golden Braid* is full of metaphorical thinking, precisely because things like number theory, artificial intelligence, and musical fugues are hard to understand without the help of metaphor. Again, the metaphor can reside in a single word, for example the "bootstrapping" of computers, or grow to an elaborate analogy. In *Gödel, Escher, Bach*, Hofstadter prepares us to think about the contradictions or "failures" of mathematical systems—a rather unfamiliar and intimidating idea—by talking about record players: "For each record player there is a record which it cannot play." Like the notion of mathematical paradoxes it helps to clarify, the analogy of a record player recurs throughout the book.

You can learn to use metaphors the same way you learn most things about writing: observe other writers, imitate them, practice on your own. And since the key to metaphor is the flash of insight that links two different ideas, you can practice without even putting pen to paper. The easiest place to start is with thinking about what things around you look like and sound like. Record these thoughts in your journal; then begin to work them into your essays.

Irony

Consider this statement by Anatole France: "The law, in its infinite majesty, forbids rich and poor alike to sleep under bridges." If you understand what France is really saying, then you understand irony, and that's an amazing accomplishment. (How long will it be before a computer will understand such a sentence?) Think about how tricky the communication is here. Taken at face value, the statement is true, but its significance lies in the writer's and reader's shared recognition that prohibiting rich people from sleeping under bridges is a moot point. The sentence critiques the hypocrisy of celebrating equality before the law when actual social circumstances are grotesquely unequal—plus the sentence is short and witty and rhythmic, too.

You won't learn irony from Dick and Jane going to the zoo, but you will learn it by reading and listening. Everyone's favorite example of extended irony is Jonathan Swift's "A Modest Proposal," one of the most widely anthologized essays in Western history. College graduates are expected to know this essay, so if you don't, you may as well find it and read it sooner rather than later. Studying examples from Swift or France may help, but primarily, you need to accumulate an ear for irony through long exposure to thousands of examples. Choosing ironical parents may be your best bet, but both highbrow reading (poems, plays) and lowbrow art (cartoons, TV) can hone your sense of irony.

Using irony in college writing is a risky business because much academic writing demands a serious tone and because inept attempts at irony may simply puzzle or confuse readers. On the other hand, if you can pull it off, this trope can add tremendous energy in appropriate pieces such as personal essays, argumentative writing, and letters to the editor.

Selected Schemes

Parenthesis

Remember, schemes are stylistic devices having to do with the *structure* of a sentence. We'll start with one you already know. Parenthesis is the interruption of a sentence's grammatical flow with another word or phrase. You are familiar (I'm sure) with the use of parentheses as punctuation marks; the *scheme* called parenthesis is merely a structure that features this kind of (parenthetical) interruption. You can also use dashes to create this scheme, as in this sentence by Katherine V. Forrest:

> Temporarily ignoring her reason for arriving early—the mountainous filing she had sorted through yesterday—she ran a hand over coarse fabric the color of bamboo which covered the walls and elevator doors, and admired two sculptured sofas with chairs of dusky brown and salmon-pink surrounding a coffee table of stark glass and silver.

Students seem to shy away from using dashes, but they are tremendously useful. You can scarcely make a mistake with them, and aside from letting you vary the pace—seldom a bad move—they let you put a needed idea virtually anywhere you want it.

Parallelism

This is another scheme you undoubtedly use in one form or another already; it simply refers to constructing two or more structurally parallel elements. Novelist Kaye Gibbons provides a simple example: "I do not think of anything but the flowers on the sheets and the bubbles in the bath water." A former student—Steve Gold, was it you?—wrote about these favorite pastimes: eating Italian food, drinking German beer, and chewing American antacids. Parallelism can also raise the energy and emotion of a passage, as in this sentence by Randy Shilts:

> The story of politics, people, and the AIDS epidemic is, ultimately, a tale of courage as well as cowardice, compassion as well as bigotry, inspiration as well as venality, and redemption as well as despair.

Isocolon (¯-sō-cṓ-lon)

Isocolon is turbo-charged parallelism, specifically parallelism in which the elements are not only grammatically similar, but also equal in length. Like tea and the Church-Turing Thesis, isocolon may be given in various strengths. Often, each parallel element has the same number of words; in extreme examples, even the number of syllables may be equal. Here is a mild example of isocolon—Mercutio describing his fatal wound in *Romeo and Juliet:*

> No, 'tis *not so deep as a well, nor so wide as a church-door;* but 'tis enough, 'twill serve.

The difference between simple parallelism and isocolon may be seen in an example from Hawthorne's *The Scarlet Letter;* it's essentially a parallel list, but the parallelism of the italicized portion is tight enough to be considered isocolon:

> …the intricate and narrow thoroughfares, the tall, gray houses, the huge cathedrals, and the public edifices, *ancient in date and quaint in architecture,* of a Continental city…

A third example features multiple parallel structures, some very tight, others looser. Here is fire-and-brimstoner Jonathan Edwards urging sinners to repent before it's too late:

> Many that were very lately in the same miserable condition that you are in, are now in a happy state, with their hearts filled with love to Him who has loved them and washed them from their sins in His own blood, and rejoicing and singing for

joy of heart, while you have cause to mourn for sorrow of heart and howl for vexation of spirit!

Note that if it's overdone, isocolon can seem contrived, old-fashioned, or "precious"—that is, too clever by half. It is perhaps more effective in speeches, where it provides a real burst of energy, than in prose, but it sometimes finds a humbler home: "No shirt, no shoes, no service."

Antithesis (an-tith́-ə-səs)

[Winston Churchill] searched always to end a sentence with a climax. He looked for antithesis like a monkey looking for fleas.
—Harold Laski

Antithesis is the arrangement of words or ideas to point out contrasts. Note in the example above from Jonathan Edwards that while some elements form a list or sequence (e.g., "loved them and washed them"), others are juxtaposed to emphasize a contrast:

"miserable condition" versus "happy state"
"very lately" versus "now"
"joy of heart" versus "sorrow of heart" and "vexation of spirit"
"rejoicing and singing" versus "mourn…and howl"

Anaphora (ə-naf́-ə-rə)
Anaphora is the repetition of a phrase at the beginning of adjacent sentences. Here's an example, again from Shilts:

People died while Reagan administration officials ignored pleas from government scientists and did not allocate adequate funding for AIDS research until the epidemic had already spread throughout the country.

People died while scientists did not at first devote appropriate attention to the epidemic because they perceived little prestige to be gained in studying a homosexual affliction....

People died while public health authorities and the political leaders who guided them refused to take the tough measures necessary to curb the epidemic's spread, opting for political expediency over the public health.

> And people died while gay community leaders played politics with the disease, putting political dogma ahead of the preservation of human life.
>
> People died and nobody paid attention because the mass media did not like covering stories about homosexuals....

Anaphora heightens the rhetorical energy of a passage. In a purely physical way, I suspect, the rhythm of anaphora pleases listeners/readers. At the same time, the repetition lets the writer emphasize a key phrase or image, in this case, "people died." For these reasons, anaphora works best when the subject matter can accommodate a somewhat emotional or impassioned tone.

Asyndeton (ə-sin´-di-ton) and
Polysyndeton (pol-ē-sin´-di-ton)

Asyndeton is the omission of connective words a reader would or-dinarily expect; its opposite, polysyndeton, is the use of many con-nective words:

> *No scheme:* He loves rap music, crossword puzzles, and naps.
>
> *Asyndeton:* He loves rap music, crossword puzzles, naps.
>
> *Polysyndeton:* He loves rap music and crossword puzzles and naps.

Obviously, these slight variations from the conventional ways of list-ing things have different rhythms. When you have a list of some kind in your writing, try reading the sentence aloud with conventional connectives, and then with suppressed connectives and exaggerated connectives. One version will usually sound best in terms of tone and rhythm. If in doubt, vary the pace a bit by using these schemes occa-sionally. Note that these schemes can work with longer phrases, not just single words, as in this sentence by Thomas Pynchon:

> Inside the carriage...he sits in velveteen darkness, with noth-ing to smoke, feeling metal nearer and farther rub and connect, steam escaping in puffs, a vibration in the carriage's frame, a poising, an uneasiness, all the others pressed in around, feeble ones, second sheep, all out of luck and time: drunks, old veter-ans still in shock from ordnance 20 years obsolete, hustlers in city clothes, derelicts, exhausted women with more children

than it seems could belong to anyone, stacked about among the rest of the things to be carried out to salvation.

Remember, using schemes and tropes in your own writing may seem a little unnatural or forced at first, but that's a sign of growth. You can begin by working on the assignments on pages 158–163, or by using schemes and tropes in low-risk situations such as journal writing, or by developing schemes or tropes at the revision stage of a paper. Before long, these figures of speech will begin to occur naturally in your writing.

The readings for this chapter, aside from being well worth reading on their own, are paired to emphasize the vastly different styles writers can employ for different audiences and purposes. Jesse Jackson's speech was delivered in August 1993 on the thirtieth anniversary of the March on Washington, led by Martin Luther King, Jr.; written as an address to an assembly of 75,000 people, it makes bold use of schemes and tropes such as parallelism and antithesis. Jamaica Kincaid's "In History"—chosen for the prestigious Houghton Mifflin collection of 1998's best essays—also concerns momentous historical events (Columbus's discovery of the New World and Carl Linnaeus's classification of plants) but is otherwise quite different. "In History" is personal, reflective, subtle, unhurried; in it, we see the writer's mind at work. The two pieces are very different kinds of excellent writing, in ways that the discussion questions and writing assignments will help you explore. Be prepared to switch gears as you move from Jackson's rousing rhetoric to Kincaid's intricate contemplations.

ADDRESS ON THE THIRTIETH ANNIVERSARY OF THE MARCH ON WASHINGTON

Jesse Jackson

To the faithful remnant who have kept the Covenant and returned thirty years later to the spot where our forefathers and foremothers sighed and to a new generation of freedom fighters—welcome.

We gather today—ardent messengers of an urgent petition, crying out with our very bodies for jobs, for justice, for equal opportunity and equal protection. Many despair. The day is hot. The road is long. The mountain too steep. The people too tired. The powerful too distant. But do not despair. We have come a long way.

When we came there thirty years ago, we had no right to vote. We could not stop along the road and find room in an inn for sleep or to relieve our bodies. In every valley at every stop, there was a prevailing terrorism against blacks and browns sanctioned by the government. In every valley, there were Bull Connors to avoid, Klan to fear.

But we did not stop. We won our civil rights. We won the right to vote.

We helped lift a people from segregation, and a nation from shame. We have come a long way. But we can't stop now.

Thirty years ago, we came seeking jobs and justice. We sought to redeem a check that had bounced, Dr. King told us, marked "insufficient funds." We urged America to honor the sacred obligation to all Americans. Sorry, we were told, "there was a Cold War to fight." The Soviet bear was in the woods. The conservative Congress would not help. A young president could not help.

But Dr. King did not stop. With the younger generation fired up with a passion for justice and a will to suffer and sacrifice for an authentic new world order, young America changed the course of the world with human rights as its centerpiece.

Now thirty years later, there are more poor people, more working poor people than thirty years ago. The ghettos and barrios of our cities are more abandoned and more endangered than thirty years ago. Jobs have gone. Drugs and guns have spread. Hope is down; violence is up.

We come down this road again. The need is there. The opportunity is clear. The Soviet bear is gone. A new administration promised a Covenant to rebuild America, to put people back to work.

Once again, the check has bounced. Insufficient funds they say. The deficit must be addressed. The military must police the world. A conservative Congress will not help. A young president cannot deliver.

So just as thirty years ago—the march was a beginning, not an end, so this march is a beginning, too. We cannot sit on our hands when so many of our brothers and sisters are forced to their knees. And so we march.

We march to challenge despair, and raise up hope. We march to challenge the moral and ethical collapse that engulfs our society. Our young lost to despair, to drugs and guns, to a culture that puts a price on everything and a value on nothing. This is not a racial or an urban problem only—it is as true in the suburbs as the city, among the affluent young as among the poor, among white as well as black and brown. We need a moral movement to help regenerate hope, to renew the will to live, the desire to struggle.

We must end the killing. The fruits of despair. If death has merely changed its name from rope to dope, from genocide to fratricide to homicide; that's retrogression. Brothers and sisters, we must go forward by hope and life, not backward by fear and death. We must reclaim, project and secure our youth. And so we march.

We march to demand a program to rebuild America, to save our children, to put people back to work. Fulfill the Covenant. Put people first. No more broken promises. And so we march.

We march to demand justice. We've come a long way. But, today, justice is still not colorblind. Black males are arrested and jailed at four times the rate of white. There are four times as many young black males in US jails than in South African prisons. More black men in jail than in college. Black, brown and poor people receive more time for less crime than those who are affluent or white. Forty-six thousand cases of police brutality reported to the Justice Department since 1986. Fewer than two hundred prosecuted. Injustice abounds, so we march. Too often, it seems the more things change the more they stay the same.

In an attempt to gain the conscience and attention of the nation, I left jail, thirty years ago, to come here fighting for public accommodations. This week along with other citizens of the nation's capital, we had to face jail again while urging the president to honor his covenant and the Congress to be as committed to democracy here at home as it is in the world.

We march to demand the right to vote. DC remains the last colony. Its citizens pay more taxes than forty-eight states. It has more residents than five states. Its citizens pay taxes in dollars that are green. Its soldiers shed blood that is red. But we are taxed and serve without the right to vote largely because our skin color is black. We demand DC statehood.

We march to reverse the assault on equal protection and equal opportunity laws. Attempts to turn back the clock abound. A conservative Supreme Court has challenged reapportionments that gave long-excluded minorities some measure of representation. And yet today, neither a Democratic Congress nor a Democratic president has spoken clearly on the continuing wounds caused by racism and the need for affirmative action if this nation is to remain one. Indifference and cynical posturing abound. And, so we march.

We march for jobs, for an economic plan that puts people first. For a trade accord with Mexico that lifts their workers up, not an investor's treaty like NAFTA that will drag our workers down, and drain our jobs South.

For a single payer national health care plan that makes health care a right for everyone; not a plan that sacrifices care for some to protect profits for a few. In order to achieve these ends, politics as we know it is not working for us. Too often, we're rounding up votes to empower people to humiliate us and be indifferent to our legitimate interest. We must see more clearly from this mountain than we saw from the valley.

We must unleash the strength of our freedom struggle in new political forms. Our legitimate needs and interests are beyond the reach and boundaries of concern for both parties. But, the waters of justice must not be dammed up and become stagnant while urban Americans and family farmers perish in valleys of neglect. The levee is breaking.

We must unleash the flood gates, waters of deep passion yearning to break free roll over the rocks of broken Covenants and deceit. We must become free political agents bound only by principles not limited by party. There were twelve million African Americans alone who voted for change and legal protection, yet we do not have an attorney general for civil rights that we can call on to fight our cause.

Through it all, don't let them break your spirit. Though the tide of fascist racism is on the rise, though the arrogant forces of indifference expand jails, underfund our schools, and warehouse our youths as they languish unemployed and unskilled with broken dreams. Don't let them break your spirit. KEEP HOPE ALIVE! Though the media stereotypes us as less worthy, less intelligent, less hardworking, less universal, less patriotic, and more violent. Don't let them break your spirit. KEEP HOPE ALIVE!

Though the plant gates are closing and jobs are shifting to cheap labor markets subsidized by our own government. Though the White House and the Congress offer a crime bill to contain the people rather than an economic stimulus plan to develop the people. Don't let them break your spirit. KEEP HOPE ALIVE! It's tough but thirty years ago, it was tougher. The sun was hotter and there was no shade. The winters were colder and there was no place of warm refuge. When torrential rains poured, we were trapped in the lowlands. Yet, we did not let it break our spirits. We must be caring not callous, loving not rejecting, putting character over color, ethics over ethnicity. We must trust in God's word.

Let's go forward back to our towns and hamlets to build new structures for freedom, new vehicles for hope in our quest to redeem the soul of America and make our world more secure. From Angola to Alabama, New York to Nigeria, Birmingham to Brazil, let the world know that we will stand fast and never surrender.

Hear this biblical admonition and promise: If my people were called by my name, will humble themselves and pray, and seek my face and turn from their wicked ways, God will forgive their sins and they will hear from heaven. Then, God will heal their land.

KEEP HOPE ALIVE!!!

IN HISTORY

Jamaica Kincaid

What to call the thing that happened to me and all who look like me?

Should I call it history?

If so, what should history mean to someone like me?

Should it be an idea, should it be an open wound and each breath I take in and expel healing and opening the wound again and again, over and over, or is it a moment that began in 1492 and has come to no end yet? Is it a collection of facts, all true and precise details, and, if so, when I come across these true and precise details, what should I do, how should I feel, where should I place myself?

Why should I be obsessed with all these questions?

My history began like this: in 1492, Christopher Columbus discovered the New World. Since this is only a beginning and I am not yet in the picture, I have not yet made an appearance, the word "discover" does not set off an alarm, and I am not yet confused by this interpretation. I accept it. I am only taken by the personality of this quarrelsome, restless man. His origins are sometimes obscure; sometimes no one knows just where he really comes from, who he really was. His origins are sometimes quite vivid: his father was a tailor, he came from Genoa, he as a boy wandered up and down the Genoese wharf, fascinated by sailors and their tales of lands far away; these lands would be filled with treasures, as all things far away are treasures. I am far away, but I am not yet a treasure: I am not a part of this man's consciousness, he does not know of me, I do not yet have a name. And so the word "discover," as it is applied to this New World, remains uninteresting to me.

He, Christopher Columbus, discovers this New World. That it is new only to him, that it had a substantial existence, physical and spiritual, before he became aware of it, does not occur to him. To cast blame on him now for this childlike immaturity has all the moral substance of a certificate given to a schoolgirl for good behavior. To be a well-behaved schoolgirl is not hard. When he sees this New World, it is really new to him: he has never seen anything like it before, it was not what he had expected, he had images of China and Japan, and, though he thought he was in China and Japan, it was not the China or Japan that he had fixed in his mind. He couldn't find enough words to describe what he saw before him: the people were new, the flora and fauna were new, the way the water met the sky was new, this world itself was new, it was the New World.

"If one does not know the names, one's knowledge of things is useless." This is attributed to Isidorus, and I do not know if this is the Greek Isidorus or the other Isidorus, the bishop of Seville; but now put it another way: to have knowledge of things, one must first give them a name. This, in any case, seems me to have been Christopher Columbus's principle, for he named and he named: he named places, he named people, he named things. This world he saw before him had a blankness to it, the blankness of the newly made, the newly born. It had no before—I could say that it had no history, but I would have to begin again, I would have to ask those questions again: What is history? This blankness, the one Columbus met, was more like the blankness of paradise; paradise emerges from chaos, and this chaos is not history; it is not a legitimate order of things. Paradise, then, is the arrangement of the ordinary and the extraordinary. But in such a way as to make it, paradise, seem as if it had fallen out of the clear air. Nothing about it suggests the messy life of the builder, the carpenter, the quarrels with the contractor, the people who are late with the delivery of materials, their defense which, when it is not accepted, is met with their back chat. This is an unpleasant arrangement; this is not paradise. Paradise is the thing just met when all the troublesome details have been vanquished, overcome.

Christopher Columbus met paradise. It would not have been paradise for the people living there; they would have had the ordinary dreariness of living anywhere day after day, the ordinary dreariness of just being alive. But someone else's ordinary dreariness is another person's epiphany.

The way in which he wanted to know these things was not in the way of satisfying curiosity, or in the way of correcting an ignorance; he wanted to know them, to possess them, and he wanted to possess them in a way that must have been a surprise to him. His ideas kept not so much changing as evolving: he wanted to prove the world was round, and even that, to know with certainty that the world was round, that it did not come to an abrupt end at a sharp cliff from which one could fall into nothing; to know that is to establish a claim also. And then after the world was round, this round world should belong to his patrons, the king and queen of Spain; and then finding himself at the other side of the circumference and far away from his patrons, human and other kind, he loses himself, for it becomes clear: the person who really can name the thing gives it a life, a reality, that it did not have before. His patrons are in Spain, looking at the balance sheet: if they invest so much, will his journey yield a return to make the investment worthwhile? But he—I am still speaking of Columbus—is in the presence of something else.

His task is easier than he thought it would be; his task is harder than he could have imagined. If he had only really reached Japan or China, places like that already had an established narrative. It was not a narrative that these places had established themselves; it was a narrative that someone like him had invented, Marco Polo, for instance; but this world, China or Japan, in the same area of the world to him (even as this familiarity with each other—between China and Japan—would surprise and even offend the inhabitants of these places), had an order, and the order offered a comfort (the recognizable is always so comforting). But this new place, what was it? Sometimes it was just like Seville; sometimes it was like Seville but only more so; sometimes it was more beautiful than Seville. Mostly it was "marvelous," and this word "marvelous" is the word he uses again and again, and when he uses it, what the reader (and this is what I have been, a reader of this account of the journey, and the account is by Columbus himself) can feel, can hear, can see, is a great person whose small soul has been sundered by something unexpected. And yet the unexpected turned out to be the most ordinary things: people, the sky, the sun, the land, the water surrounding the land, the things growing on the land.

What were the things growing on the land? I pause for this. What were the things growing on that land, and why do I pause for this?

I come from a place called Antigua. I shall speak of it as if no one has ever heard of it before; I shall speak of it as if it is just new. In the writings, in anything representing a record of the imagination of Christopher Columbus, I cannot find any expectation for a place like this. It is a small lump of insignificance, green, green, green, and green again. Let me describe this landscape again: it is green, and unmistakably so; another person, who would have a more specific interest, a painter, might say it is a green that often verges on blue, a green that often is modified by reds and yellows and even other more intense or other shades of green. To me, it is green and green and green again. I have no interest other than this immediate and urgent one: the landscape is green. For it is on this green landscape that, suddenly, I and the people who look like me made an appearance.

I, me. The person standing in front of you started to think of all this while really focused on something and someone else altogether. I was standing in my garden; my garden is in a place called Vermont; it is in a village situated in a place called Vermont. From the point of view of growing things, that is the gardener's, Vermont is not in the same atmosphere as that other place I am from, Antigua. But while standing in that place, Vermont, I think about the place I am from, Antigua. Christopher Columbus never saw Vermont at all; it never entered his imagination. He saw Antigua, I believe on a weekday, but if not, then it would have been a Sunday, for in this life there would have been only weekdays or Sundays, but he never set foot on it, he only came across it while passing by. My world then—the only world I might have known if circumstances had not changed, intervened, would have entered the human imagination, the human imagination that I am familiar with, the only one that dominates the world in which I live—came into being as a footnote to someone just passing by. By the time Christopher Columbus got to the place where I am from, the place that forms the foundation of the person you see before you, he was exhausted, he was sick of the whole thing, he longed for his old home, or he longed just to sit still and enjoy the first few things that he had come upon. The first few things that he came on were named after things that were prominent in his thinking, his sponsors especially; when he came to the place I am from, he (it) had been reduced to a place of worship; the place I am from is named after a church. This church might have been an important church to Christopher Columbus, but churches are not important, originally, to people who look like me. And if people who look like me have an inheritance, among this inheritance will be this confusion of intent; nowhere in his intent when he set out from his point of embarkation (for him, too, there is not origin: he originates from Italy, he sails from Spain, and this is the beginning of another new traditional American narrative, point of origin and point of embarkation): "here is something I have never seen before, I especially like it because it has no precedent, but it is frightening because it has no precedent, and so to make it less frightening I will frame it in the thing I know; I know a church, I know the name of the church, even if I do not like or know the people connected to this church, it is more familiar to me, this church, than the very ground I am standing on; the ground has changed, the church, which is in my mind, remains the same."

I, the person standing before you, close the quotation marks. Up to this point, I and they that look like me am not yet a part of this narrative. I can look at all these events: a man setting sail with three ships, and after many, many days on the ocean, finding new lands whose existence he had never even heard of before, and then finding in these new lands people and their things and these people and their things, he had never heard of them before, and he empties the land of these people, and then he empties the people, he just empties the people. It is when this land is completely empty that I and the people who look like me begin to make an appearance, the food I eat begins to make an appearance, the trees I will see each day come from far away and begin to make an appearance, the sky is as it always was, the sun is as it always was, the water surrounding the land on which I am just making an appearance is as it always was; but these are the only things left from before that man, sailing with his three ships, reached the land on which I eventually make an appearance.

When did I begin to ask all this? When did I begin to think of all this and in just this way? What is history? Is it a theory? I no longer live in the place where I and those who look like me first made an appearance. I live in another place. It has another narrative. Its narrative, too, can start with that man sailing on his ships for days and days, for that man sailing on his ships for days and days is the source of many narratives, for he was like a deity in the simplicity of his beliefs, in the simplicity of his actions; just listen to the straightforward way many volumes featuring this man sailing on his ships begin: "In fourteen hundred and ninety-two..." But it was while standing in this other place, which has a narrative mostly different from the place in which I make an appearance, that I began to think of this.

One day, while looking at the things that lay before me at my feet, I was having an argument with myself over the names I should use when referring to the things that lay before me at my feet. These things were plants. The plants, all of them and they were hundreds, had two names: they had a common name—that is, the name assigned to them by people for whom these plants have value—and then they have a proper name, or a Latin name, and that is a name assigned to them by an agreed-on group of botanists. For a long time I resisted using the proper names of the things that lay before me. I believed that it was an affectation to say "eupatorium" when you could say "joe-pye weed." I then would only say "joe-pye weed." The botanists are from the same part of the world as the man who sailed on the three ships, that same man who started the narrative from which I trace my beginning. And in a way, too, the botanists are like that man who sailed on the ships: they emptied the worlds of things animal, mineral, and vegetable of their names, and replaced these names with names pleasing to them; the recognized names are now reasonable, as reason is a pleasure to them.

Carl Linnaeus was born on May 23, 1707, somewhere in Sweden. (I know where, but I like the highhandedness of not saying so.) His father's name was Nils Ingemarsson; the Ingemarssons were farmers. Apparently, in Sweden then, surnames were uncommon among ordinary people, and so the farmer would add "son" to his name or he was called after the farm on which he lived. Nils Ingemarsson became a Lutheran minister, and on doing so he wanted to have a proper surname, not just a name with "son" attached to it. On his family's farm grew a linden tree. It had grown there for generations and had come to be regarded with reverence among neighboring farmers; people believed that misfortune would fall on you if you harmed this tree in any way. This linden tree was so well regarded that people passing by used to pick up twigs that had dropped from it and carefully place them at the base of the tree. Nils Ingemarsson took his surname from this tree: Linnaeus is the Latinized form of the Swedish word *lind*, which means *linden*. Other branches of this family who also needed a surname drew inspiration from this tree; some took the name Tiliander— the Latin word for linden is *tilia*—and some others who also needed a surname took the name Lindelius, from the same Swedish word *lind*.

Carl Linnaeus's father had a garden. I do not know what his mother had. His father loved growing things in this garden and would point them out to the young Carl, but when the young Carl could not remember the names of the plants, his father gave him a scolding and told him he would not tell him the names of any more plants. (Is this story true? But how could it not be?) He grew up not far from a forest filled with beech, a forest with pine, a grove filled with oaks, meadows. His father had a collection of rare plants in his garden (but what would be rare to him and in that place, I do not know). At the time Linnaeus was born, Sweden this small country that I now think of as filled with well-meaning and benign people interested mainly in the well-being of children, the well-being of the unfortunate no matter their age—was the ruler of an empire, but the remains of it are visible only in the architecture of the main square of the capital of places like Estonia. And so what to make of all this, this small detail that is the linden tree, this large volume of the Swedish empire, and a small boy whose father was a Lutheran pastor? At the beginning of this narrative, the narrative that is Linnaeus, I have not made an appearance yet; the Swedes are not overly implicated in the Atlantic slave trade, not because they did not want to have a part in it, only because they weren't allowed to do so; other people were better at it than they.

He was called "the little botanist" because he would neglect his studies and go out looking for flowers; if even then he had already showed an interest in or the ability to name and classify plants, this fact is not in any account of his life that I have come across. He went to university at Uppsala; he studied there with Olof Rudbeck. I can pause at this name, Rudbeck, and say rudbeckia, and say, I do not like rudbeckia. I never have it in my garden, but then I remember a particularly stately, beautiful yellow flower in a corner of my field garden, *Rudbeckia nitida,* growing there. He met Anders Celsius (the Celsius scale of temperature measurement), who was so taken with Linnaeus's familiarity and knowledge of botany that he gave Linnaeus free lodging in his house. Linnaeus became one of the youngest lecturers at the university. He went to Lapland and collected plants and insects native to that region of the world; he wrote and published an account of it called *Flora Lapponica.* In Lapland, he acquired a set of clothing that people native to that region of the world wore on festive occasions; I have seen a picture of him dressed in these clothes, and the caption under the picture says that he is wearing his Lapland costume. Suddenly I am made a little uneasy, for just when is it that other people's clothes become your costume? But I am not too uneasy, I haven't really entered this narrative yet, I shall soon. In any case, I do not know the Laplanders, they live far away, I don't believe they look like me.

I enter the picture only when Linnaeus takes a boat to Holland. He becomes a doctor to an obviously neurotic man (obvious only to me, I arbitrarily deem him so; no account of him I have ever come across has described him so) named George Clifford. George Clifford is often described as a rich merchant banker; just like that, a rich merchant banker, and this description often seems to say that to be a rich merchant banker is just a type of person one could be, an ordinary type of person, anyone could be that. And now how to go on, for on hearing that George Clifford was a rich merchant in the eighteenth century, I now am sure I have become a part of the binomial-system-of-plant-nomenclature narrative.

George Clifford had glass houses full of vegetable material from all over the world. This is what Linnaeus writes of it:

> I was greatly amazed when I entered the greenhouses, full as they were of so many plants that a son of the North must feel bewitched, and wonder to what strange quarter of the globe he had been transported. In the first house were cultivated an abundance of flowers from southern Europe, plants from Spain, the South of France, Italy, Sicily and the isles of Greece. In the second were treasures from Asia, such as Poincianas, coconut and other palms, etc.; in the third, Africa's strangely shaped, not to say misshapen plants, such as the numerous forms of Aloe and Mesembryanthemum families, carnivorous flowers, Euphorbias, Crassula and Proteas species, and so on. And finally in the fourth greenhouse were grown the charming inhabitants of America and the rest of the New World; large masses of Cactus varieties, orchids, cruciferea, yams, magnolias, tulip-trees, calabash trees, arrow, cassias, acacias, tamarinds, pepper-plants, Anona, manicinilla, cucurbitaceous trees and many others, and surrounded by these, plantains, the most stately of all the world's plants, the most beauteous Hernandia, silver-gleaming species of Protea and camphor trees. When I then entered the positively royal residence and the extremely instructive museum, whose

collections no less spoke in their owner's praise, I, a stranger, felt completely enraptured, as I had never before seen its like. My heartfelt wish was that I might lend a helping hand with its management.

In almost every account of an event that has taken place sometime in the last five hundred years, there is always a moment when I feel like placing an asterisk somewhere in its text, and at the end of this official story place my own addition. This chapter in the history of botany is such a moment. But where shall I begin? George Clifford is interesting—shall I look at him? He has long ago entered my narrative; I now feel I must enter his. What could it possibly mean to be a merchant banker in the eighteenth century? He is sometimes described as making his fortune in spices. Only once have I come across an account of him that says he was a director of the Dutch East India Company. The Dutch East India Company would not have been involved in the Atlantic trade in human cargo from Africa, but human cargo from Africa was a part of world trade. To read a brief account of the Dutch East India trading company in my very old encyclopedia is not unlike reading the label on an old can of paint. The entry mentions dates, the names of Dutch governors or people acting in Dutch interest; it mentions trade routes, places, commodities, incidents of war between the Dutch and other European people; it never mentions the people who lived in the area of the Dutch trading factories. Places like Ceylon, Java, the Cape of Good Hope, are emptied of their people as the landscape itself was emptied of the things they were familiar with, the things that Linnaeus found in George Clifford's greenhouse.

"If one does not know the names, one's knowledge of things is useless." It was in George Clifford's greenhouse that Linnaeus gave some things names. The Adam-like quality of this effort was lost on him. "We revere the Creator's omnipotence," he says, meaning, I think, that he understood he had not made the things he was describing, he was only going to give them names. And even as a relationship exists between George Clifford's activity in the world, the world as it starts out on ships leaving the seaports of the

Netherlands, traversing the earth's seas, touching on the world's peoples and the places they are in, the things that have meant something to them being renamed and a whole new set of narratives imposed on them, narratives that place them at a disadvantage in relationship to George Clifford and his fellow Dutch, even as I can say all this in one breath or in one large volume, so too then does an invisible thread, a thread that no deep breath or large volume can contain, hang between Carolus Linnaeus, his father's desire to give himself a distinguished name, the name then coming from a tree, the linden tree, a tree whose existence was regarded as not ordinary, and his invention of a system of naming that even I am forced to use?

The invention of this system has been a good thing. Its narrative would begin this way: in the beginning, the vegetable kingdom was chaos; people everywhere called the same things by a name that made sense to them, not by a name that they arrived at by an objective standard. But who has an interest in an objective standard? Who would need one? It makes me ask again what to call the thing that happened to me and all who look like me? Should I call it history? And if so, what should history mean to someone who looks like me? Should it be an idea, should it be an open wound and each breath I take in and expel healing and opening the wound again and again, over and over, or is it a long moment that begins anew each day since 1492?

DISCUSSION QUESTIONS AND WRITING ASSIGNMENTS

On the Readings by Jackson and Kincaid

1. Jesse Jackson's speech was written to be delivered orally to a huge audience. In what ways is the writing tailored to that setting? How effective is the piece as a *written* document, in your opinion? Point to any specific features of the text that you think would work better in oral delivery than in silent reading. Are there any features that are better suited to private reading?

2. Identify ten or more examples of schemes and tropes in Jackson's speech. Also point to any additional figures of speech you can see in Jackson's speech that aren't defined in this book. Save your notes for question 6.

3. The 1975 *New Columbia Encyclopedia* entry on Antigua includes this passage:

> Hilly, with a much indented coast, Antigua has farms that grow mostly sugarcane and cotton. Tourism is a major industry; the island provides many hunting and fishing resorts. Discovered by Columbus in 1493, Antigua was named for a Spanish church in Seville. Unsuccessful Spanish and French settlements on the island were followed by a fruitful British effort in 1632, when sugarcane was introduced from St. Kitts. After a brief French occupation in 1666, Antigua passed permanently to Britain. The abolition of slavery in 1834 hurt the sugar industry; in the early 19th century cotton was introduced. The United States has a military base on the island.

What do you think Kincaid would say is wrong with this description?

4. Is there a thesis in "In History"? What is it, and where is it most specifically expressed? Why doesn't Kincaid include a straightforward declaration of her thesis in her opening paragraphs?

5. Explain the importance of the concepts of naming and of narratives to Kincaid's essay. Begin by carefully rereading passages about narratives and names. What points do you think Kincaid is making?

6. Kincaid's use of stylistic devices such as artful repetition is gentler than Jackson's, but is nevertheless in evidence. Identify Kincaid's most noteworthy stylistic devices and compare their tone, structure, and effect to those you noted in Jackson's speech.

7. Examine the vocabulary, sentence length, and sentence structure in the two readings. How important are these to the "voice" of each selection?

8. Write a journal entry in which you begin to explore your own relationship to history. Ask yourself, as Kincaid does, "When I

come across these true and precise details, what should I do, how should I feel, where should I place myself?"

On Chapter 3

9. Write a journal entry or short paper in response to one or two of the quotations included in this chapter. Possible approaches include the following:

   - Explain the meaning of the quotation. For example, what does Brossard mean by "taking down the patriarchal posters" (page 120)?
   - Use the quotation as a starting point for your own reflections or experience relating to the topic. In response to the Lodge quotation on page 122, for example, write about any differences you have noted between writing with a pen and writing at a keyboard.
   - Amplify on the quotation: develop it; provide examples.
   - Explain why you agree or disagree with the quotation.
   - Compare and contrast two or more quotations.

10. Structural imitation exercise: for one or more of the passages below, write an imitation that mimics the grammar and sentence structure of the original as precisely as possible. For examples and further explanation, see pages 115–116.

   > I visited that house only once. It was low and covered with tiles shaped like fish scales. There were big wooden doors and a veranda that had been perched high on layers of stone above the dampness of the ground. Attached were three outbuildings: one for raising silkworms, one for threshing and pounding rice, and the third for storing farming tools. It was a traditional house, solidly built, but dimly lit and sinister. (Duong Thu Huong, translated by Phan Huy Duong and Nina McPherson)
   >
   > *Suggested approach: Describe a house or apartment.*

   > I lit the lamp beside the bed, turned off the gas, and opened the wide windows. The bed was far back from the windows, and I sat with the windows open and undressed by the bed. Outside a night train, running on the street-car

tracks, went by carrying vegetables to the markets. They were noisy at night when you could not sleep. Undressing, I looked at myself in the mirror of the big armoire beside the bed. That was a typically French way to furnish a room. Practical, too, I suppose. (Ernest Hemingway)

Suggested approach: Describe getting ready for bed in a hotel or motel.

The boy was a tall fourteen, hunched with his sudden growth and very pale. His mouth was sweetly curved, his skin fine and girlish. His sister was only eleven years old, but already she was so short and ordinary that it was obvious she would be this way all her life. Her name was square and practical as the rest of her. Mary. She brushed her coat off and stood in the watery wind. Between the buildings there was only more bare horizon for her to see, and from time to time men crossing it. (Louise Erdrich)

Suggested approach: Describe a pair of related characters, or perhaps animals.

It is, of course, the responsibility of every butler to devote his utmost care in devising a staff plan. Who knows how many quarrels, false accusations, unnecessary dismissals, how many promising careers cut short can be attributed to a butler's slovenliness at the stage of drawing up the staff plan? Indeed, I can say I am in agreement with those who say that the ability to draw up a good staff plan is the cornerstone of any decent butler's skills. (Kazuo Ishiguro)

Suggested approach: Describe the key skill to some job or activity.

At such a time I found out for certain, that this bleak place overgrown with nettles was the churchyard; and that [...] the dark flat wilderness beyond the churchyard, intersected with dykes and mounds and gates, with scattered cattle feeding on it, was the marshes, and that the low leaden line beyond was the river; and that the savage lair from which the wind was rushing, was the sea; and that the small bundle of shivers growing afraid of it all and beginning to cry, was Pip. (Charles Dickens)

Suggested approach: Describe a series of discoveries.

Across a blue tile patio, in through a door to the kitchen. Routine: plug in American blending machine won from Yank last summer, some poker game, table stakes, somewhere in the north, never remember now.... Chop several bananas into pieces. Make coffee in urn. Get can of milk from cooler. Puree 'nanas in milk. Lovely. *I would coat all the booze-corroded stomachs of England....* Bit of marge, still smells all right, melt in skillet. Peel more bananas, slice lengthwise. Marge sizzling, in go long slices. Light oven *whoomp* blow us all up someday oh, ha, ha, yes. (Thomas Pynchon)

Suggested approach: Describe a routine of some sort.

11. Examine a 500-to-1,000-word sample of your own writing. What schemes and tropes, if any, can you find already there? Where could you add schemes and tropes, and what effect would they have? A hint for beginners: despite their long names, asyndeton and polysyndeton are extremely easy to use.

12. Using a 500-to-1,000-word sample of your own writing, practice the scheme called parenthesis by inserting some new idea into the middle of several of your original sentences: using dashes or parentheses to set off the addition. Experiment with clarity and rhythm by inserting the new material in more than one spot.

   Example

   Original sentence
   Yo-Yo Ma is the world's greatest living cellist.

   First revision
   Yo-Yo Ma is—the experts seem to agree—the greatest living cellist.

   Second revision
   Yo-Yo Ma—the experts seem to agree—is the greatest living cellist.

   Third revision
   Yo-yo Ma is the world's greatest—the experts seem to agree—living cellist. (To learn what works and what

doesn't, don't be afraid to produce some ugly sentences like this one.)

Tip: Learn how to type a true dash on your computer, or use two hyphens--like those around this phrase--with no spaces.

13. Working with one of the two sentences below, experiment to see how many different places you can insert a parenthetical interruption.

    University policy once allowed students to drop classes without penalty up to the moment they began the final exam, but that policy has changed dramatically.

    Americans who are used to wide open spaces may be shocked to witness the population density in Switzerland or Italy, much less India or Pakistan.

    ### Example

    Original sentence
    Most of Thomas Mangelson's photographs feature not only a stunning landscape, but also some animal in its natural environment.

    Expanded versions
    Most—but not all—of Thomas Mangelson's photographs feature not only a stunning landscape, but also some animal in its natural environment.

    Most of Thomas Mangelson's photographs—at least those displayed in the Images of Nature galleries—feature not only a stunning landscape, but also some animal in its natural environment.

    Most of Thomas Mangelson's photographs feature not only a stunning landscape—whether Arctic icefield or tropical rainforest—but also some animal in its natural environment.

    Most of Thomas Mangelson's photographs feature not only a stunning landscape, but also—this is why he wins awards—some animal in its natural environment.

14. Practicing anaphora is simplicity itself. All you need is the beginning of a sentence; then simply use this opening (or a variation

on it) in two or three or four sentences in a row. Try using these sentence openings or others of your own creation:

On a good day,...

When I think of a child being kidnapped,...

Before anyone else was awake,...

Because we are a free nation,...

It is not our duty...

If you believe in yourself,...

After midnight,...

In happy families,...

Forget...

15. To practice creating parallel structures, complete the following sentences by adding two or more phrases parallel to the italicized portions:

Natasha spends her weekends *painting her nails*...

Can you remember the first time you heard *the twang of a steel guitar*...

I plan to visit Europe some day, not only to *see the old museums and the latest fashions*, but also to...

16. Write a paragraph comparing and contrasting two clearly different things, like youth and old age, spring and fall, city life and rural life, or cooperation and competition. Write and revise your passage to include as many parallel phrases as possible.

17. Find a sample of writing, such as a news story, that is unlikely to feature many schemes and tropes. Rewrite a 100-word chunk of it, introducing as many schemes and tropes as possible. Use your imagination, and aim for excess.

Abbreviated example

Original version
The body was discovered in the woods.

Ridiculously expanded version
The body—its eyes hollow, its heart stopped, its limbs cold—was discovered (so I've been told) in the serene and

quiet and peaceful woods, the ancient, sacred, unchanging woods.

18. Below are the openings of two student essays. Working in small groups if possible, identify the two or three most important ways each could be improved. Then revise the paragraphs according to these goals.

> Will women ever get the respect that they deserve? Unfortunately, women in history have always been oppressed, and up to this day, women are still not getting the equality they have been wanting. What is obvious is that women today have a better chance to survive in the working world than they did in the fifties. Women have advanced at many positions that could not be reached by a woman fifty years ago....

> While I would like to say that I have not allowed myself to be pressured into gender role association, and to some extent that is true, I know that as much as I try to resist, my opinions have been influenced by this. I think this is true of most all people. It is hard, if not impossible, to live within a society your entire life and not be influenced at all by it, though some allow themselves to be influenced more than others.
>
> I would like to say that I am more open to things that are "different." I do not feel the need to hate those who fit the description of "different" in our society. I suppose that this makes me "different" as well, but that doesn't bother me....

REFERENCES

Bizzell, Patricia and Bruce Herzberg. *The Rhetorical Tradition: Readings from Classical Times to the Present.* New York: St. Martin's Press, 1990.

Corbett, Edward P. J. *Classical Rhetoric for the Modern Student.* New York: Oxford University Press, 1990.

Gates, Henry Louis, Jr. *The Signifying Monkey: A Theory of Afro-American Literary Criticism.* New York: Oxford University Press, 1988.

Hofstadter, Douglas R. *Gödel, Escher, Bach: An Eternal Golden Braid.* New York: Vintage Books, 1979.

Lanham, Richard A. *Revising Prose.* New York: Macmillan, 1992.

Smitherman, Geneva. *Talkin and Testifyin: The Language of Black America.* Boston: Houghton Mifflin, 1977.

Wharton, Edith. *The Age of Innocence.* 1920. New York: Macmillan, 1987.

◧ Part 2

Rhetoric in
Cultural Context

4

Rhetoric in Historical Context: An Introduction and Critique

How forcible are right words!
—JOB 6:25

When people see the word *rhetoric*, they often think of negative ideas such as "mere rhetoric" or "political rhetoric" or "empty rhetoric." Because such negative ideas are so common, some students graduate from American high schools without any broader notion of what rhetoric is or how it has affected—and continues to affect—global civilization. Sadly, it's easy to graduate from many colleges and universities without knowing much more; in keeping with the wisdom that you can't know where you are unless you know where you've been, this chapter offers a quick overview of the history of rhetoric—a history that has strongly influenced your education and that has helped shape our most important cultural institutions, including Congress, the courts, the media, and many religious organizations. The chapter also critiques some serious problems, such as the all-too-common exclusion of women from rhetorical study and practice.

There are some very good reasons to see your own studies in the broader context of the history of rhetoric. First, rhetoric, defined as the art of effective speaking, has been absolutely fundamental to Western education, public life, politics, and law for twenty-five centuries; you can't truly understand concepts such as democracy or Caesar or impeachment without some knowledge of rhetoric. Second, and just as important, rhetoric hasn't so much disappeared as dispersed, in the last century or so, into a myriad of fields, including linguistics, political science, feminism, and philosophy, not to mention advertising, marketing, public relations, and lobbying. Once you develop a broad, sophisticated notion of rhetoric, you will see it everywhere, in your studies and in the world around you, from the pulpit to the Web. Finally, most of the academic prose that you will read and write has its roots in this rhetorical heritage.

This chapter whizzes through the history of rhetoric from about 2,500 years ago to the present, giving special emphasis to rhetoric in the United States. I can't avoid using a few names and dates, but presumably you won't be tested on these; focus on the principles— ideas you might remember for a few years—such as how women were largely excluded from the study of rhetoric, or how *rhetoric* can mean much more than niceties of style, how it can point to a broad theory of how people use language. These principles, I believe, you will find easy to understand and remember.

After the historical survey and critique, as well as some speculations about the state of rhetoric today, the chapter reprints two brief essays on the role of rhetoric in the 1996 United States presidential election. These essays, Michael Kelly's "Running On" and Hendrik Hertzberg's "Big Talk," serve two functions: first, they demonstrate the continuing importance of rhetoric in national affairs; second, they are models of rhetorical analysis, examples of how to think critically about issues by carefully observing people's use of language. The chapter concludes with questions and assignments related to these readings and to the chapter as a whole.

⊠ FEATURED PAPER TOPIC

Write a detailed rhetorical analysis of a short piece of writing that aims to *persuade* its audience of something. The passages on pages 191–194 by Harriet Beecher Stowe and Frederick Douglass are examples of such writing and could be used for this paper. (See assignment 10 in the Discussion Questions and Writing Assignments. Elsewhere in this book, you could turn to the speech by the Rev. Jesse Jackson in the Chapter 3 Readings or the argument by Patricia J. Williams in the Chapter 1 Readings, or look forward to the selections by Eldridge Cleaver and James Baldwin in the Chapter 6 Readings. And, of course, there is a whole world of such writing beyond this book, in magazine articles, essays, speeches, ads, letters to newspaper editors, and other forums. Whatever text you choose—or are assigned—show your understanding of what the writer has done to make her or his ideas as appealing as possible. Begin by determining what text you will work with and jotting down some initial reactions. As you read the chapter, you will learn some terminology (e.g., *logos, pathos,* and *ethos*) that should help you; you will also see elements of rhetorical analysis in the readings by Kelly and Hertzberg.

RHETORIC AS A UNIVERSAL CULTURAL VALUE

All human societies have valued rhetoric, if rhetoric is broadly defined as the ability to communicate with special effectiveness. So many aspects of human life depend on communication that it's hardly surprising that people who can speak or write wisely, powerfully, precisely, or beautifully would be appreciated, whether or not they are called rhetoricians. This is not much different from the observation that all cultures value beauty, courage, strength, patience, creativity, and intelligence. Scholars cannot examine the rhetoric of *every* human culture (some nonliterate societies, for example, have vanished, leaving nothing to study), but everywhere researchers find human language, they find rhetoric at work— whether in aboriginal peoples of Australia, the ancient Chinese and Egyptians, or Native American tribes. One of the world's foremost authorities on rhetoric, George A. Kennedy, even argues that a kind of very basic rhetoric exists in the communications of social animals such as deer and monkeys, in which different sounds can signal sexual interest, warning, aggression, and other basic messages.

Though rhetoric is apparently fundamental to every culture, it is certainly not identical in all societies. Like cuisine, like gender roles, like notions of beauty, like taste in music and art, rhetoric varies widely among cultures and can also change dramatically within a single society over time. For example, language that you might consider excessively fancy or "flowery" has often been the norm in western Europe and even the plain-talking United States. Sometimes wit may be highly valued, sometimes emotional impact, sometimes intricacy and ingenuity in phrasing, sometimes rigorous logic, but all societies have a rhetorical culture, a shared sense of what kinds of speech and writing work best in various situations.

To illustrate this with a very simple example, consider the rhetoric of e-mail. Although electronic mail is a very recent invention, a very new rhetorical environment compared to something like a political speech or a eulogy, people around the world have already internalized "guidelines" for e-mail—for example, that such messages should ordinarily be short, that they may be relatively informal, that they need not contain a salutation like "Dear Kichung" (because the computers provide the necessary information), and so on.

Whether or not you know the rhetoric of e-mail, you certainly have a sense of what kinds of language you would expect to encounter in different cultural environments such as a courtroom, a synagogue or temple or church, a racetrack, MTV, Shakespeare in the Park, or talk radio. Speakers and writers succeed when they are highly sensitive to these different environments and are adept at shaping their language for particular audiences, contexts, and purposes. Miscommunication and conflict occur when people hold different beliefs or assumptions about what kind of language or rhetoric is best in a particular setting.

CLASSICAL RHETORIC: GREECE AND ROME

Oh, for my dear old Greeks, who talked everything—not to shine as in the Parisian salons, but to learn, to teach, to vent the heart, to clear the mind!—Margaret Fuller

The Birth of Rhetoric

It's no coincidence that the birth of Western rhetoric and the rise of the Greek empire occurred at the same time; indeed, the two phenomena fed off one another. In classical Greece, using language skillfully was of the utmost importance both in practical matters like political survival and in any number of more philosophical matters, from education to metaphysics.

Note the connection of rhetoric to the emergence of democracy. A tyrant with near-absolute power does not have to speak eloquently to persuade those around him; in many city-states before the rise of Athens, the most powerful individuals and families simply commanded, eloquent or not. In the emerging democracy, however, the Greeks quickly recognized that artful language could greatly enhance the attractiveness of one's ideas. And the stakes were high, ranging from opportunities to amass personal wealth all the way to the most important civic issues imaginable, such as who should govern and when he should lead the nation into war. Training in rhetoric helped men (almost never women, alas) think carefully and speak persuasively and thus prosper in a competitive and rapidly changing society.

On the more philosophical side, the Greeks were trying to figure out a whole series of complicated questions: how best to educate their youth, how to distinguish between truth and falsity, how to reason about the gods and the afterlife, and so on. As in affairs of state, rhetoric helped people imagine various arguments, test them, and communicate them persuasively to others.

The Greeks also recognized—they could scarcely have missed this—that skillful speaking could make unwise thinking look wise and that clever speakers could intentionally deceive their audiences. Thus, rhetoric itself was not simply an accepted method or system for speaking well, but was a matter of serious controversy addressed by virtually every major thinker. Plato, for example, sharply criticized the "sophists," whose rhetoric in his opinion was empty and amoral and swayed people with fancy language instead of teaching them with more reliable logic. Though he was a masterful rhetorician himself, Plato would have liked somehow to get beyond the effective use of language, beyond rhetoric, and dwell in a land of pure idea and pure logic. Plato's attack on the sophists was so successful that only in the twentieth century has this group of thinkers been widely respected as shrewd observers of how language really works, complete with inconsistency, ambiguity, and irrationality. Unfortunately, few writings of the sophists survive, and we know many of their ideas only through secondhand and often hostile summaries.

Aristotle, who studied under Plato for some twenty years, carried on the Platonic tradition to the extent that he agreed that "logic" and "proof" were higher than rhetoric and mere "belief," but he recognized that rhetoric, for all its problems, could not be avoided. Political and military decisions, for example, often have to be made without any proof of what the best course of action is. It would be nice always to reason deductively from clearly established premises, but life is messier than that, Aristotle knew, and he thus embraced rhetoric as a method of communication for people seeking the truth when it could not be absolutely proved.

Aristotle is generally credited with first systematizing Greek ideas about persuasive speech—though he did not invent them—in a work known simply as the *Rhetoric*. Although we lack a completely authoritative manuscript of the work, Aristotle's presentation of Greek rhetoric established the foundation of rhetorical practice for centuries to come; Western writers and teachers of all eras have typically accepted much of the Greek system. The subsequent sections summarize some of its most important ideas.

The Canons

The Greeks divided rhetoric into five areas called the *canons* of rhetoric. The first, and the one that most interested Aristotle, was "invention" or "discovery," that is, the business of figuring out what there is to say about a given topic. Aristotle considered invention so important that he virtually equated it with rhetoric itself. "Rhetoric," he said, "may be defined as the faculty of observing in any given case the available means of persuasion." It's not surprising, then, that some of the methods you saw in Chapter 2 for gathering ideas date back to classical Greek times; from its origins, rhetoric was much more than honeyed words: the first canon of rhetoric was concerned with how to develop the raw materials for argument, with how to think analytically, broadly, and precisely about an issue.

The second canon is usually called "arrangement"; you can think of it as "organization." Some classical rhetoricians devised elaborate rules for organizing different kinds of speeches, but Aristotle's favored approach still works very well: simply state your case and begin arguing it. As Chapter 2 points out, writers today must also take into account the conventions of various genres of writing, such as scientific papers, business letters, psychological case studies, televised speeches, and so on. See pages 79 to 86 to review some of the most basic and powerful principles of organization or arrangement.

The third canon, and the last that relates directly to college writing, is "style"; this area is concerned with the particular language you use to express your ideas. Under this umbrella come concerns with crafting language that is clear, direct, and appropriate to the audience and the situation. This is bound to be one of the major focuses of your college education, not only in your writing classes, but also in your reading and writing in other academic disciplines. The stylistic methods now used in a broad range of cultures and languages were first codified by classical rhetoricians. Some of these techniques (for example, the use of metaphor and other schemes and tropes) were introduced in Chapter 3; Chapter 6, Dialects and Composition, also has much to do with style.

The orator, as we have seen, must be a substantial personality. Then, first, he must have power of statement,—must have the fact, and know how to tell it.—Ralph Waldo Emerson

Lacking teleprompters, Greek speakers often memorized their speeches (and those of others, as a method of study), though notes were apparently acceptable for long speeches. Unless you are a drama student, you can gratefully ignore this aspect of the fourth canon, "memory." On the other hand, memory also refers to a rhetorician's storehouse of knowledge, and in this respect you might think of your entire education and personal experience as a stockpile of materials—what novelist William Faulkner called his "lumber yard." Good speakers and writers always seem to *know* a lot. Your campus library is an immensely useful backup system, but the more you have in your head, in your memory, the better you will write. If the cupboard is a little bare right now, stocking it is what college is for.

The fifth canon, "delivery," will probably not show up in your writing courses, though you may run into it in Oral Communication or other speech classes. Delivery is the ability to breathe life into words in a speech, debate, or other oral presentation. This includes enunciation, the pace of speaking, vocal dynamics, gestures, and facial expressions. To the extent that you are writing and not speaking publicly, you have somewhat different responsibilities from a Greek student. The energy he might have devoted to delivery you could perhaps expend on careful proofreading. (Try reading paragraph by paragraph beginning at the *end* of your paper.)

Moving an Audience

The five canons provide an overview of rhetoric in action from the writer's or speaker's point of view. They define in general terms the processes an effective orator must complete, and within this simple framework, teachers of rhetoric could introduce more and more detailed advice, such as how to discredit a hostile witness or how to choose between a fancy, a straightforward, or a markedly casual style. The Greeks also looked at rhetoric from the audience's point of view and generally recognized three main ways listeners could be persuaded: by appeals to reason (*logos*), by appeals to the emotions (*pathos*), and by appeals to the audience's sense of the speaker as a moral and reliable person (*ethos*). You will quickly recognize a dilemma that the Greeks saw as well: appeals to reason seem the best, the most honest, but appeals to emotions or to the trustworthiness of the speaker may often prove the most effective. Moreover, in practice, these three types of appeal cannot always be neatly divided: a writer's meticulous reasoning certainly contributes to our sense of her as a reliable, trustworthy person, and even obvious appeals to emotion, if we are sympathetic to them, probably make a writer seem more real, more human, and more believable than a "coldly" logical argument. To the dismay of philosophers from Plato to the present, most people prefer Captain Kirk's fuzzy logic to Mr. Spock's rigid thought.

Logos, pathos, and *ethos* may overlap, but the terms remain useful, especially in extreme cases in which an "argument" can be revealed as lacking reason and entirely dependent on appeals to emotion. Such arguments appear regularly on the editorial pages of campus and other newspapers and are often betrayed by their broad generalizations, their reliance on stereotypes, or their name calling. Rhetoricians have frequently condemned such tactics as il-

---

⊠ **WRITING BREAK**

Logos, Pathos, Ethos

If you are working on the Featured Paper Topic for Chapter 4, try using the concepts of *logos, pathos,* and *ethos* to help explain how your chosen text is attempting to persuade its readers. Note that doing this three-pronged analysis might or might not produce three paragraphs for your essay.

---

legitimate, arguing that appeals to emotion are inevitable and even valuable, but only in support of a reasoned position on an issue. Good readers are quick to distinguish between different types of appeal; use the Writing Break above not only to help write one specific paper, but also to help establish a habit of critical reading and thinking. Note also how Michael Kelly's essay in the Readings carries out this kind of analysis as he seeks to explain President Clinton's rhetorical appeal.

Aspasia of Miletus

> *To ask questions about Aspasia's life is to ask questions about half of humanity.*—Madeleine Henry

One woman in ancient Greece managed to etch her presence into the history of rhetoric so deeply that she has not been forgotten. Her name was Aspasia, and her story is both tragic and inspiring.[1]

Relatively little is known about Aspasia (this is part of the tragedy), but she came to Athens from a colony called Miletus in approximately 445 B.C.E. ("before the common era"). She took full advantage of her remarkable education—she was trained in rhetoric and music, among other subjects—and became a famous, powerful, and controversial figure. Not only did she meet and influence such major thinkers as Socrates, but also she wielded (or was accused of wielding) considerable political power.

---

1. I am indebted to Kevin O'Brien, a former student, for his help in researching Aspasia.

One key to her unequalled importance was, no doubt, her relationship with Pericles, the preeminent Athenian leader of the fifth century. She lived with Pericles, bore his son, and is given credit for helping him become the greatest orator of classical times. Some suggest that she was the ghost writer of his magnificent speeches. Though the story of Pericles and Aspasia has been told and retold throughout history, it is extremely difficult to separate fact from fiction or to bring Aspasia out from the shadow of Pericles, partly because her sex has inclined writers of most eras to doubt or denigrate her accomplishments. Her reputed status as a *hetaera*—a professional female companion—led in the past to her characterization as a kind of high-class whore. In her own time, the playwright Aristophanes made fun of her influence on Pericles. Novelists of Victorian England, on the other hand, preserved her purity by portraying her as married to Pericles. One sculpture shows her as a dignified, serene figure, almost like a goddess, whereas an eighteenth-century painting emphasizes her individuality, learning, and sexuality. None of her own writing remains, at least not under her name, and it is only within the last decade that scholarly reconstructions and reconsiderations of Aspasia have begun to claim a prominent and, one hopes, permanent place for Aspasia in the annals of rhetoric.

> *History has largely considered only Plato and other men to be philosophers; women philosophers are footnotes, freaks, groupies, and martyrs.—Madeleine Henry*

The twentieth-century writer Virginia Woolf emphasized the limitations placed on women by arguing that if Shakespeare had had a sister of equally immense talent, we would know nothing of her: she would have had no chance to cultivate and display her genius. In Aspasia of Miletus we have a kind of real-life "Shakespeare's sister," a woman we scarcely know whose genius may well have matched that of Socrates, Plato, and Pericles. Although Aspasia did make her mark against all odds, she is a powerful reminder of what Western culture has lost by restricting roles for women throughout the centuries.

Rhetoric in Rome: Cicero and Quintilian

For our limited purposes, rhetoric in Rome may be thought of as a Greek import. In fact, educated Romans spoke Greek as well as Latin, just as European scholars used Latin rather than their native languages for centuries after the fall of the Roman empire. In the interest of brevity, and given the fundamental similarity of Greek and Roman rhetoric, I would like merely to make a few comments about the two most important Roman rhetoricians, Cicero (106 to 43 B.C.E.) and Quintilian (ca. 35 to 96 C.E., "of the common era").

The high point in the whole history of rhetoric may have come early on with the multifaceted career of the Roman leader Cicero. The crucial link between rhetoric in Greece and in Rome, Cicero studied with Greek teachers in both Rome and Athens. He wrote a highly influential text on rhetoric, *Of Oratory;* complaining that some writers reduced rhetoric to superficial rules, he argued that rhetoricians should be concerned instead with "the organization of States, or the drafting of laws, or…the topics of fair-dealing, justice, loyalty, or the subduing of the passions or the building of human character." Most importantly, he applied his rhetorical knowledge successfully and honorably in such fields. In politics, he rose to the highest public office, that of consul. He was a splendid and prolific writer, and for centuries after his death, stylists studied his Latin in order to imitate its grace and power. He pursued educational and even cultural reform, maintaining ambitious goals for a highly literate society. Last but not least, he was the most brilliant lawyer of his day, a position he established early in his career with his dazzling prosecution of a corrupt governor of Sicily. In this case, Cicero's attack was so overwhelming that Hortensius, the hot-shot lawyer for Governor Verres, gave up without even speaking for the defense, leaving his client to go into exile. In all of this, Cicero's prowess as a rhetorician was fundamental to his public life. Power in Rome was all about rhetoric.

> *In an orator we must demand the subtlety of the logician, the thoughts of the philosopher, a diction almost poetic, a lawyer's memory, a tragedian's voice, and the bearing almost of the consummate actor.*—Cicero

Unfortunately, Roman politics grew bloody in the coming years (Cicero himself was assassinated—a sure sign of his potential danger to his enemies), and sheer force ruled. Some eighty years after Cicero, Quintilian—the other Roman rhetorician you might want to know about—confined his public argument primarily to legal cases, wisely risking no involvement in politics. (Just to show how dicey things got, in "the year of the four emperors," two were assassinated and another committed suicide.) The contrast between Cicero's era and Quintilian's is the contrast between the pen and the sword. Despite being shut out of politics, Quintilian kept alive Ciceronian ideals and, most important, created a blueprint for rhetorical education that lasted for two thousand years. Most of his ideas in *The Education of an Orator* came from Cicero and the Greek rhetorical tradition, but Quintilian arranged them into a clear and very comprehensive package that offered advice on everything from childhood education to literary criticism. Quintilian's admirers have included Martin Luther King, Jr., Erasmus, Alexander Pope, and John Quincy Adams, and students who learned according to his system include Churchill, Shakespeare, Milton, and Augustine.

Women's roles were severely restricted in Rome, and clearly no woman rivaled the activity or influence of Cicero or Quintilian. On the other hand, women's influence was not entirely absent, even in this highly masculinized world. On at least one occasion, Hortensia (daughter of the lawyer mentioned above) argued publicly and successfully against a new tax on women's wealth. Another remarkable woman, Cornelia, was bilingual in Greek and Latin and directed the rhetorical education of two sons (nine of her children died!) who became successful statesmen.

> *Let woman share the rights, and she will emulate the virtues of man.—Mary Wollstonecraft*

Classical Rhetoric Problematized

To be quite clear about it, let me state explicitly my hypothesis that a system of rhetorical education that survived for two thousand years—adapting itself in the process to social and political conditions ranging from medieval warfare to the French Revolution to abolitionism—and that produced hundreds of brilliant thinkers and writers, might have a few things to teach us even now. That's why this book contains some traditional ideas as well as modern ones. Though I greatly value the rhetorical tradition, here I'd like to introduce three absolutely fundamental problems with it. The first, introduced above, is that rhetoric was almost exclusively a male activity. Whenever sexism first arose—presumably in prehistoric times—it was firmly entrenched well before Aristotle. For the most part, rhetoric in ancient Greece and Rome was of the men, by the men, and for the men. Moreover, rhetoric remained primarily the province of males until well into the nineteenth century; throughout Western civilization, women were generally denied rhetorical education, just as they were denied access to the political processes, the courts, the universities, and the pulpits where such an education could be used directly and powerfully.

> *You pretend to admire me as a female prodigy, but there lurks sugared deceit in your adulation.—Laura Cereta*

A closely related problem is that rhetoric was essentially a *contest* between *individuals.* Rhetoric has always been about winning, whether a court case, an election, or simply a debate. It's a kind of ritualized combat, an intellectual and verbal game of king-of-the-hill. Rhetorical handbooks don't often teach compromise, conciliation, and collaboration. Chapter 5, Authority and Gender in Student Writing, discusses the implications for students of these first two problems.

The third problem with classical rhetoric is that it can't seem to get around the possibility, even the likelihood, that rhetorical power can be used for evil purposes. This issue concerned all of the great rhetorical thinkers, but none really solved the problem. At one extreme, Plato banned rhetoric from his imagined Republic because, compared to philosophical reasoning ("dialectic"), it was unreliable and subject to abuse. His student Aristotle, who was more of a pragmatist, settled for rhetoric as an imperfect but powerful method that helped people think carefully about what was true and good; according to Aristotle, truth supported by rhetoric would generally win out over the false or the evil, no matter how many rhetorical strategies these latter employed. As noted above, Cicero set very worthy goals for orators, and prominent among Quintilian's requirements for an orator is that he be a good man. Unfortunately, it seems clear that the scales are at best tipped only very slightly in favor of the moral speaker.

DECLINE, REVIVAL, EXPANSION

One thing I learned in college was that everything is inextricably connected to its historical, cultural, and political setting. The history of music, for example, continually reflects reactions not only to previous music, but also to the political climate, to technological advances that improve instruments, to patterns of human migration, and so on. Rhetoric is no exception to this rule of connection, and if you happen to know the broad outlines of European history, you will have a good idea of what happened to rhetoric after the fall of the Roman Empire. The three words that head this section—*decline, revival, expansion*—tell much of the story.

As for *decline*, though some historians object to calling the Middle Ages the Dark Ages, the term well suits the history of rhetoric at this time. As Europe struggled for a thousand years just to retain basic literacy—imagine that world if you can—classical rhetoric suffered every kind of problem imaginable. Manuscripts were abbreviated, corrupted, badly translated, misattributed, forgotten, lost, and destroyed. Most people, even nobles, were illiterate, as were nearly all women in western Europe. The Catholic Church, the most stable and powerful institution of this era, was ambivalent at best about rhetoric; deeming most classical Greek and Roman texts immoral, dangerous, or superfluous, the Church suppressed many such works. Athens became a backwater town, at least compared to its former glory. As a measure of how bad things got, consider that while Cicero and Quintilian were not entirely forgotten, their key works were not available for about a thousand years until their rebirth in the fifteenth century when, for example, a full text of Quintilian's *The Education of an Orator* was unearthed in a monastery.

Despite these woes, a couple of notable positive events occurred. First, the arts of letter writing and preaching developed. These were the first steps in the expansion of rhetoric into fields of communication beyond law, politics, and ceremonial speeches. Second, in what little education was going on, the seven liberal arts were established. These arts were based on classical knowledge and became the mold for education for centuries to come—hence, our "liberal arts" colleges. I list here the seven arts to emphasize that rhetoric was at one time at the heart of advanced education: grammar, dialectic ("logical argumentation," roughly), *rhetoric*, geometry, arithmetic, astronomy, music. Rhetoric held this prominent position until about a hundred years ago.

Composing and delivering a sermon...could not be done by the unlettered preacher, the overemotional revivalist, the self-seeking

*"professional," the lopsided esthete, the audience-ignoring techni-
cal theologician, or the morally weak orator. It required the holy
man skilled in speaking….—Russel Hirst*

Many of the tensions and problems surrounding rhetoric in the
Middle Ages are captured in the career and writing of Augustine, who
lived in the fourth and fifth centuries and was the most influential religious scholar of his time. First, his people were frequently fighting
pagan German tribes; he died, in fact, during a Vandal siege of Hippo
in North Africa. Second, he had taught rhetoric, including the ideas of
his hero, Cicero, for ten years before his conversion to Christianity; he
knew rhetoric was "profane," not sacred, but he couldn't unlearn
what he knew. He recognized that rhetorical persuasion could help
convert people to Christianity, but he also believed that the credit had
to go to God or to Biblical truth, *not* to the preacher/rhetorician or to
the canons of rhetoric. The Bible, meanwhile, was supposedly sacred
but presented all kinds of problems, from difficulties with translation
to the seeming redundancy of four gospels to the mixture of widely
diverse styles and genres (history, law, poetry, letters, and so on).
These problems would be understandable in a purely human product,
but shouldn't God be a better writer? And, of course, the "heretics"
who "misinterpreted" the Bible were sometimes very skillful rhetoricians. Despite Augustine's best efforts to subsume rhetoric into a
Christian context, it remained an unwelcome guest in the Church.
There was no home for it at all with pagan warriors, of course, and
there was no place else for it to go, except into hiding.

*Since through the art of rhetoric both truth and falsehood are
pleaded, who would be so bold as to say that against falsehood,
truth ought to stand unarmed?—Augustine*

Female rhetoricians were quite rare in medieval times, for they
faced all the problems discussed above plus a presumption of
women's intellectual inferiority and a host of legal and cultural barriers. Indeed, it is only thanks to researchers such as Cheryl Glenn
that the status of female rhetoricians in the Middle Ages can now be
upgraded to "rare" from "nonexistent." In the brief comments that
follow on Julian of Norwich and Margery Kempe, I am greatly indebted to Glenn's eye-opening *Rhetoric Retold*. Both women's stories are remarkable.

But because I am a woman, ought I therefore to believe that I should not tell you of the goodness of God, when I saw at that same time that it is his will that it be known?—Julian of Norwich

Julian of Norwich (1343 to 1415), a Benedictine nun, expressed herself in one of the very few ways allowed to women of her era—as a theological writer; her only known work describes her visionary and mystical religious experience. We know little of her education, though she was clearly familiar with the theological writings of Augustine and Gregory. Her description of herself as "unlettered" means that she probably did not know French or Latin, and it's possible that she dictated her own work. This much we do know: she asserted her right to speak, to address a Christian audience on matters of profound importance; she set a high value on women's prayer and worship; she envisioned God as inclusive, not male; she produced the earliest extant writing in English by a woman; and she was important to keeping English alive when French and Latin threatened to overwhelm it following the Norman Conquest. That's a pretty impressive record for someone living a life of pious seclusion. She was not a rhetorical theorist, but Glenn makes a strong case for considering her a highly accomplished, important, and innovative practitioner. She is a precursor of women like Sojourner Truth, women relegated to the margins of mainstream discourse who then wrote themselves into those margins in indelible ink.

The same could be said of Margery Kempe (died ca. 1438), who met and was guided by Julian. Kempe is a fascinating figure whose sole work, a spiritual autobiography, was dictated to two scribes late in her life. *The Book of Margery Kempe* found a small audience in its own day but disappeared for centuries until a single preserved copy was discovered in 1934. That's the kind of thing that happens when people don't support libraries! Like Julian, Kempe can lay claim to a bit of literary history: hers is the earliest extant autobiography written in English. Also like Julian, Kempe was a mystical writer, and her visions have sometimes been dismissed as hysteria rather than religious revelation. The autobiography is strange to modern sensibilities; it is written in the third person, for example, and events are not recorded in chronological order. But what a life it reveals! A middle-class, uneducated woman, Kempe had fourteen children, ran a brewery, traveled throughout Europe, made a pilgrim-age to the Holy Land, and had religious visions. She eventually turned to chastity and describes telling her husband, who insisted on knowing, that she would indeed rather see him beheaded than re-sume sexual relations. Her book, like Julian's, is not rhetorical theory, but it is the invention, from scratch, of a rhetorical vehicle which well suits both her humble audience and her spiritual message.

Rhetoric emerged from hiding in the Renaissance (the period lasting roughly from the fourteenth to the seventeenth centuries, depending on the country), along with other aspects of classical learning and culture, and it multiplied like rabbits in the outback. Where little had happened for centuries, suddenly everything hap-pened at once, in areas ranging from letter writing to literature to courtly politics. Where there had existed only about 100 texts before 1500, there were now 800 editions by a single scholar, Peter Ramus. Thousands of authors, writing in at least a dozen languages, inves-tigated every aspect of rhetoric, and they disputed about them all ("systematics" versus Ramists versus Senecans versus scholastics versus Ciceronians versus anti-Ciceronians). Writers best known for other accomplishments—Petrarch and Machiavelli in Italy, Eras-mus in northern Europe, Sir Thomas More and Francis Bacon in England—were well educated in rhetoric and wrote theoretical works about it. Also, a few more women gained access to good ed-ucations and, thus, rhetoric. Behind all this activity is a newfound recognition of rhetoric as the study of language at work in human society.

> *The speech of man is a magnificent and impressive thing when it surges along like a golden river, with thoughts and words pouring out in rich abundance.*—Erasmus

> *Few words, but to effect.*—King Lear

Ever since the Renaissance, this study of language has intensified and become more and more specialized. Modern universities, though variously organized, typically contain many departments that study issues that are, historically speaking, rhetorical—philosophy and En-glish, most obviously, but also linguistics, communications, psychol-ogy, journalism, speech, radio/TV/film, advertising, marketing, and

---

☒ Writing break

Exploring Modern Theories of Language

The section Classical Rhetoric Problematized contains several generalizations about modern theories of language. Try applying them to one or more of the words/ideas listed below—not to produce a polished analysis, but merely to suggest interesting points of view or hypotheses about language and meaning.

addiction	heaven
liberal and conservative	right to life
cult	pro-choice
AIDS	homelessness
Third World	welfare reform
native	illegal alien
queer	ravish
angels	

To point this activity toward the chapter's featured paper topic, choose one or two key words or phrases from the persuasive writing you are analyzing.

As an example, I have used modern theories about language to generate these thoughts about the word *feminist*:

- Although a dictionary might give you some rough idea of what *feminist* means, it could not provide anything like a full understanding. The word's meaning depends on how people use it, and this might change.
- This word could imply condemnation or praise depending on the speaker and the audience. Because people disagree about what the word means, it might be explicitly or implicitly defined by different writers and speakers almost every time it is used.
- Can a man be a feminist? Does it mean the same thing when a woman and a man say, "I am a feminist"?
- Virtually any use of the word positions the speaker as either a supporter or an opponent of full equality for women.
- Feminism could become a powerful social force only when it adopted a name for itself.
- Negative connotations of *feminist* are strong enough that many people who strongly believe in women's complete equality hesitate to accept this label.
- The word is a young or recent one, but it has changed meaning significantly already with changing political agendas and public perceptions.
- *Feminist* has spawned at least one new term, Alice Walker's stronger concept associated with *womanist*. These quick language developments reflect or maybe help produce social change.

some areas of law, anthropology, political science, women's studies, and many others. Like rhetoric in the Renaissance, rhetoric today defies summary. In lieu of summary, then, I would like to try to suggest the flavor of modern thought about language with a handful of nonobvious claims about rhetoric and communication. Some of these may seem as strange to you as the notions that gravity bends time or that some infinities are bigger than others, but they may also be just as true.

- Meaning does not exist in a dictionary or in any other written definition; meaning exists only in social and cultural contexts, in conversations (oral or printed) between people.
- *All* language is rhetorical, that is, has aims and purposes that determine its precise form; there is no such thing as a neutral description or an objective account of something. To use Richard Weaver's term, *all* language is "sermonic"—that is, it preaches, it promotes certain values.
- Language is not logical, never has been, never will be.
- The meaning of language does not reside in words themselves or in rules about how to string words together. *All* language use is interpretation, with all the ambiguity interpretation implies.
- Language does not report knowledge, it creates knowledge. Communities make things "true" through the way they talk about them. We pretend language is neutral in order to hide how the prevailing language supports the prevailing power structure of a society.

These are abstract, difficult concepts, and in trying to explain them and trace their implications, scholars tend to write book-length studies. I won't ask you to go swimming in that ocean, but the Writing Break on the previous page invites you to wade along its beaches. (You can think and write profitably on your own about these issues, but it can really help to have a class conversation: The instructor can clarify or complicate the issues, as appropriate.)

RHETORIC IN THE UNITED STATES

Rhetoric has been especially important in the United States for a couple of reasons. First, it was central to education in the liberal arts, for American universities imitated the course of study in English and European universities, which in turn owed a great deal, so far as rhetoric is concerned, to Quintilian and the classical scholarship he systematized. A writer such as Ralph Waldo Emerson, the most admired American essayist of the nineteenth century, then, was well steeped in a classical tradition, even as he championed distinctively American literature and arts.

In a similar way, American preachers studied the techniques of their European predecessors, who had been refining the rhetorical arts in religious contexts since Augustine. One could argue that the rhetorical tradition of preaching—the homiletic tradition—has continued uninterrupted from the time of the first European settlement to the present, however great a gap may seem to exist between Puritan fire-and-brimstone sermons and today's slick televangelism. Lots of religious traditions have arrived on American soil since Jamestown was settled in 1607 (to say nothing of the survival of Native American belief systems), but you don't have to look far to find preaching whose rhetorical strategies come straight out of a centuries-old European heritage.

As you can see around you, though, the rhetorical tradition in higher education *has* been very much interrupted; rhetoric is no longer a unified and prestigious discipline, but has apparently given up some of its most interesting aspects to other fields—for example, mass communications—leaving only composition, or academic writing, as a vestige of rhetoric's 2,500-year history. What happened, and why?

> *Too much is said of women being better educated, that they may become better companions and mothers for men.... A being of infinite scope must not be treated with a view to any one relation.*
> —*Margaret Fuller*

In an article entitled "Women's Reclamation of Rhetoric in Nineteenth-Century America," Robert J. Connors makes a strong case that what triggered the decline of rhetoric in American education was the entrance of women into male colleges and universities. Connors points out that until the nineteenth century, rhetoric was an all-male activity, and the thought of women rhetoricians was "either frightening or humorous to male orators." Stereotypes of women as fragile, illogical, and intellectually inferior made them seem ill-suited for an activity that was in essence a war of words and, in addition, a preparation for careers in law and politics, fields off limits to women. Connors emphasizes the competitive or "agonistic" nature of oratory: "Classical rhetoric is, plain and simple, about fighting, ritual fighting with words." As American women made their way into higher education, something had to give; either people had to reformulate their understanding of what women could do or the educational system had to change so that women were not tainted by unseemly, intellectually violent activities like debating.

The latter occurred, and the change was rapid. Connors writes that while there were no women in college in 1830, three quarters of American colleges admitted women by 1900. As a result, rhetorical education changed in four key ways:

- student/teacher relationships became less judgmental, more nurturing;
- the emphasis shifted from oral to written performance;
- the emphasis shifted from argumentative to explanatory writing; and
- personal assignments replaced abstract subjects for writing.

These shifts occurred because the institutions could not imagine pitting men against women in verbal contest. There was no glory, only shame, in defeating a female opponent—and the idea that women might routinely win was unthinkable. Written composition about personal topics, on the other hand, was considered safe territory. Since 1900, *rhetoric* in American higher education has meant "composition." To make a long story short, it has been marginalized in many ways, most notably, perhaps, by becoming conceptualized as "women's work"—tedious, unglamorous work—taught largely by women without Ph.D.s or tenure, by women with heavy teaching loads and low salaries (perhaps working at multiple institutions), by women with limited or no health benefits.

If that's the bad news, the good news is exactly the same: composition is women's work. Because college writing instruction has depended so heavily on women, it has been in a good position to take advantage of the revelations of recent feminist thought.

> *The cheapness of writing paper is, of course, the reason why women have succeeded as writers before they have succeeded in the other professions.*—Virginia Woolf

More than many academic fields, lowly composition has critiqued traditional "knowledge" and "ways of knowing," to borrow a phrase from Mary Belenky and her colleagues. Composition has also done a lot to welcome students of nontraditional backgrounds to higher education and has been a leader in implementing innovative methods of teaching such as collaborative learning. The field is in good hands, then, and as I argue below, there's at least some hope that in the next century rhetoric will regain a higher status, not just as rewarmed Quintilian, but as an art of inquiry and communication regarding matters of enduring importance.

Although rhetoric has fallen on tough times within American higher education, it has always been extremely important in American public life. You will recall that rhetoric emerged in Greece along with democratic government and that it flowered in Rome before the later emperors took all power into their own hands. Rhetoric flourishes, then, when persuasive speech and writing can exert a real influence on a nation's course. Certainly, the United States has been such a country more than most others, however short we have fallen of democratic ideals. To illustrate the significance of rhetoric in the practical affairs of the nation—not just in classrooms—the next two sections ask you to consider the role of rhetoric during two important historical eras: the founding of the nation and the abolitionist struggle against slavery.

Rhetoric and the Birth of the United States

It would be absurd to argue that the colonies broke free from England merely because some folks spoke persuasively, but it is reasonable to argue that the break could not have occurred without the rhetoric of people like Patrick Henry, Thomas Paine, Samuel Adams (a "brewer and patriot," as the beer bottle says, *with a Harvard education*), and a host of other orators and rabble-rousers. Public oratory played an important role in the widespread riots protesting the Stamp Act of 1765, for example, which were "rehearsals" for the Boston Tea Party and the Declaration of Independence, itself a work of immense rhetorical sophistication—and one whose strategies Aristotle and Cicero would have fully understood. The Continental Congress, which cemented the colonies' resistance to England and spread Bostonian radicalism throughout the nation, was a rhetorical battle royal, as delegates debated courses of action ranging from conciliation to economic boycott. Most famous of all colonial pamphlets, but just one among thousands, was Thomas Paine's *Common Sense,* which appeared in Philadelphia on January 9, 1776. This incendiary piece of rhetoric is often credited with moving the Second Continental Congress irreversibly down the path toward independence. Here is a sample of what historian Gary Nash has called its "muscular language":

> But if you say, you can still pass the violations over [that is, if you can forgive the violations of the British against the colonists], then I ask, hath your house been burnt? Hath your property been destroyed before your face? Are your wife and children destitute of a bed to lie on, or bread to live on? Have you lost a parent or a child by their hands, and yourself the ruined and wretched survivor? If you have not, then you are not a judge of those who have. But if you have, and can still shake hands with the murderers, then are you unworthy of the name of husband, father, friend, or lover, and whatever may be your rank or title in life, you have the heart of a coward, and the spirit of a sycophant.

Them's fightin' words.

Note that this whole enterprise—trying to reach a public concensus, through the use of rhetoric, on a matter of civic importance—mirrors Greek and Roman assumptions about rhetoric and an educated populace. Put simply, people figured out what to do by debating issues in various public forums. You may feel so distant from our federal government today that this concept seems implausible, but it was strong in the United States until about 1850. Rhetoricians were men of action and power, not mere scholars: John Quincy Adams, before he was our sixth President, taught rhetoric at Harvard. I've described above how the entry of women into higher education helped changed the role of rhetoric after the Civil War. Scholars also point to the emergence of increasingly specialized fields of knowledge as the country became more urban, industrialized, and commercial; they also cite the country's cultural shift toward individualism rather than community values. These two trends diminished the relevance of classical rhetoric both in the university and in public life.

Rhetoric and Slavery

I do not wish to think, or speak or write, with moderation. No!
no! tell a man whose house is on fire to give a moderate alarm;
tell him to moderately rescue his wife from the hands of the ravisher.
—William Lloyd Garrison

My second example of rhetoric's sway in the nation's history also comes from before the Civil War: the abolitionist movement to end slavery. Again the very existence of the Union was at stake. And again, as in the founding of the republic, actual war followed the rhetorical war. In the decades leading up to the shelling of Fort Sumter, rhetoric was exercised in every conceivable way, by pro- and antislavery groups. The Clay–Calhoun–Webster debate of 1850, for example, galvanized the country as three aging but powerful senators exchanged their last verbal broadsides on slave territories, the Fugitive Slave Act, and the possible secession of Southern states. Rhetoric was not confined to Congress, however, or to election-year stump speeches, or even to antislavery publications such as *The Liberator*, founded by William Lloyd Garrison in 1831, or the *North Star*, founded by ex-slave Frederick Douglass in 1847. Preachers, too, were expected to make their views clear—to "guide their flocks" on the country's most divisive moral issue; to make his sermons not only clear, but also unforgettable, abolitionist Henry Ward Beecher repeatedly spoke from the pulpit with a chained slave on display.

It's hard to imagine the scope and intensity of the slavery debate, but one measure of its prominence in public discourse is that the total number of abolitionist sermons, speeches, pamphlets, and books numbered over 1 million. By far the most rhetorically powerful of all these works—it outsold every book but the Bible in the nineteenth century—was a novel, *Uncle Tom's Cabin*, by Harriet Beecher Stowe. You may not be accustomed to thinking of novels as rhetorical works, but *Uncle Tom's Cabin* is unmistakably a story with a moral message. It is designed to persuade its audience that slavery must end, and it does so by using all the techniques recommended by classical rhetoricians: it appeals to the reader's emotions with tear-jerking scenes of slaves being mistreated (*pathos*); it appeals to her reason, offering explanations of why slavery offends Christianity (*logos*); finally, it is permeated with the aura of Stowe's reliability as a trustworthy, moral speaker (*ethos*)—not surprising when you consider that she came from a family in which you couldn't swing a dead cat without hitting a minister.

What happens in the novel—its plot—systematically lays bare the moral bankruptcy of slavery: mothers are separated from their children without warning; slaves are bartered like cattle; the meek, mild, Christ-like Uncle Tom dies at the hand of a brutal master (and Stowe compares his patient suffering explicitly to Christ's crucifixion). The shape of the story itself, constructed as it is to teach a moral lesson, is fundamentally rhetorical in nature. In addition, the novel accommodates many other occasions for oratory. For example, Stowe lets us listen in on Northerners trying to rationalize slavery, revealing as she does so the superficiality of their self-serving arguments. At another point, a kind woman named Mrs. Bird berates her husband for voting for the Fugitive Slave Act, which outlawed assistance to runaway slaves:

> "You ought to be ashamed, John! Poor, homeless, houseless creatures! It's a shameful, wicked, abominable law, and I'll break it, for one, the first time I get a chance; and I hope I shall have a chance, I do! Things have got to a pretty bad pass, if a woman can't give a warm supper and a bed to poor, starving creatures, just because they are slaves, and have been abused and oppressed all their lives, poor things!"

It's not hard to see a character like Mrs. Bird as a mouthpiece for Stowe. And at other times, Stowe speaks to the reader directly, lecturing the reader for a few moments, as in the passage below from her final chapter, Concluding Remarks. I quote at some length because Stowe typically wrote at some length:

> Nothing…can be written, can be spoken, can be conceived, that equals the frightful reality of scenes daily and hourly acting on our shores, beneath the shadow of American law, and the shadow of the cross of Christ.
>
> And now, men and women of America, is this a thing to be trifled with, apologized for, and passed over in silence? Farmers

of Massachusetts, of New Hampshire, of Vermont, of Connecticut, who read this book by the blaze of your winter-evening fire,—strong-hearted, generous sailors and ship-owners of Maine,—is this a thing for you to countenance and encourage? Brave and generous men of New York, farmers of rich and joyous Ohio, and ye of the wide prairie states,—answer, is this a thing for you to protect and countenance? And you, mothers of America,—you, who have learned, by the cradles of your own children, to love and feel for all mankind,—by the sacred love you bear your child; by your joy in his beautiful, spotless infancy; by the motherly pity and tenderness with which you guide his growing years; by the anxieties of his education; by the prayers you breathe for his soul's eternal good;—I beseech you, pity the mother who has all your affections, and not one legal right to protect, guide, or educate the child of her bosom! By the sick hour of your child; by those dying eyes, which you can never forget; by those last cries, that wrung your heart when you could neither help nor save; by the desolation of that empty cradle, that silent nursery,—I beseech you, pity those mothers that are constantly made childless by the American slave-trade! And say, mothers of America, is this a thing to be defended, sympathized with, passed over in silence?

Though this passage remains moving, if old-fashioned, most of Stowe's speeches have not stood the test of time very well because of the underlying racism in her views. Despite her opposition to slavery, she clearly did not see Africans as equal to Europeans and Americans, but more as unfortunate, childlike people to be pitied, rescued, and Christianized. The insulting name Uncle Tom, as you may know, comes from Stowe's portrait of a slave who meekly and piously accepts every outrageous action of his cruel master, never resisting but patiently awaiting his reward in heaven.

To balance the attention given here to *Uncle Tom's Cabin*, my discussion of rhetoric and abolitionism concludes with a look at a related but quite different African American genre, the slave narrative. The stories of ex-slaves, like Stowe's novel, are essentially narrative works, not speeches. Taken as a whole, though, they are perfect examples of Richard Weaver's claim that all language is "sermonic": They are sermons in a different form, rhetorical arguments against slavery fleshed out and made dramatic, visual, almost palpable.

The rhetorical occasion, or context, of slave narratives was complex and delicate. If one key to persuading an audience is subtly to impress upon them your reliability and morality, that's a tough challenge for a black speaker addressing a white audience in the 1840s. In addition, even the most ardent abolitionists did not see Africans as equals, so the kind of claims made a century later in the Civil Rights Movement could not be publicly voiced. The narratives could not afford to offend white allies who might have the power to end slavery, so writers and speakers had to conceal some of the worst things they knew, because Northern audiences would not believe that their fellow citizens could be so cruel. Finally, the veracity of slave narratives was routinely challenged by advocates of slavery North and South, as people tried to dismiss them as sensational, dishonest pieces of Northern propaganda. Because he was such an effective speaker, many people doubted that Frederick Douglass, author of the best-known slave narrative, could ever have been a slave. To combat such criticism, whether in print or at meetings, ex-slaves and their narratives were often introduced by white abolitionists who would vouch for their truthfulness.

For the most part, slave narratives recounted stories in seemingly straightforward ways, following chronological order, avoiding flowery writing, and letting the facts speak for themselves. Of course, this does not necessarily lessen the rhetorical effectiveness of the prose. Here is an example of very plain writing from the *Narrative of the Life of Frederick Douglass, an American Slave* that is quite powerful even out of context:

> I was seldom whipped by my old master, and suffered little from any thing else than hunger and cold. I suffered from hunger, but much more from cold. In hottest summer and coldest winter, I was kept almost naked—no shoes, no stockings, no jacket, no trousers, nothing on but a coarse tow linen shirt, reaching only to my knees. I had no bed. I must have perished with cold, but that, the coldest nights, I used to steal a bag which was used for carrying corn to the mill. I would crawl into this bag, and there sleep on the cold, damp, clay floor, with my head in and feet out. My feet have been so cracked with the

frost, that the pen with which I am writing might be laid in the gashes.

Douglass was quite capable of shifting rhetorical gears when the occasion called for it; here is a rather different passage asking readers to imagine the predicament even escaped slaves found themselves in, given the Fugitive Slave Act:

> The motto which I adopted when I started from slavery was this—"Trust no man!" I saw in every white man an enemy, and in almost every colored man cause for distrust. It was a most painful situation; and, to understand it, one must needs experience it, or imagine himself in similar circumstances. Let him be a fugitive slave in a strange land—a land given up to be the hunting-ground for slaveholders—whose inhabitants are legalized kidnappers—where he is every moment subjected to the terrible liability of being seized upon by his fellowmen, as the hideous crocodile seizes upon his prey!—I say, let him place himself in my situation—without home or friends—without money or credit—wanting shelter, and no one to give it—wanting bread, and no money to buy it,—and at the same time let him feel that he is pursued by merciless men-hunters, and in total darkness as to what to do, where to go, or where to stay,—perfectly helpless as to the means of defence and means of escape,—in the midst of plenty, yet suffering the terrible gnawings of hunger,—in the midst of houses, yet having no home,—among fellow-men, yet feeling as if in the midst of wild beasts, whose greediness to swallow up the trembling and half-famished fugitive is only equalled by that which the monsters of the deep swallow up the helpless fish upon which they subsist,—I say, let him be placed in this most trying situation.... Then, and not till then, will he fully appreciate the hardships of, and know how to sympathize with, the toil-worn and whip-scarred fugitive slave.

American Rhetoric Today and Tomorrow

State of the Union speeches never mention the health of rhetoric in the United States, but if they did, it would have to be admitted that the prognosis is rather dire at the moment. The level of our political rhetoric was abysmally low even before President Clinton's impeachment. Principles take a back seat to reelection, and while speech making, campaigning, and fund raising grow increasingly sophisticated, expediency reigns; campaigns are about images, sound bites, hollow promises, and, too often, appeals to fear and prejudice. Of course, politics has never been a gentle art, but perhaps only in recent times have its dramas been played out with such scientific precision and such deep cynicism. Political campaigns differ little from advertising campaigns—thus, our fondness for "policies" that can be reduced to slogans (Read my lips, no new taxes; It's the economy, stupid; Just say no). It's an MTV, bumper-sticker world.

We face some serious challenges in areas beyond politics, as well. Think of talk radio, of court cases that become media spectacles, of con artists posing as preachers. While the vast majority of the people involved in radio, law, and religion are honest and reasonable, there are enough unscrupulous, deceptive, and manipulative speakers to make us all a little suspicious. Rhetoric becomes news most often when it's abused.

Part of the problem lies, no doubt, with the power and nature of media today (I only remind you of what you know and ask you to connect it to rhetoric). In contemporary culture, a picture may be worth far more than a thousand words, we are so easily swayed by images and so impatient with complex reasoning. And even when the focus is on words, not images, we have plenty to be embarrassed about: think of the worst talk shows you've seen on television.

Nevertheless, there are some signs that the nation might yet recover its health. For one thing, our understanding of language and communication has never been better. Twentieth-century scholarship in linguistics, sociology, philosophy, mass communications, English, and other fields has given us a much more sophisticated and accurate knowledge of how language works. Such knowledge makes propagandists and demagogues more dangerous, but it can also be used to resist them. As in Lincoln's day, it remains impossible to fool all of the people all of the time.

For anyone who wants to be informed and thoughtful beyond the nightly news level, there are plenty of sources of information and varying perspectives available. Although a relatively small number of media conglomerates are threatening to control an ever-larger share of American and international publications, we still have access to more informed, well-reasoned, and diverse perspectives than any previous era has enjoyed. The Internet, too, offers ordinary citizens extremely low-cost access to both information and audience, to a degree unprecedented in human history.

Within the field of rhetoric itself, the (re)gendering of both the historical record and current theory bodes well for the future and is just one sign of the deep and lasting benefits of feminism. Indeed, the most hopeful thought of all is that a kind of political activism concerning language seems to be chalking up real gains in innumerable areas, from the way textbooks are written to water-cooler conversations to alternative Webzines. Despite our problems, then, it may be a little early to write off the twenty-first century.

⊠   ⊠   ⊠

The two essays that follow speak to the crucial role rhetoric still plays in the public life of the United States. Both are rhetorical analyses of the Clinton/Dole presidential campaign of 1996. (Recall that before President Clinton used rhetoric to defend his presidency, he used it to gain office.) Michael Kelly's "Running On" compares and contrasts Clinton's rhetorical sophistication with challenger Bob Dole's shortcomings and all but predicts the easy victory Clinton eventually achieved. Hendrik Hertzberg's "Big Talk" is a humorous but ultimately dark look at some details of the campaign rhetoric. Both pieces appeared originally in *The New Yorker*.

RUNNING ON

Michael Kelly

On Wednesday of last week, the morning in Pueblo, Colorado, was nearly perfect. The sky was blue and the sun was bright and hot, and there wasn't a drop of humidity in the air. The Pueblo County courthouse, which was built in 1908, is a handsome block of white sandstone, fronted with massive Corinthian columns and topped by a tin dome of vaguely Byzantine parentage. On the pediment above the columns are chiseled the words "Vox Populi Vox Dei" ("the

Voice of the People, the Voice of God"), testimony to a time when the passion for democracy was so strong it tempted men to blasphemy. On this later day, when President Clinton stopped by the courthouse in a campaign swing arcing across Missouri, Colorado, Arizona, and California, there wasn't much emotion evident. The street in front of the courthouse and a parking lot behind it were pretty well packed, and up against a row of heavy steel crowd-control fences in front of the speaker's platform people were crammed body to body, but it was a happy, unthreatening crowd: the average age of those in the front was about eleven. Students from public schools all over Pueblo had been excused from classes, given specially stamped tickets that allowed them access to the area directly in front of the stage, and bused to the courthouse before most adults arrived. They filled the area in the front, and, although they had been waiting for hours by the time Clinton arrived, they were still full of exuberant good cheer, waving "Clinton-Gore '96" posters and "U.S.A." balloons that they had been given by the campaign, and yelling "Hi, Bill!" and "Look at me, Bill!" Behind the children, the ranks were thinner, but they had been cunningly arranged by rope lines and riot fences to form masses in the right places, so that the event seemed larger and more festive than it was.

The President appeared before the people suddenly and theatrically, walking out of the dark open front door of the courthouse, framed visually by the large white columns on either side and aurally by the amplified strains of "Hail to the Chief." He strode down the stone steps, which had been lined with flags, and up to the platform and onto the podium. He gave a long speech. It was not a good speech in any classical sense—it was, as most of his speeches are, too multitudinous in specifics, and lacking in coherence—but it was casual and fluid, moving from one part to another with an internal rhythm. It was likable, and the man who was delivering it was likable, too. Above all, it was relentlessly sunny, assuring those who were listening that they lived in a great and good time.

Sitting on the steps of the half-empty press platform, enjoying the sun on my face and the sight of a performing politician going through his paces with such easy, lazy strength, I had a feeling I had been there before, and, of course, I had. Bill Clinton in the early autumn of 1996 is exactly where he planned to be, and where his smart strategists planned to have him. He has run not as George Bush in 1988 but as Ronald Reagan in 1984, and this campaign is "Morning in America II." The carefully built crowds, the insistently Presidential nature of the President in his public appearances, the heavy reliance on human props in the form of local heroes or hardluck stories (in Phoenix later that day he added to his schedule a hospital visit to the conservative icon Barry Goldwater; in St. Louis the night before, he had spoken movingly of a "beautiful ten-year-old boy" who had died in the crash of T.W.A. Flight 800, and whom, incredibly, he presented as a martyr of sorts because the child had declined to appear in a political advertisement against Clinton), and even the personal mannerisms (Clinton's formerly limp salute has become a Reaganesque beauty, crisp and snappy without being pompous)—it is all Reagan '84, the candidate as the leader of an America that is a shining city on a hill. And Bob Dole is all Walter Mondale, the dark man in the corner carping that it isn't morning at all—it's evening, and night is approaching fast.

A year ago, Clinton's strategists thought that the President was going to have to run on the strength of relatively minor claims of nation-improving—he had signed the Family Medical Leave Act and the Brady Bill, had banned some species of assault weapons, had put more police officers on the streets, and so on. What's more, they felt sure that even these modest assertions would have to fight against a prevailing public sentiment that the nation was, in the language of the pollsters, "on the wrong track," not "heading in the right direction." It appeared that the argument to reëlect Clinton would have to be based on fear of the alternative, rather than on a positive rationale. Two things happened to change this. The first was that the economy, which had been running at a modestly strong clip, got stronger and stayed that way. The second was that Clinton waged the fear campaign, and won it, in the context of the 1995 budget face-off with Newt Gingrich's 104th Congress. This victory, due almost entirely to Clinton's superior demagogic abilities, utterly changed the dynamic between the White House and Congress. Gingrich and company argued that the Republicans were saving the children from coming of age in a bankrupt America, while Clinton and the Democrats argued that *they* were saving the old folks from being tossed in the gutter, and Clinton made the more convincingly frightening case. Blamed for shutting down the government, the Republicans' need for accomplishments suddenly outweighed their desire to deny Clinton accomplishments of his own. Thus, the election year saw the passage of the first minimum-wage increase in five years, the end of welfare as a federal entitlement, and the Kennedy-Kassenbaum health-insurance-reform act.

By the summer of 1996, Clinton's pollsters, the New York firm of Penn & Schoen, had evidence that the balance of belief was reversing itself: for the first time in years, as many voters believed that the country was heading in the right direction as believed the contrary. Clinton saw the change coming early, and recognized its significance.

The President decided that, while he would not abandon fear as a campaign theme (the phrase "Dole-Gingrich" recurs endlessly), he would subordinate it. Partly hidden within the Morning campaign's sunny positivism is a relentlessly attacking negative campaign. Although Clinton frequently proclaims, in Reaganesque terms, that he will not stoop to "the politics of who is to blame," he does just that, all the time. In his St. Louis speech, he told the voters that when the Republicans had their turn in power "they said, 'We'll balance the budget by giving people like the President, who didn't need it, a tax cut, and cutting Medicare, destroying Medicaid's guarantee of thirty years to poor children and pregnant women, and middle-class families with members with disabilities, and the elderly in nursing homes, by cutting back on education when we need to be investing more, by weakening our environmental protection when we need to be doing more.'" The Clinton campaign's massive program of television advertising has overwhelmingly featured negative ads, and has been notable for its rawness. A commercial attacking Dole for his opposition to the Family Medical Leave Act that was released last week in a number of battleground states juxtaposed Dole's opposition with the death from cancer of a twelve-year-old girl called Melissa. "Melissa lived every moment," her mother says. "She maintained that positive attitude until the last day," her father adds. "Bob Dole led a six-year fight against Family Leave," the announcer declares. "President Clinton understands the struggle that families go through," the mother says.

Dole did not see the climate change coming and did not react when it arrived. The tonal parameters of the contest between him and Clinton were set in what amounted to their first debate—Clinton's 1996 State of the Union Address and Dole's response. Clinton played his prolix version of Reagan, accentuating the positive as he ran through his long laundry list of America's successes in the past four years and his promises of more successes in the next four, calling on heroes in the audience, and stressing the themes of unity and progress. Dole played his dour version of Mondale, standing uncomfortably before the camera to warn the people that they lived in a dangerous and foreboding time, and in a nation at risk.

It is in theory possible for a Midnight in America argument to beat a Morning in America argument, if the former is very strong and the latter is very weak. That is the faint hope of the Dole campaign as it prepares for its last chance—the Presidential debates of late September and October. In this regard, it is getting difficult not to simply feel pity for Dole. Clinton's great ability as a political performer lies in his talent for cloaking his negative message with a positive one. It is a talent for weaving conflicting and disparate elements into a disparate, intricate whole. Merely addressing what Clinton says is an exhausting, endless chore, as George Bush found, because he says so much and because the things he says are all so mixed together—some are true, some not; some are important, some are meaningless; some have nothing to do with Clinton; some are real, some are vapor.

The speech that Clinton gave the afternoon of Tuesday, September 10th, at Samuel Shephard Gateway Educational Park, in St. Louis, is a fair example of the President in action. Here is a partial list of the things the President claimed, or seemed to claim, credit for: the vote that day by the United Nations to ban nuclear testing, which Clinton suggested was the result of his determination "to lift the cloud of nuclear threats from our children and our future" (in reality, it had little to do with Clinton); the "lowest unemployment rate in seven and a half years, ten point five million new jobs, wages going up again for the first time in a decade" (true, and partly due to Clinton); passage of an expanded earned-income tax-credit program (true), which meant that "fifteen million hardworking American families got a tax cut, so they would always want to stay off welfare and keep working" (vapor); passage of the Family Medical Leave Act (true), which meant that "twelve million families got to take a little time off from work without losing their jobs for the birth of a baby or the illness of a parent" (true); passage of an increase in the minimum wage, which meant that "ten million Americans on October the first are going to get an increase in minimum wage" (true); a "crime bill that put one hundred thousand police on the street" (false) "and banned assault weapons" (partly true; not all are banned); cleaning up "more toxic-waste sites in the last three years than were cleaned up in the previous twelve years" (true); bringing the deficit down "in each of the four years that I've been President" (true) "for the first time since before the Civil War" (meaningless: for several decades after the Civil War the government ran surpluses); a "dramatic" reduction in the murder rate in St. Louis and the crime rate generally in the nation (nothing to do with Clinton).

To mount a successful counter to a cotton-candy confection of this sort requires an ability to argue on Clinton's level, and on his terms—to argue both thematically and particularly, and to do so with a suppleness of mind and a facility of tongue matching Clinton's. Dole did this in his superb acceptance speech at the Republican Convention, but that was an atypical performance. Dole's favorite recourse when he is faced with the task of explaining an idea beyond two clauses is to mutter "whatever" and shut up. He can't grasp the idea that his opponent is operating on two contradictory levels at once, running a Terror Stalks the Nursing Home within a larger Morning in America campaign.

Last week, as Clinton was touring the West, Dole was back in Washington delivering what was billed as a pep talk. He talked about the campaign against him. "Fear," he said. "That's all they've got. They don't have any ideas. They don't have any agenda.... All they have is fear."

They do have that, and they use it. But they now have a good deal more as well. And Bob Dole seems to be the only man in politics who doesn't know it.

BIG TALK

Hendrik Hertzberg

So many words! At the national political conventions just completed, a couple of hundred thousand of them issued from the podiums—and that was on top of millions more poured forth at caucus meetings, delegation meetings, press conferences, and panel discussions, and into the microphones of an immense journalistic horde. Cascades of words, cataracts of words, great rolling tsunamis of words—all spoken for the purpose not of enlightening or entertaining, or even tricking, the public but of persuading it, by any verbal means necessary (including enlightenment, entertainment, and trickery, if that's what it takes), to vote the right way come November.

So little meaning! For when the object of the game is to sway the emotions of the largest possible masses of people vagueness is a precision tool. Politicians are not essayists; their purpose is not to make themselves clear but to make themselves, and their ideas, acceptable to a fleeting majority. The more precise a formulation is, the more it invites disagreement. If the essayist is a sculptor, chipping away at each thought until its significance is exact and unmistakable, the politician is a truck driver, hauling as much raw granite as his vehicle will hold. Both follow honorable trades, but each of them bears watching by the other.

In the verbal war for political domination, the big guns are the focus-group-tested "themes"—the Republicans' "Restoring the American Dream," the Democrats' "Putting Families First," the endlessly repeated references to values, strength, community, opportunity, diversity, work, responsibility, and the like. As Michael Kelly reports elsewhere in this issue, the parties invest enormous quantities of energy, ingenuity, and money in trying to create associations in the public mind between themselves and feel-good bromides of this kind. But there's some small-calibre ordnance lying around, too.

For example, the minute Bob Dole selected Jack Kemp as his running mate, a drumbeat went up from operatives of the Clinton campaign. Senator Christopher Dodd, the Democratic Party's general chairman, immediately went around describing Kemp's views as "totally out of the mainstream." George Stephanopoulos, a senior adviser to the President, added, "His economic ideas, while interesting, are certainly outside the mainstream, and in some cases even flaky." And deputy campaign manager Ann Lewis, speaking of Kemp's hard line on abortion, chimed in, "Let us be clear: that is an extreme position. That is not in the mainstream." The chorus continued right through the Democratic Convention, and it shows no signs of letting up.

It's not true, of course. Kemp's views may indeed be flaky (as is, arguably, his attachment to the gold standard). They may even be extreme (as is, certainly, his support for a constitutional amendment that would criminalize abortion in all instances). But, by definition, the long-held, well-known views of a major-party candidate for national office cannot be outside the mainstream. Beyond that, though, this sanctification of the mainstream as a political Ganges, a sacred river whose waters cleanse all impurities, is a thoroughly bad business. Mainstream-mongering suggests that the test of an idea is not logic, reason, or merit but conventionality. It implies that an unpopular, or even an unfamiliar, idea is per se a bad idea. Yet the list of ideas that were good many years before they were mainstream is a long and distinguished one—it includes abolitionism, woman suffrage, social security, child-labor laws, and the income tax. Without tributaries, after all, the mainstream dries up.

The season's most noticeable vogue word, however, is an innocent-sounding preposition. Having been thoroughly tested by the advertising and fashion industries, "about" has now become the new universal solvent of political language. Everything is about something, and, by contrast, is not about something else. The Republican Party is about inclusion. The Democratic Party is about working families. The Reform Party is about—or not about—Ross Perot. The beauty of "about" is that it suggests some sort of causal or programmatic relationship without having to specify one. "About" represents a technological leap over its predecessor, the verb "to address." Addressing problems long ago became the rhetorical substitute for solving them. But "addressing" calls a little too much attention to its own cluelessness. If "addressing" is a vacuum tube, the far speedier and more versatile "about" is a silicon chip.

The country's leading aboutnik, of course, is Bob ("That's what Bob Dole's all about") Dole. Yet the Republican nominee's acceptance speech in San Diego contained not a single instance of that invidious usage. More remarkably, it contained scarcely a single cliché, even in the pedestrian—and occasionally (such as an attack on United Nations Secretary-General Boutros Boutros-Ghali for having a foreign-sounding name) vulgar—passages that had obviously been shoehorned into the original draft, which, as was widely reported, was the work of the novelist Mark Helprin. Dole offered little of the usual vacant blather about "dreams," especially "the American dream," which the Republicans are "about" "restoring." On the contrary, Dole won the hearts of at least a few skeptical listeners by declaring that "facts are better than dreams," thus trashing the whole carefully devised theme of the Convention. The speech was a beautifully written exercise in old-fashioned rhetoric—so old-fashioned that it owed more to Pericles than to, say, Daniel Webster. In simple, elevated, rather archaic language, Dole embraced "God, family, honor, duty, country," and expressed a dignified contempt for money: "The triumph of this nation lies not in its material wealth but in courage, sacrifice, and honor."

Fine words, but the virtues they praise are martial, civic, public virtues. The great flaw in the speech was the absence of any connection between those virtues and the program they supposedly require: a huge, unfinanced tax cut skewed to the already well-off. Yes, Dole's was a wonderful speech, but its formal style was so remote from the candidate's usual way of talking, and its charm so much a result of its literary qualities, that one is hard put to imagine how it can endure and be replicated on the stump. What's more likely to endure in the public mind is the program: that great big tax cut, which Dole argued would simultaneously spur people to work harder and allow them more time to spend at home with their families—a neat trick, but perfectly manageable, no doubt, in the supply-side fantasy world Dole has chosen to enter, where cutting taxes raises revenues.

President Clinton, in accepting renomination two weeks later in Chicago, used up his opponent's allotment of clichés as well as his own. The President's speech was interminable and uninspiring. Its try for the vision thing, "a bridge to the future," was lifted directly from Dole's far more eloquent paean to the past: "Let me be the bridge to an America that only the unknowing call myth." But Clinton's lengthy list of modest, practical specific proposals—here a community-development bank and a bit of gun control, there a flextime law and an extra day in the hospital—is truer to his tinkerer's heart, and is probably more in tune with a public made wary of big promises and big plans. In any case, all was back to normal the next day. "It's about America," Dole told his first post-Convention rally. "It's about America's children. It's about the future."

DISCUSSION QUESTIONS
AND WRITING ASSIGNMENTS

On the Readings by Kelly and Hertzberg

1. Michael Kelly begins his essay by carefully describing the setting for President Clinton's appearance in Pueblo, Colorado. Why do you think he begins this way, and what elements of the setting seem most significant?

2. Which elements of Kelly's analysis echo ideas about rhetoric that you have encountered in this chapter or earlier in this book? Explain.

3. According to Kelly, in what specific ways did Clinton's rhetorical achievements contribute to his successful campaign? In what ways might Dole's failures be considered rhetorical weaknesses?

4. Describe Hertzberg's fundamental attitude toward the rhetoric of the 1996 campaign. How closely does it resemble your own attitude toward political campaigning? If you are cynical about politics, what would it take to change your attitude?

5. Hertzberg focuses on the words *mainstream* and *about*. Explain his objections to how these words were used in the campaign. In the coming week or two, pay attention to how often you hear these words and in what contexts. Compare notes with classmates. Do you find any evidence that the usages Hertzberg describes are still in vogue?

6. Hertzberg's essay contains a lot of effective metaphorical language. Some of Hertzberg's similes and metaphors are easy to spot, such as the statement "If 'addressing' is a vacuum tube, the far speedier and more versatile 'about' is a silicon chip"; others are quite subtle, such as the use of *spur* in the phrase "spur people to work harder" (which is metaphorical because no one is being physically prodded with actual spurs). Reread the essay and underline all the language that you consider metaphorical. Compare notes with classmates, focusing on Hertzberg's best metaphors and on the most subtly metaphorical words or phrases.

7. Hertzberg says that Dole's acceptance speech at the Republican convention was a "beautifully written exercise in old-fashioned

rhetoric." Obtain a copy of the speech, perhaps from the Internet, and analyze its rhetoric, attempting to understand precisely what Hertzberg means by his observation.

On Chapter 4

8. Write a journal entry or short paper in response to one or two of the quotations included in this chapter. Possible approaches include the following:

   - Explain the meaning of the quotation.
   - Use the quotation as a starting point for your own reflections or experience relating to the topic.
   - Amplify the quotation: develop it, provide examples.
   - Explain why you agree or disagree with the quotation.
   - Compare and contrast two or more quotations.

9. Classical rhetorical theory recognized three kinds of appeals in persuasive writing: appeals to the audience's reason (*logos*), to its emotions (*pathos*), and to its sense of the writer as a moral person (*ethos*). Examine one or more of the passages by Harriet Beecher Stowe and Frederick Douglass in the Rhetoric and Slavery in the Rhetoric in the United States section with this three-fold division in mind. Identify specific phrases, words, images, arguments, and so on as appeals to one or more of these three faculties.

10. Analyze the stylistic strategies of one or more of the passages by Harriet Beecher Stowe and Frederick Douglass in the Rhetoric and Slavery section of Rhetoric in the United States. How would you describe the style of each passage? For example, how would you characterize the writers' word choice, their sentence structures, their images? What words, images, and ideas are repeated, and why? In what specific ways does the language differ from "everyday" language, or from contemporary language? What effect does each passage seek to achieve, and how successful do you think it is? Do you see any connection between the specific stylistic choices and the writers' appeals to *logos, pathos,* and *ethos*?

11. Write a rhetorical analysis of one interesting document or speech related to the impeachment of President Clinton. You

might look, for example, at testimony by his legal defense team before the House Judiciary Committee, or at the House's actual articles of impeachment, or at statements made by your own senators or representative.

REFERENCES

Benson, Thomas W., ed. *American Rhetoric: Context and Criticism*. Carbondale: Southern Illinois University Press, 1989.

Bizzell, Patricia and Bruce Herzberg. *The Rhetorical Tradition: Readings from Classical Times to the Present*. New York: St. Martin's Press, 1990.

Clark, Gregory and S. Michael Halloran, eds. *Oratorical Culture in Nineteenth-Century America: Transformations in the Theory and Practice of Rhetoric*. Carbondale: Southern Illinois University Press, 1993.

Connors, Robert J. "Women's Reclamation of Rhetoric in Nineteenth-Century America." In Louise Wetherbee Phelps and Janet Emig, eds. *Feminine Principles and Women's Experience in American Composition and Rhetoric*. Pittsburgh: University of Pittsburgh Press, 1995.

Enos, Theresa, ed. *Learning from the Histories of Rhetoric: Essays in Honor of Winifred Bryan Horner*. Carbondale: Southern Illinois University Press, 1993.

Glenn, Cheryl. "Refiguring Aspasia in the History of Rhetoric." *College Composition and Communication* 45 (1994) 180–199.

———. *Rhetoric Retold: Regendering the Tradition from Antiquity through the Renaissance*. Carbondale: Southern Illinois University Press, 1997.

Golden, James L., Goodwin F. Berquist and William E. Coleman. *The Rhetoric of Western Thought* (5th ed.). Dubuque: Kendall/Hunt, 1992.

Henry, Madeleine M. *Prisoner of History: Aspasia of Miletus and Her Biographical Tradition*. New York: Oxford University Press, 1995.

Hirst, Russel. "The Sermon as Public Discourse: Austin Phelps and the Conservative Homiletic Tradition in Nineteenth-Century America." In Gregory Clark and S. Michael Halloran, eds., *Oratorical Culture in Nineteenth-Century America*. Carbondale: Southern Illinois University Press, 1993.

Horner, Winifred Bryan and Michael Leff. *Rhetoric and Pedagogy: Its History, Philosophy, and Practice; Essays in Honor of James J. Murphy*. Hillsdale, NJ: Lawrence Erlbaum Associates, 1995.

Julian of Norwich. *Julian of Norwich: Showings*. New York: Paulist, 1978.

Kempe, Margery. *The Book of Margery Kempe*, trans. by John Skinner. New York: Doubleday, 1998.

Kennedy, George A. *Classical Rhetoric and Its Christian and Secular Tradition from Ancient to Modern Times*. Chapel Hill: University of North Carolina Press, 1980.

Knoblauch, C. H. and Lil Brannon. *Rhetorical Traditions and the Teaching of Writing*. Boynton/Cook, 1984.

Lunsford, Andrea A., ed. *Reclaiming Rhetorica: Women in the Rhetorical Tradition.* Pittsburgh: University of Pittsburgh Press, 1995.

Murphy, James J. *A Short History of Writing Instruction from Ancient Greece to Twentieth-Century America.* Davis, CA: Hermagoras Press, 1990.

Nash, Gary B. et al. *The American People: Creating a Nation and a Society.* New York: Harper & Row, 1986.

Phelps, Louise Wetherbee and Janet Emig, eds. *Feminine Principles and Women's Experience in American Composition and Rhetoric.* Pittsburgh: University of Pittsburgh Press, 1995.

Reynolds, John Frederick. *Rhetorical Memory and Delivery: Classical Concepts for Contemporary Composition and Communication.* Hillsdale, NJ: Lawrence Erlbaum Associates, 1993.

Schiappa, Edward, ed. *Landmark Essays on Classical Greek Rhetoric.* Davis, CA: Hermagoras Press, 1994.

Waggenspack, Beth. "Women's Role in Rhetorical Traditions." Preliminary manuscript issued with Golden et al., *The Rhetoric of Western Thought* (5th ed.). Dubuque: Kendall/Hunt, 1992.

Welch, Kathleen E. *The Contemporary Reception of Classical Rhetoric: Appropriations of Ancient Discourse.* Hillsdale, NJ: Lawrence Erlbaum Associates, 1990.

Young, Richard E. and Yameng Liu. *Landmark Essays on Rhetorical Invention in Writing.* Davis, CA: Hermagoras Press, 1994.

5

Authority and Gender in Student Writing

In a world where language and naming are power,
silence is oppression, is violence.
—ADRIENNE RICH

Because the world contains more ideas and things than it does words, some words must have several meanings. *Authority* will be such a word in this chapter. Early in the chapter, authority will be presented as a worthy goal for a writer. You will learn ways to assert a healthy control over your writing—ways to make sure it feels like it really belongs to you. You'll find advice on choosing among paper topics, for example, and on quoting and using detail. Next, as an extended example of a writer's choices, the chapter focuses on gender issues (e.g., the choice of masculine or feminine pronouns), which are very much a matter of who decides what is appropriate in college or other writing.

Later in the chapter, *authority* will take on darker overtones as I show how scholarly, "authoritative" writing can be seen as *male* writing designed to exert control and thus inhibit or exclude many voices, in particular those of women. I'll point to ways some women have resisted or subverted traditional expectations and broadened the range of voices and strategies available to all professional writers, male or female, and I'll ask you to consider how you can find similar freedom as a student. Throughout the chapter, the ideas of authority and gender are linked by the question of who has the power to define acceptable or prestigious forms of language.

Before closing with Discussion Questions and Writing Assignments, the chapter features a piece that explores the idea of feminist writing, Gloria Anzaldúa's "Speaking in Tongues: A Letter to 3rd World Women Writers." The piece is also an excellent example of a writer asserting her authority in both traditional and untraditional ways.

⊠ FEATURED PAPER TOPICS

Write a personal essay about a specific person, event, or situation that taught you something important about gender roles in American society. Establish a tight focus so that you can provide both details of your experience and well-developed reflections about or insights into its significance. Your essay must of course grow out of your own unique experience, but here are examples of topics students have written on successfully: switching from an all-girls to a "coed" high school, the different rules and freedoms for boys and girls within the student's nuclear family, experiences in athletic competition against the opposite sex, the discovery that a family member is gay or lesbian, travel to a foreign country having different gender expectations, and changes in religious practices to expand roles for women.

* * *

For a more academic and analytical writing task, study the topic of gender and authority in your immediate environment, namely, your college or university. The indispensable steps of this process are to gather information, to report it, and to discuss it in writing. This topic can be tailored for group or individual work as follows.

Continued

(continued)

Group Work

Brainstorm the areas where you might be able to observe or quantify gender differences at your school. Assign individuals or pairs to gather information on specific topics; then, pool your resources and write up the results either individually or collaboratively. Here are a few ideas to get you started:

- makeup of the Academic Senate in terms of women and men
- number of female/male tenured faculty, full professors
- budget and facilities for women's and men's athletic programs
- ratio of female/male professors in specific academic areas such as physics, nursing, aviation, social work, philosophy, information sciences, mathematics, and engineering
- ratio of female/male students in various majors

Once you've gathered such information, carefully consider the possible causes of what you've discovered as well as the implications for students, the school, and the broader society. If any of your findings point to problems, what could be done to remedy them?

Individual Work

Look into three or four ideas such as those listed under Group Work before choosing one for close study. Learn everything you can; then, write a short paper presenting your data or observations and discussing their significance.

THE NOVICE/EXPERT DILEMMA

Outside of educational settings, virtually all writing addresses an audience of readers who know *less* than the author. Most writers— be they journalists, technical writers, businesswomen, essayists, or scholars—enjoy the tremendous advantage of knowing more about their topic than their readers do. That's as it should be, of course, but if you are only accustomed to writing in the role of student, you may not appreciate how unusual a situation your classes put you in. Imagine trying to say something interesting about the Civil War to a historian who has read several books and articles on the subject or trying to summarize the relationship of the stock and bond markets for the economist who wrote your textbook. Students face such tasks routinely, often with disheartening consequences. When things go wrong, novices (students) writing to experts (teachers) may start to think of writing as test-taking or mere intellectual exercise rather than important communication. Limited knowledge undermines the student writer's authority over her text, and the lack of authority erodes self-confidence, motivation, and purpose. In the worst-case scenario, bored teachers read the half-hearted efforts of bored writers. Many teachers will help you avoid this predicament, but it will sometimes be up to you.

> *Because direct criticism is embarrassingly impolite or even politically dangerous in many cultures, expecting world majority students to feel at home critiquing the authors they read is somewhat unrealistic.—Helen Fox*

As the quotation above by Helen Fox indicates, issues of authority can be especially perplexing for students from non-Western cultures, who may be understandably reluctant to comment on the published work of acknowledged experts until they have themselves gained considerable expertise. If this is true of the graduate students Fox has interviewed, one would expect the challenge to be even more daunting for a younger and less educated student. To try on the role of expert, then, is not a simple matter, and it is not merely an intellectual exercise: it has important cultural dimensions, too. All this being recognized, the intellectual assertiveness and confidence that might seem presumptuous or rude elsewhere remain cherished values in most classes at American colleges.

Fortunately, there are several things you can do to build, retain, or regain a sense of ownership and control over what you write. Below are several tips—some easy, some challenging—to help you assert your authority even in a school setting.

Become an expert yourself
I don't mean a world expert, obviously, but make sure you're well informed. Listen to the three voices below from three very different disciplines—biology, history, and music—and note how each asserts its authority through its use of specific detail and precise, sometimes specialized vocabulary:

- Biology: "Marine biologists are particularly interested in sea-horses because they provide the rare case in which the male of the species becomes pregnant: in each of the roughly three dozen species (all in the genus *Hippocampus*) females deposit eggs into a brood pouch on the male, where the eggs are fertilized and nourished."
- History: "Teddy Roosevelt's charge up San Juan Hill has become the most celebrated event of the Spanish American War (1898)—a war in which more soldiers died from disease than from enemy fire—but rarely is it mentioned that Roosevelt's flank was protected by black troops."
- Music: "Jazz is truly the music of improvisation, but not all jazz is free-form; 'ragtime' jazz, for example, achieved its distinctive sound through its emphatic and systematic use of syncopation, that is, the accentuation of a beat that would normally be weak."

These passages exemplify good academic writing, but they display no genius or uncanny wisdom. All students can claim similar authority by virtue of their knowledge, no matter how new that knowledge is. Also, keep in mind that there is plenty your teachers *don't* know, however well educated they may be. Learn some of this, teach it to your teachers, and you'll both benefit. That brings us to the next strategy...

Choose your topics carefully

When presented with a choice of topics, forget about looking for the "easiest" one (it's very hard to guess this anyway). Instead, seek out a topic that you care about or that will help you later in your major or that you can connect somehow with other classes. Above all, consider the connections between the topic and your personal experience—an area in which you are indeed the world expert. You will find specific advice about writing personal essays below, but even when your assignment seems highly *im*personal, merely thinking about topics in relationship to your experience, and your family's, may spark your most creative thinking. Whatever the particulars of the writing task, your goals early on should include actively choosing and shaping the assignment, not just passively receiving it. Don't trivialize your prior knowledge and experience!

Traditional power arrangements in the classroom are counterpro-ductive and...learning is much more likely to occur when stu-dents are active participants in their own education—that is, when a significant portion of the teacher's "authority" is trans-ferred to the students themselves.—Gary A. Olson

Many college courses address enduring human issues—marriage and divorce, birth and death, immigration, religious conversion, sickness and health, warfare, struggle/success/failure, and so on. Whether the approach is economic, psychological, literary, historical, or even chemical, the issues are still human issues, and you should develop the habit of connecting your firsthand experience (or your family's) with the more theoretical approaches found in your classes. Such connections can form two-way streets, in which academic study and personal experience are enriched by one another.

Learn to "bend" topics

As suggested in the previous paragraph, you may be able to turn certain topics toward your individual interests. There's no foolproof recipe for doing this, but try asking these questions:

- Can I take advantage of my special perspective on this issue as a woman or as a Texan or as a parent or as an environmentalist or as an orphan or as a Jew, etc.? (This can be quite a deep, com-plex question—one that might guide your entire essay.)
- How might this topic relate to my other studies, past, present, or future? How can I capitalize on such connections?
- How does this topic relate to my personal experiences or those of my family and close friends? Could my personal experience provide useful examples for my essay or perhaps an opening or closing paragraph?
- What reading have I already done that might inform my writ-ing? Does the topic lend itself to a bit of research that I would enjoy or benefit from?

The knack of gently bending topics is well worth acquiring, but be-ware of straying from the topic. When in doubt, consult with your instructor, early and often. Finally, don't become a "one-trick pony": I recently had a student who wanted to turn *every* assignment, from research paper to review to personal essay, into a paper about hula.

Negotiate the topic

Sometimes you won't be given a choice or you won't much like the choices presented. This may not be the end of the road. Think of an alternative topic that meets these criteria:

- it's of greater interest or value to you, in a way you can articulate clearly and tactfully;
- it calls for somewhat similar types of reading, thinking, and writing as the original assignment; and
- it is at least as ambitious as the original assignment.

Then, schedule an appointment with your instructor to propose your topic, *not to complain about hers.* Avoid hurried requests before, after, or during class. About the worst that can happen is that she will say no, but even then, you may learn more about the instructor's goals for the assignment, and you may be justifiably proud of showing some initiative.

Favor the narrow and specific

It's almost impossible to write a good short essay on "abortion"; the topic is simply too complex, and virtually all readers know more already than anyone could explain in four or five pages. A better option might be something like "physician privacy and the 'morning-after' pill" or "health risks of second abortions." Whatever your topic area, the idea is to get beyond what most people already know, to write something more probing and complex than what you could toss off in a fifty-minute timed essay. Good writing usually goes beyond merely expressing an opinion and attempts to teach, to entertain, or to persuade; accomplishing such goals with overly broad topics is extraordinarily difficult.

Personalize the style

Near the beginning of her first novel, *The Bluest Eye,* and again in *Paradise,* Toni Morrison uses the expression "quiet as it's kept...." As she has explained in an interview, probably only readers who grew up in rural Ohio will recognize this phrase as one that often introduces some piece of outrageous gossip, so her use of it is a kind of private joke. There can be more to your writing than meets the eye, too: you can easily work in a favorite expression or a newly learned word or a reference to a favorite author or some such detail as a way of "signing" your work internally, the way Alfred Hitchcock played cameo roles in the movies he directed. For example, on the rare occasions I use the odd phrase "I don't know him from Adam's off ox," I think of my father, and when I found a way to use *feng shui* in Chapter 3, I thought of Sydney Leung, the student philosopher who explained it to me. When you can see a little bit of yourself in the writing, you'll have taken one step toward developing a written voice rather than just echoing a bland generic style. As Maria Irene Fornes points out, "Writing is an intellectual process, so it's good to *root* the process into your stomach, your heart, your bowels."

Save all your work

It's yours, and it's valuable. Keep your work *after* it's been returned to you by an instructor, but of course you should also save draft versions as you work. For important work, keep one copy on a diskette, one on a hard drive (if available), and one on paper.

Write for a real audience

Options include journals, school or other newspapers, letters, classroom peer groups, and the Internet. Writing is a social activity, not simply an intellectual exercise.

SHAPING SO-CALLED PERSONAL ESSAYS

> *Tongue, mother tongue. Tongue, and the mother. We generate ourselves through speech.*—Nicole Ward Jouve

Why "so-called" personal essays? Because outside the artificial world of classrooms, there's no clear boundary between personal essays and other essays (just as there is no distinct line between "research" papers and other papers). If you were to read a thousand randomly chosen essays from America's most respected publications, you could line them up according to how extensively they used personal experience. At one end would be highly introspective, reflective, idiosyncratic pieces, seemingly written for the author alone or for his closest friends; at the other end, you might find things such as a scholarly paper on statistics that reflects no personal experience at all and has a highly formal, impersonal voice. Most important, though, most pieces would fall somewhere in the middle: a writer's decision to use personal experience is not usually an On/Off, Yes/No decision. Instead, it's a matter of how much, when, and how.

To some extent, you will have to answer these questions for yourself, negotiating between your own aims as a writer and the particular demands of your assignment, your teacher, and your writing program. It is not uncommon, for example, for a writing curriculum to ask students to *begin* by writing about their personal experience and to proceed to more abstract, analytical writing or to writing based more heavily on library research. Though no textbook can anticipate every writing situation you will face, the general guidelines below should help.

First, note that "personal essays" automatically solve the novice/expert dilemma described above. You are, of course, the ultimate authority on your experience: readers are free to interpret your experience as they like, but they can't rewrite it. Moreover, if you're like most people, you've thought more carefully and more energetically about your own experience than you have about anything else. Thus, you may have "rehearsed" stories and ideas from your life—in thought, in speech, or even in previous writing—so that they flow more coherently and energetically onto the paper (or screen) than the brand-new ideas that you might be trying out in other assignments. It's perhaps for this reason that many teachers find personal essays the most interesting and illuminating.

> *What sort of diary should I like mine to be? Something loose knit and yet not slovenly, so elastic that it will embrace anything, solemn, slight, or beautiful that comes into my mind.—Virginia Woolf*

A second built-in advantage to writing that draws heavily on personal experience is that good readers will often learn things and imagine things well beyond what you as the author consciously try to communicate. Given half a chance, they will find something interesting in the dullest report. This habit—you might think of it as "thick reading" to emphasize its density and richness—is particularly strong in English teachers because by nature and training they read imaginatively, actively, energetically; they are eager to see patterns and to interpret behavior.

In keeping with this idea, one productive way of looking at personal writing is to think of it as giving good readers a chance to exercise their imaginations. At some point in the revision process, stop worrying for a moment about telling your story and focus instead on what you are giving a reader to work with. Above all, be aware of what kind of *details* you are providing: they are the lifeblood of personal writing. It *is* possible to clutter your writing with needless detail, but the inclination of most student writers is to reveal too little. Consider how a reader can respond to an essay that begins with this sentence:

> My parents grew up in different areas of the country, but they shared the same religion.

It's difficult for a reader to go very far with this. She can store this information for future reference; she might guess that religion will be important to the essay; she might wonder where the parents grew up. But there's simply not much to go on yet.

In contrast, this alternative opening sentence lets a reader put her imagination to work:

> Soon after her marriage in St. Patrick's Cathedral, my mother found herself riding seven miles every Sunday to go to Mass in Laramie, Wyoming.

Now the astute reader knows that the religion mentioned is Catholicism. She may be able to picture St. Patrick's Cathedral, having seen it on TV or even visited it in New York. She knows that the two places mentioned—Manhattan and a ranch (perhaps) in Wyoming—are immensely different settings. She may well wonder how the parents met and what attracted them to one another. She may sense that the mother is remarkably devout to ride to Mass every week (on horseback? through Wyoming snowstorms?). In short, the writer of the second sentence has made it easier for the reader to engage herself in the essay. It's more fun to read the more detailed sentence, and it may be as easy or easier to write. (If you don't believe this, try tonight to write one memorable abstract sentence or ten effective descriptive sentences.)

To generate a wealth of details from which to choose, you may want to use brainstorming or other prewriting activities as described in Chapter 2. Because personal essays give writers the most freedom to plumb their memories and exercise their creativity, creative prewriting activities can prove especially useful here.

A final important consideration is choosing between "showing" and "telling." Highly personal essays, which can have a lot in common with short stories or other forms of fiction, allow writers the leeway to work less directly than they would in analytical or argumentative pieces, to be less obvious and explicit.

Being explicit is never wrong: it's common practice—and often a much-appreciated courtesy to your reader—to state your main ideas directly. For example, you might write, "My mother and I were getting on one another's nerves." A more sophisticated way of handling this, however, is to tell a story or work details into your

---

⊠ WRITING BREAK

Focus, Detail, Showing versus Telling

Quickly review the chapter up to this point and determine what advice you can apply to a current writing task. For example, if you are writing the personal essay on gender roles in the Featured Paper Topics, you might try one or more of the following activities:

- Consider or reconsider your focus. Think of several possible approaches to this writing task—for example, several experiences you could describe—and choose the best.
- Check that your topic is sufficiently narrow. If you have a length requirement, can you cover the topic adequately in the allotted number of pages, or should you restrict your focus or negotiate extra pages to work with?
- Consider the kinds of details that will make your experience seem real, important, and individual. Brainstorm a list of visual details you might want to include.
- Try applying the idea of showing versus telling to your topic. What will you need to explain, and what will readers understand if you simply report what happened, what was said, and so on?

---

essay that show this without any explicit statement. Look, for example, at this sentence from *Dreaming in Cuban,* by Cristina Garcia:

> Now, whenever I'm in the bathroom, my mother knocks on the door like President Nixon's here and needs to use the john.

Even taken totally out of context, this humorous remark suggests something about the mother and the daughter and their relationship. It is also much more alive than the dull phrase "getting on one another's nerves." You have to decide when you're ready to risk an indirect approach; because many beginning writers both show *and* tell their key ideas, one way to begin is to examine a draft of an essay and ask about each sentence, "Have I made this clear or implied it elsewhere in the essay?" Cut the sentences that tell and let the sentences that show do their work.

CONTROLLING THE SURFACE OF YOUR WRITING

Obviously, you can exert a good deal of authority over your writing in the area of content—for example, by choosing what to write about and, most fundamentally, what to say. But you can also make powerful choices regarding *how* you say things. In fact, most language theorists would claim that you can never truly separate "content" from the specific language that communicates it. This section offers advice on two worthwhile goals for your writing—quoting effectively and avoiding gender bias in your style.

QUOTING, RESEARCH, AND AUTHORITY

I quote others only in order the better to express myself.—Montaigne

Authority points in two directions here—to your authority as a writer and to the "authorities" whom you choose to quote. The principle is simple: *you are who you quote.*

What do I mean by this exaggeration? Simply this: whenever you quote to support or illustrate your points (rather than to differ with whomever you're quoting), you are letting someone else speak for you. Be sure that that's what you want. Now, unless you happen to be a spectacularly gifted writer, it can be quite advantageous to turn over the microphone, so to speak, to Toni Morrison or Gabriel García Márquez or Mother Teresa or Confucius. Obviously, consulting what great writers or important figures have said can add spice to your writing as well as lend it authority; moreover, quotations may help you express a complex idea quickly or even help you get your own creative juices flowing. The key danger lies in sharing your authority with a too-restricted group of famous people in Western history. I recently attended a graduation ceremony in which a well-meaning colleague quoted dozens of writers; all the writers were male, and all had been dead for at least 200 years.

Anthologies of quotations can be extremely useful, but many show a strong bias toward white men. One aging *Dictionary of Quotations* on the shelves of my local library contains 143 quotations about "Woman"—every single one of them written by a man! Even more alarming are the subheadings in this list, including "Woman: all alike" and "Woman: frail, shifting, treacherous" and "Woman: illogical and trivial" and "Woman: should be subject to man" and "Woman: vices." (Let this serve as a reminder that quotations are usually claims, not facts.) Fortunately, many good sources of quotations have appeared in recent years, and your library is likely to have them, perhaps in the Reference section. Here are a few you might look for:

- *The New Quotable Woman,* by Elaine Partnow. This volume is arranged chronologically, from 2300 B.C.E. to 1990, and contains 15,000 quotations by 2,500 women. To help you find what you want, entries are indexed by subject matter, occupation of author, and ethnicity/nationality of author. See also Partnow's *The Quotable Woman from Eve to 1799* and *The Quotable Woman: 1800–1981.*
- *Feminist Quotations: Voices of Rebels, Reformers, and Visionaries,* by Carol McPhee and Ann Fitzgerald. This book features 1,500 quotations by 300 feminists, mostly Britons and Americans of the last two centuries.
- *Classical and Foreign Quotations,* by W. Francis H. King. This volume lists Latin, Greek, French, German, and Italian quotations, with English translations.

- *In Few Words/En Pocas Palabras: A Compendium of Latino Folk Wit and Wisdom,* by José Antonio Burciaga, author of "What's in a Spanish Name?" in Chapter 1. This bilingual collection is arranged by theme (e.g., "food," "education,") and is also indexed.
- *Bartlett's Familiar Quotations.* This is the grand-daddy of them all. It has a general focus, not a multicultural one, but it's much broader now than in its original 1855 edition.
- *Simpson's Contemporary Quotations,* by James B. Simpson. This volume emphasizes quotations from the past forty years.
- *Voices of Multicultural America: Notable Speeches Delivered by African, Asian, Hispanic, and Native Americans, 1790–1995,* edited by Deborah Gillan Straub. This contains 230 speeches or excerpts, not just short quotations; the keyword index lets you find promising materials quickly.

In addition to checking such reference works, you may glean quotations from the research you undertake on a given topic. These are likely to be more up-to-date and more precisely relevant than what the anthologies offer. If you someday work on a long-term project such as a master's thesis, or if you are considering writing as a career, you may want to establish your own files of quotations, just as you might save articles, bibliographies, cartoons, photographs, and other materials.

Can Language Be Neutral?

Lots of people think of language as a powerful human tool but also as an inherently *neutral* one. From this point of view, language itself does not influence us as we use it: In order to persuade, command, inquire, and so on, we control language much as we might control a computer program or some complex piece of machinery, but we aren't deeply affected by it. But consider the possibility—a much more likely one in my estimation—that language *does* shape us; that people's languages and dialects are very closely intertwined with their beliefs, their values, their very perceptions of the world; and that the relationship of language to the rest of our being is dynamic and everchanging.

We are beginning to understand that theories which talk about "language" and "gender" as if they were free-floating, separate entities are misleading. As children, we become language users and, through using language, become gendered members of the community: both language and gender are developed through our participation in everyday social practice. In other words, language and gender are inextricably linked.—Jennifer Coates

For centuries, the connections between language, thought, and behavior have occupied philosophers, not to mention more recent specialists such as psychologists, anthropologists, and linguists; it's hard to prove anything, but there are many indications that the specific language(s) that we read, hear, and use every day constitute a sort of lens through which we see the world. Change the lens and you change the world.

Consider, for example, how the world was transformed by Darwin's insights into natural selection, the mechanism of evolution. Science changed, surely, but so did human languages and, perhaps, our very notion of the universe. Because of Darwin, students today are less likely to know the expression "Great Chain of Being" but more likely to know concepts such as ecosystem, survival of the fittest, and gene pool. Such developments not only reflect scientific progress but may in fact deeply influence our perceptions of our environment (to use a handy Darwinian term). Your familiarity with the idea of an ecosystem, for example, may make your experience of the world different from that of my parents, who grew up without that idea and without the notion of "environmentalism," which has "evolved" into a powerful political force.

Another example comes from the experience of African Americans, who have repeatedly noted the negative connotations of *black* in many traditional English expressions, such as "black as sin," "black as night," "black-ball," "black magic," and others. Given the overwhelmingly negative connotations of such phrases, using "black" to describe a wide range of skin colors was, I believe, a powerful and racist act of naming. Moreover, the connotations of phrases such as "black magic" may exert a powerful influence over all those, black or not, who grow up using this language. (On a more positive note, African American writer James Baldwin noted that the language and thinking of our country have been unalterably affected—and enriched—by black contributions, such as the terms *jazz, whipped, with it, funk, uptight,* and many others.)

Because the relationships between language, thought, and behavior are complex and multifaceted—the examples above merely scratch the surface—it makes sense to pay careful attention to all the details of language that may not only suggest but also insidiously promote racial, gender, and other kinds of bias. Chapter 1, Names and Labels, touches on these issues; the pages that follow look specifically at some of the basic gender issues in American English.

Gender and Pronouns

One of the unfortunate effects of the origins of English in a fundamentally sexist culture is that masculine pronouns have traditionally been used to refer to people who could be either male or female. An example is the sentence "Every successful novelist must understand the psychology of the characters *he* creates," which in effect erases female novelists from the literary scene. You have to make up your own mind, but it's hard to pretend that this is "just" a convention of language (sometimes called the generic *he*); many readers are offended by this old-fashioned usage, and with good reason. Some handbooks treat this as a problem to be solved or circumvented, but it is also an opportunity: you have several choices, a couple of which are quite good:

Use **they** *to replace* **he** *or* **she**
It has become acceptable to mix singular and plural forms in sentences such as "Every*one* has a right to *their* own opinion," and you will certainly hear sentences like this spoken all around you, even in relatively formal settings such as national news broadcasts. Though some professors will object to this usage, you may use the "singular *they*" in all but the most formal writing, and some scholars believe you should be able to use it anywhere.

Use combination forms such as **s/he**
You've probably seen lots of these combinations—*his or her, she/he, he/she, s/he,* even *her(him)self.* These can work, but they can become awkward and confusing when a writer needs to use lots of them, as in the sentence "If a chemist is assigned by her or his supervisor to carry out a procedure which she or he considers environmentally dangerous, she or he has the responsibility to ask her(him)self about moral as well as legal issues."

Make everything plural
This is the most elegant and least obtrusive way to circumvent the issue, and it is certainly a strategy you ought to have, literally, at your fingertips. Instead of writing about *a* doctor and *her* or *his* patients, write about *doctors* and *their* patients. Instead of writing "Everyone has a right to *their* own opinion," write, "All individuals have a right to their own opinions."

Alternate between female and male pronouns
Simply write sentences such as "A scuba diver must trust *her* partner" even when the gender of the diver is indefinite. After a few pages, or in the next section of your paper, switch to the masculine pronouns for a while. This strategy works best in long pieces, which afford ample opportunities to use both masculine and feminine forms. The huge advantage of this option is that you deliver a complex message to your audience simply by writing *she* where the traditional usage would be *he*: you show that you are aware of the issue of sexism in language, that you are sensitive to your readers, and that you are sophisticated and ambitious enough to adopt a strategy to avoid gender bias.

Always use feminine pronouns
This fight-bias-with-bias strategy makes similar points, but a little more assertively. You may have noticed by now that this book uses feminine pronouns almost exclusively.

Use pronouns subversively
Subversive is a rather strong term for such a mild act, but you may occasionally have (or create) an opportunity to surprise readers with a pronoun. I have in mind sentences such as "A boxer fights not only, or even primarily, with *her* fists, but also with *her* legs and *her* head" or "Jean was the gentlest, most soft-spoken, most courteous nurse in the hospital, and even the terminally ill patients appreciated *his* demeanor."

Gender, Nouns, and Adjectives
Gender bias also shows up in the way careless writers use certain nouns. The most common way, surely familiar to you, is the use of *man* or *men* to refer to people of both sexes, as in phrases such as

"for the good of mankind" or "men working" or "sufficient man-power." Again, even if you feel such terms are neutral and convenient, you cannot change the fact that they offend some readers and make them skeptical about your attitudes—or even hostile toward you. If you find such expressions in a draft of a paper, why not revise them? *Crew working* can replace *men working*, for example; *police officer* is preferable to *policeman; fireman* should ordinarily become *fire fighter*. Avoid ludicrous terms such as *personholecover*, concoctions that are sometimes used to mock those of us who attempt to avoid sexism in our speech and writing. The needed revisions are usually quite minor, but if you must rewrite a whole passage, do so rather than offend readers.

> *If the pen is a metaphorical penis...then what is the site of female expression?*—Carol J. Singley

Throughout the 1996 Summer Olympics, NBC commentators frequently referred to female athletes—particularly gymnasts and swimmers—as ladies or girls. When the athlete in question is fourteen, calling her a girl can be defended, but some of the "girls" were in their twenties. Unless you are truly referring to a girl, or a Lady (as in Lady Brett Ashley), throw such choices on the scrap heap along with *gal* and *little gal*—usages that I've encountered in speech, though not in writing, quite recently. You will find it easy to use terms such as *women, young women, gymnasts, vaulters, backstrokers, the Ukrainian team*, and so on.

Also, avoid nouns such as *actress, aviatrix*, and *waitress*. The feminine endings of such nouns, aside from suggesting that the words are derived from and thus secondary to the "normal" male nouns, call undue attention to gender, as if it's odd that an aviator is a woman. In the same vein, think twice before using terms such as *female jockey* or *women's athletics*. Such terms are sometimes necessary, but rarely. Finally, if you attend a school that still uses sexist names, such as Lady Vols or Lady Techsters, start a dialogue about this issue in the school paper.

A Caution about Sports Analogies

An analogy is a comparison of two fundamentally different things that nevertheless share several common features; for example, complex computer software might be compared to a simple recipe, or the stages of human life might be compared to the seasons.

Once student writers grow sophisticated enough to begin using analogies to explain their points, many begin to rely on analogies drawn from the world of sports. For example, two candidates beginning their campaigns might be compared to boxers "feeling each other out," as they say. As a sports enthusiast myself, I'm sorry to report that you should employ sports analogies in moderation, if at all, for at least three reasons:

1. Sports analogies are so common that people who don't care much about sports are getting very, very tired of hearing them constantly. And while it's too simple to say that such analogies appeal to men and not to women, that surely will be the case in some settings.
2. These analogies typically imply competitive settings and behaviors, thus subtly skewing our perceptions of the situation.

⊠ WRITING BREAK
Gender, Quotations

Apply the ideas discussed on the previous pages to one of your papers that is currently in the draft stage. Specifically, try one or more of the following:

- Check your draft carefully to see how you have handled pronouns. Are you following a conscious and consistent strategy in choosing between *she, he,* and other options? Try rewriting a page employing a different strategy; then, read both versions aloud to consider the effect of the revisions.
- Skim your draft looking for sports analogies. If you find any, decide whether you should keep them in light of the problems they sometimes cause.
- Get to know the sources for quotations available in your library's reference section. Try to find one or two quotations that you can weave into your current draft or that simply give you a new perspective on your topic.

It's hard to pursue a line of thought based on cooperation, for example, while using metaphors that all imply competition.

3. Many of the analogies turn out to be clichés, overused phrases that sap the energy of your writing; it's no longer original to compare a business deal to a slam dunk or a failure to a strike-out.

GENDER, AUTHORITY, AND RHETORIC

There is always within [woman] at least a little of that good mother's milk. She writes in white ink.—Hélène Cixous

Is Western Rhetoric "Masculine"?

It's relatively easy to reform your own use of nouns, pronouns, and adjectives, if necessary, but doing so is only a small step in the right direction. Some scholars argue that most public speech and writing—most discourse, to use the scholarly term—is fundamentally masculine, at least in Western cultures.[1] As we saw in Chapter 4, Western rhetoric, throughout its two-thousand-year history, has been primarily concerned with political debate, law, and, to a lesser extent, preaching. These areas have been predominantly male, and female voices have rarely been heard.

In addition to the fact that men have been doing most of the talking for two millennia, it can be argued that the very nature of discourse in Western culture is masculine. That is, law and politics, which gave rise to the study of rhetoric, are arenas of argumentation, dispute, competition, conflict—activities that some scholars label male or masculine; this discourse values logic, reason, hard evidence, and proof, and it has certainly tolerated bullying and namecalling. Much academic publishing falls into the same category of fundamentally *adversarial* writing. The theory is that all ideas will be subjected to intense intellectual scrutiny and that only the best ideas—the true ideas—will survive. In practice it's clear

---

1. In the interest of brevity, this chapter does not attempt to cover the differences between men's and women's *speech,* but they do exist. For example, research by Jennifer Coates showed that men interrupt more and are more likely to shout, to threaten, or to insult others. Women are more likely than men to discuss personal feelings and are better at aiding conversations with "minimal responses" such as "yeah."

that for centuries many folks' ideas were given considerably less than half a chance, precisely because the thinkers were women, or members of minority groups, or "commoners" or "heretics" or "savages" or "perverts" or "commies" or whatever other label would suffice to silence or marginalize them.

> *Although it's not the same thing to savage a person's book as it is to kill them with a machine gun, I suspect that the nature of the feelings that motivate both acts is qualitatively the same.—Jane Tompkins*

Most college professors are aware of such problems, but you should recognize that many of them nevertheless have a deep personal and professional commitment to the way academia works. In this world, *fighting* for one's ideas and *defending* one's territory are commonplace notions. Writers must anticipate *attacks* on their ideas and do their best to *undermine* any *opposition*. Feminist observers have also noted that much scholarly debate, if one cuts through the polite euphemisms, is incredibly harsh, rude, and exaggerated, as rival scholars gently point out each other's ignorance, stupidity, and carelessness. As the next section suggests, a feminine rhetoric might conceivably be quite different.

What Would a "Feminine" Rhetoric Look Like?

> *If it is true every national language has its own dream language and unconscious, then each of the sexes—a division so much more archaic and fundamental than the one into languages—would have its own unconscious wherein the biological and social program of the species would be ciphered in confrontation with language, exposed to its influence, but independent from it.—Julia Kristeva*

Women's responses to cultures and languages that preferred their silence have been as varied as the women who accepted the challenge to speak and be heard. As we saw in Chapter 4, a magnificently educated woman named Aspasia astounded Athens with her prowess in philosophy, rhetoric, and other intellectual endeavors; defying the reigning cultural stereotypes, she exerted a powerful influence on the key thinkers and leaders of her time, including Socrates, Plato, and Pericles. Much later, the first professional female writer in Europe hid her identity by signing an early work with the meaningful name Creintus ("fearful"), a near anagram of her name, *Christine* de Pisan. Some women wrote anonymously or, like the Brontë sisters, used male pen names. Excluded from male libraries and universities, some formed private reading and writing clubs that later became the cornerstones of public libraries. Some collaborated (usually invisibly) with their husbands, like Elizabeth Fernea, who contributed information on Iraqi women in the harem to her husband's scholarly work, and Carobeth Laird, who typed, translated, cooked, drove, and gathered plant samples for her spouse, John Harrington. In nineteenth-century America, ex-slave Sojourner Truth and Quaker abolitionists Angelina and Sarah Grimké argued openly and powerfully for their right to join the culture's conversation. Lucy Stone and Antoinette Brown, forbidden to debate in public, formed a secret debate society and protected its meetings by posting sentinels. Oberlin graduate Harriet Keeler, allowed in 1870 to read quietly at commencement ceremonies, shocked the crowd by discarding her written speech and addressing the audience directly. In France, a woman named Colette wrote about her girlhood sexual experiences in a series of books which her husband published under his own name; she finally published a novel under her own name at age fifty. The first Native American woman to publish a novel, Christine Quintasket (who used the pen name Mourning Dove), had to wait eleven years for her book, *Co-ge-we-a, the Half-Blood*, to appear; she supported herself by cooking, housekeeping, and picking apples as a migrant worker. Sioux writer Ella Deloria died before her novel, *Waterlily*, finally reached print in 1988, forty-four years after she finished it; despite her substantial contributions to the work of world-famous anthropologist Franz Boas, she lived in poverty on a reservation in South Dakota.

> *Perhaps if we had left these pages blank, we should have had a better understanding of what feminine writing is all about.*
> —Xavier Gauthier

Beyond struggling to be heard, women have been experimenting in many ways to refashion traditional forms of Western language (e.g., the novel, the essay) and even to create new ones. Although no well-defined "school" or methodology exists, such writing has earned a French title, *écriture féminine*, which has a little more panache, as they say, than the English version, "feminine (or feminist) writing." Here are some of the features often found in *écriture féminine.*

- It values women's experience, history, and points of view and shows a concern with women's social and political status.
- It does not assume that what is true for men is true for women.
- It suggests its points through experience, example, image, and metaphor.
- It invites the reader to make up her or his own mind about something, rather than pushing the writer's view single-mindedly.
- It critiques masculine power/dominance and masculine language.
- It questions male myths, such as the myth of the self-made man or the solitary hero.
- It values personal experience, emotion, and ethics.
- It shifts between personal and "academic" or "professional" voices to indicate that both are valuable.
- It acknowledges its audience as real flesh-and-blood people.
- It owns up to its weak points rather than shielding, denying, or disguising them.
- It is the result of collaborative writing rather than solitary authorship.
- It promotes cooperation rather than conflict.
- It may address a nonacademic community instead of or in addition to an academic one.
- It accentuates people in relationship to one another rather than individuals in isolation.
- It plays (seriously) with elements of language such as syntax, grammar, punctuation, and vocabulary in order to suggest a resistance against or tension with inherited (male) rules of discourse.
- It aims to change cultural games rather than win them.

In order to make these issues a little less abstract, let me briefly describe two widely admired and well-known essays that illustrate some of the strategies women writers have adopted. (You'll also see a sample at chapter's end.) In "*La conciencia de la mestiza*/Towards a New Consciousness," Gloria Anzaldúa not only writes about creating a new self, but also cobbles together a new kind of language, a new rhetoric if you will, to help her do so. First, as her title hints, she uses as many as half a dozen languages and dialects in a single essay. This strategy challenges the common assumption that English is and should be America's dominant or only language. Similarly, she mixes argument with personal narrative with poetry, refusing to place argument or scholarly analysis above other forms of communication. Her very topic, the consciousness of the mestiza (a woman of mixed cultural heritage), has to do with women negotiating the borders of various cultures—male and female, for example, as well as "American" and Mexican and Indian, straight and queer.

> *For lesbians to come abreast of who they are, what they need is a bed, a worktable to write on, and a book. A book we must read and write at the same time. This book is unpublished, but we are already quite familiar with its substantial preface. In it, we find the names Sappho, Gertrude Stein, Djuna Barnes, Adrienne Rich, Mary Daly, Monique Wittig, and others.—Nicole Brossard*

Where Anzaldúa's writing is concerned with subverting racial and cultural assumptions as well as gender bias, in "The Laugh of the Medusa," French feminist Hélène Cixous is more narrowly focused on women's writing. Cixous's essay blends the highest erudition with scathing and sometimes raunchy wit. The essay is occasionally perplexing, but always full of energy and insight. The style is vibrant, sarcastic, sensual, inspiring. In urging women to write, Cixous doesn't send them to the library, but urges them to write out of their bodies, out of their experience, out of the "infinite richness of their individual constitutions." She mocks male pontifications about the Freudian theory of penis envy, renaming the Greek *Perseid* legend the *Penisneid* and defending herself against the charge of being a castrating feminist with the following comment: "Isn't it evident that the penis gets around in my texts, that I give it a place and appeal? Of course I do." Like Anzaldúa, Cixous writes in conscious opposition to a tradition that has aimed to silence her. ("The dominant white culture is killing us slowly with its ignorance," says Anzaldúa.) Below is a single magnificent paragraph from Cixous's essay. In this purportedly casual "parenthetical remark," Cixous poses a stunning challenge to Western rhetoric:

Let me insert here a parenthetical remark. I mean it when I speak of male writing. I maintain unequivocally that there is such a thing as *marked* writing; that, until now, far more extensively and repressively than is ever suspected or admitted, writing has been run by a libidinal and cultural—hence political, typically masculine—economy; that this is a locus where the repression of women has been perpetrated, over and over, more or less consciously, and in a manner that's frightening since it's often hidden or adorned with the mystifying charms of fiction; that this locus has grossly exaggerated all the signs of sexual opposition (and not sexual difference), where woman has never *her* turn to speak—this being all the more serious and unpardonable in that writing is precisely *the very possibility of change*, the space that can serve as a springboard for subversive thought, the precursory movement of a transformation of social and cultural structures.

I have risked describing pieces you have presumably not read yet because you may very well not encounter much *écriture féminine* in college. It's important to know that the work is out there, and that if you're interested, you can find it, and perhaps imitate it. Resources available to you may include not only your campus library, but also a Women's Studies program, feminist scholars on campus, feminist bookstores, and, of course, the Internet.

> *To what extent is there really such a thing as "women's writing"?*
> *To the extent that women, for historical and biological reasons, experience a different reality than men.*—Christa Wolf

Authority in the Classroom

The extent to which you can begin to imitate some of the features of *écriture féminine*, as listed above, depends on your own courage, determination, and resourcefulness and perhaps also depends a bit on your instructors. Some teachers relish their role as experts, as arbiters of standards, as judges of student ability, and as "gatekeepers" for the university and, by extension, the culture. They will expect you to "play by the rules."

> *I had an instructor, and we had dissimilar beliefs.... I thought my*
> *way was correct, and she thought hers was correct. Well, I revised*

it so it was what she wanted, but I didn't think it was very good. I got the grade, but it lacked my point of view.—undergraduate nursing student

I'm not afraid of disagreeing with a professor.... If professors begin to tell me what I have to say, then it's their [writing], not mine anymore. And being the person I am, I would probably not conform to what they wanted me to do, and therefore, I would win for myself and lose in the course.—graduate student in anthropology (both quoted in Kirsch)

Whatever your instructor's approach, it's virtually impossible for a teacher to abdicate all authority in an American classroom— whether or not this would be desirable—and it's instructive to think consciously about the power relationships at work in your education. Even in "user-friendly" classes that feature open discussion, for example, you will easily recognize that students' rights rarely approach the teachers'. Courtney Cazden has concisely summarized some of the key differences:

> In the bluntest terms, teachers have the right to speak at any time and to any person; they can fill any silence or interrupt any speaker; can speak to a student anywhere in the room and in any volume or tone of voice. And no one has the right to object.

I am not arguing here for a classroom without teachers, but I am urging you to be aware of the power relationships in your various classrooms and of the ways authority is demonstrated and reinforced. Question 7 at the end of this chapter invites you to observe these things in a class you visit; from there it should be a short step to thinking about how much authority you can or should exert in other areas of your education, such as what you read, what you write about, what foreign language(s) you study, and so on. Developing authority over your writing is excellent practice for sharing authority in the rest of your education, a goal whose value can hardly be overstated.

Interestingly enough, your teachers, be they graduate students or professors, may be facing similar issues in their own writing. Many academics—and in particular women, minority scholars, or students of nonmalestream subjects—must make difficult choices concerning what kinds of research, teaching, and publication will be recognized and accepted by their academic communities. Tied to these choices are very tangible rewards (grants, publications, graduate assistants, tenure) and punishments (rejection slips, lack of promotions, denial of "merit pay"). Remember that academia is not a big group of like-minded people who all agree on what subjects should be studied, what projects should be supported, what research should be published, and what curricula should be taught; instead, these issues—all issues of authority—are constantly negotiated. As a student, your freedom and power are limited, but you can make important choices about what you study, and under whose guidance. Because reading assignments, lectures, labs, and tests are often tightly controlled, you are likely to find your greatest freedom when it comes to writing.

The reading for this chapter takes the form of a letter from radical writer Gloria Anzaldúa to Third World women writers. It stands in stark contrast to most academic writing you will encounter (especially textbooks) and displays rather clearly several features of *écriture féminine* as described earlier in this chapter.

SPEAKING IN TONGUES: A LETTER TO 3RD WORLD WOMEN WRITERS

Gloria Anzaldúa

21 mayo 80
Dear mujeres de color, companions in writing—
  I sit here naked in the sun, typewriter against my knee trying to visualize you. Black woman huddles over a desk in the fifth floor of some New York tenement. Sitting on a porch in south Texas, a Chicana fanning away mosquitos and the hot air, trying to arouse the smouldering embers of writing. Indian woman walking to school or work lamenting the lack of time to weave writing into your life. Asian

American, lesbian, single mother, tugged in all directions by children, lover or ex-husband, and the writing.

It is not easy writing this letter. It began as a poem, a long poem. I tried to turn it into an essay but the result was wooden, cold. I have not yet unlearned the esoteric bullshit and pseudo-intellectualizing that school brainwashed into my writing.

How to begin again. How to approximate the intimacy and immediacy I want. What form? A letter, of course.

My dear *hermanas,* the dangers we face as women writers of color are not the same as those of white women though we have many in common. We don't have as much to lose—we never had any privileges. I wanted to call the dangers "obstacles" but that would be a kind of lying. We can't *transcend* the dangers, can't rise above them. We must go through them and hope we won't have to repeat the performance.

Unlikely to be friends of people in high literary places, the beginning woman of color is invisible both in the white male mainstream world and in the white women's feminist world, though in the latter this is gradually changing. The *lesbian* of color is not only invisible, she doesn't even exist. Our speech, too, is inaudible. We speak in tongues like the outcast and the insane.

Because white eyes do not want to know us, they do not bother to learn our language, the language which reflects us, our culture, our spirit. The schools we attended or didn't attend did not give us the skills for writing nor the confidence that we were correct in using our class and ethnic languages. I, for one, became adept at, and majored in English to spite, to show up, the arrogant racist teachers who thought all Chicano children were dumb and dirty. And Spanish was not taught in grade school. And Spanish was not required in High School. And though now I write my poems in Spanish as well as English I feel the rip-off of my native tongue.

I lack imagination *you say*

No. *I lack language.*
The language to clarify

my resistance to the literate.
Words are a war to me.
They threaten my family.

To gain the word
to describe the loss
I risk losing everything.
I may create a monster
the word's length and body
swelling up colorful and thrilling
looming over my mother, *characterized.*
Her voice in the distance
unintelligible illiterate.
These are the monster's words.[1]

Cherríe Moraga

Who gave us permission to perform the act of writing? Why does writing seem so unnatural for me? I'll do anything to postpone it—empty the trash, answer the telephone. The voice recurs in me: *Who am I, a poor Chicanita from the sticks, to think I could write?* How dare I even considered becoming a writer as I stooped over the tomato fields bending, bending under the hot sun, hands broadened and calloused, not fit to hold the quill, numbed into an animal stupor by the heat.

How hard it is for us to *think* we can choose to become writers, much less *feel* and *believe* that we can. What have we to contribute, to give? Our own expectations condition us. Does not our class, our culture as well as the white man tell us writing is not for women such as us?

The white man speaks: *Perhaps if you scrape the dark off of you face. Maybe if you bleach your bones. Stop speaking in tongues, stop writing left-handed. Don't cultivate your colored skins nor tongues of fire if you want to make it in a right-handed world.*

> "Man, like all the other animals, fears and is repelled by that which he does not understand, and mere difference is apt to connote something malign."[2]

I think, yes, perhaps if we go to the university. Perhaps if we become male-women or as middleclass as we can. Perhaps if we give up loving women, we will be worthy of having something to say worth saying. They convince us that we must cultivate art for art's sake. Bow down to the sacred bull, form. Put frames and metaframes around the writing. Achieve distance in order to win the coveted title "literary writer" or "professional writer." Above all do not be simple, direct, nor immediate.

Why do they fight us? Because they think we are dangerous beasts? Why *are* we dangerous beasts? Because we shake and often break the white's comfortable stereotypic images they have of us: the Black domestic, the lumbering nanny with twelve babies sucking her tits, the slant-eyed Chinese with her expert hand—"They know how to treat a man in bed," the flat-faced Chicana or Indian, passively lying on her back, being fucked by the Man *a la* La Chingada.

The Third World woman revolts: *We revoke, we erase your white male imprint. When you come knocking on our doors with your rubber stamps to brand our faces with DUMB, HYSTERI-CAL, PASSIVE PUTA, PERVERT, when you come with your branding irons to burn MY PROPERTY on our buttocks, we will vomit the guilt, self-denial and race-hatred you have force-fed into us right back into your mouth. We are done being cushions for your projected fears. We are tired of being your sacrificial lambs and scapegoats.*

I can write this and yet I realize that many of us women of color who have strung degrees, credentials and published books around our necks like pearls that we hang onto for dear life are in danger of contributing to the invisibility of our sister-writers. "La Vendida," the sell-out.

The danger of selling out one's own ideologies. For the Third World woman, who has, at best, one foot in the feminist literary world, the temptation is great to adopt the current feeling-fads and theory fads, the latest half truths in political thought, the half-digested new age psychological axioms that are preached by the white feminist establishment. Its followers are notorious for "adopting" women of color as their "cause" while still expecting us to adapt to *their* expectations and *their* language.

How dare we get out of our colored faces. How dare we reveal the human flesh underneath and bleed red blood like the white folks. It takes tremendous energy and courage not to acquiesce, not to capitulate to a definition of feminism that still renders most of us invisible. Even as I write this I am disturbed that I am the only Third World woman writer in this handbook. Over and over I have found myself to be the only Third World woman at readings, workshops, and meetings.

We cannot allow ourselves to be tokenized. We must make our own writing and that of Third World women the first priority. We cannot educate white women and take them by the hand. Most of us are willing to help but we can't do the white woman's homework for her. That's an energy drain. More times than she cares to remember, Nellie Wong, Asian American feminist writer, has been called by white women wanting a list of Asian American women who can give readings or workshops. We are in danger of being reduced to purveyors of resource lists.

Coming face to face with one's limitations. There are only so many things I can do in one day. Luisah Teish addressing a group of predominantly white feminist writers had this to say of Third World women's experience:

> "If you are not caught in the maze that (we) are in, it's very difficult to explain to you the hours in the day we do not have. And the hours that we do not have are hours that are translated into survival skills and money. And when one of those hours is taken away it means an hour not that we don't have to lie back and stare at the ceiling or an hour that we don't have to talk to a friend. For me it's a loaf of bread."

Understand.
My family is poor.
Poor. I can't afford
a new ribbon. The risk
of this one is enough
to keep me moving
through it, accountable.
The repetition like my mother's
stories retold, each *time*

reveals more particulars
gains more familiarity.

You can't get me in your car so fast.[3]

Cherríe Moraga

"Complacency is a far more dangerous attitude than outrage."[4]
Naomi Littlebear

Why am I compelled to write? Because the writing saves me from this complacency I fear. Because I have no choice. Because I must keep the spirit of my revolt and myself alive. Because the world I create in the writing compensates for what the real world does not give me. By writing I put order in the world, give it a handle so I can grasp it. I write because life does not appease my appetites and hunger. I write to record what others erase when I speak, to rewrite the stories others have miswritten about me, about you. To become more intimate with myself and you. To discover myself, to preserve myself, to make myself, to achieve self-autonomy. To dispel the myths that I am a mad prophet or a poor suffering soul. To convince myself that I am worthy and that what I have to say is not a pile of shit. To show that I *can* and that I *will* write, never mind their admonitions to the contrary. And I will write about the unmentionables, never mind the outraged gasp of the censor and the audience. Finally I write because I'm scared of writing but I'm more scared of not writing.

Why should I try to justify why I write? Do I need to justify being Chicana, being woman? You might as well ask me to try to justify why I'm alive.

The act of writing is the act of making soul, alchemy. It is the quest for the self, for the center of the self, which we women of color have come to think as "other"—the dark, the feminine. Didn't we start writing to reconcile this other within us? We knew we were different, set apart, exiled from what is considered "normal," white-right. And as we internalized this exile, we came to see the alien within us and too often, as a result, we split apart from ourselves and each other. Forever after we have been in search of that self, that "other" and each other. And we return, in widening spirals and never to the same childhood place where it happened, first in our families, with our mothers, with our fathers. The writing is a tool for piercing that mystery but it also shields us, gives a margin of distance, helps us survive. And those that don't survive? The waste of ourselves: so much meat thrown at the feet of madness or fate or the state.

24 mayo 80

It is dark and damp and has been raining all day. I love days like this. As I lie in bed I am able to delve inward. Perhaps today I will write from that deep core. As I grope for words and a voice to speak of writing, I stare at my brown hand clenching the pen and think of you thousands of miles away clutching your pen. You are not alone.

> Pen, I feel right at home in your ink doing a pirouette, stirring the cobwebs, leaving my signature on the window panes. Pen, how could I ever have feared you. You're quite house-broken but it's your wildness I am in love with. I'll have to get rid of you when you start being predictable, when you stop chasing dustdevils. The more you outwit me the more I love you. It's when I'm tired or have had too much caffeine or wine that you get past my defenses and you say more than what I had intended. You surprise me, shock me into knowing some part of me I'd kept secret even from myself.
> —Journal entry.

In the kitchen Maria and Cherríe's voices falling on these pages. I can see Cherríe going about in her terry cloth wrap, barefoot washing the dishes, shaking out the tablecloth, vacuuming. Deriving a certain pleasure watching her perform those simple tasks, I am thinking *they lied, there is no separation between life and writing.*

The danger in writing is not fusing our personal experience and world view with the social reality we live in, with our inner life, our history, our economics, and our vision. What validates us as human beings validates us as writers.

What matters to us is the relationships that are important to us whether with our self or others. We must use what is important to us to get to the writing. *No topic is too trivial.* The danger is in being too universal and humanitarian and invoking the eternal to the sacrifice of the particular and the feminine and the specific historical moment.

The problem is to focus, to concentrate. The body distracts, sabotages with a hundred ruses, a cup of coffee, pencils to sharpen. The solution is to anchor the body to a cigarette or some other ritual. And who has time or energy to write after nurturing husband or lover, children, and often an outside job? The problems seem insurmountable and they are, but they cease being insurmountable once we make up our mind that whether married or childrened or working outside jobs we are going to make time for the writing.

Forget the room of one's own—write in the kitchen, lock yourself up in the bathroom. Write on the bus or the welfare line, on the job or during meals, between sleeping or waking. I write while sitting on the john. No long stretches at the typewriter unless you're wealthy or have a patron—you may not even own a typewriter. While you wash the floor or clothes listen to the words chanting in your body. When you're depressed, angry, hurt, when compassion and love possess you. When you cannot help but write.

Distractions all—that I spring on myself when I'm so deep into the writing when I'm almost at that place, that dark cellar where some "thing" is liable to jump up and pounce on me. The ways I subvert the writing are many. The way I don't tap the well nor learn how to make the windmill turn.

Eating is my main distraction. Getting up to eat an apple danish. That I've been off sugar for three years is not a deterrent nor that I have to put on a coat, find the keys and go out into the San Francisco fog to get it. Getting up to light incense, to put a record on, to go for a walk—anything just to put off the writing.

Returning after I've stuffed myself. Writing paragraphs on pieces of paper, adding to the puzzle on the floor, to the confusion on my desk making completion far away and perfection impossible.

26 mayo 80

Dear mujeres de color, I feel heavy and tired and there is a buzz in my head—too many beers last night. But I must finish this letter. My bribe: to take myself out to pizza.

So I cut and paste and line the floor with my bits of paper. My life strewn on the floor in bits and pieces and I try to make some order out of it working against time, psyching myself up with decaffeinated coffee, trying to fill in the gaps.

Leslie, my housemate, comes in, gets on hands and knees to read my fragments on the floor and says, "It's good, Gloria." And I think: *I don't have to go back to Texas, to my family of land, mesquites, cactus, rattlesnakes and roadrunners. My family, this community of writers. How could I have lived and survived so long without it. And I remember the isolation, re-live the pain again.*

"To assess the damage is a dangerous act,"[5] writes Cherríe Moraga. To stop there is even more dangerous.

It's too easy, blaming it all on the white man or white feminists or society or on our parents. What we say and what we do ultimately comes back to us, so let us own our responsibility, place it in our own hands and carry it with dignity and strength. No one's going to do my shitwork, I pick up after myself.

It makes perfect sense to me now how I resisted the act of writing, the commitment to writing. To write is to confront one's demons, look them in the face and live to write about them. Fear acts like a magnet; it draws the demons out of the closet and into the ink in our pens.

The tiger riding our backs (writing) never lets us alone. *Why aren't you riding, writing, writing?* It asks constantly till we begin to feel we're vampires sucking the blood out of too fresh an experience; that we are sucking life's blood to feed the pen. Writing is the most daring thing I have ever done and the most dangerous. Nellie Wong calls writing "the three-eyed demon shrieking the truth."[6]

Writing is dangerous because we are afraid of what the writing reveals: the fears, the angers, the strengths of a woman under a triple or quadruple oppression. Yet in that very act lies our survival because a woman who writes has power. And a woman with power is feared.

> *What did it mean for a black woman to be an artist in our grand-mother's time? It is a question with an answer cruel enough to stop the blood. —Alice Walker.*[7]

I have never seen so much power in the ability to move and transform others as from that of the writing of women of color.

In the San Francisco area, where I now live, none can stir the audience with their craft and truthsaying as do Cherríe Moraga (Chicana), Genny Lim (Asian American), and Luisah Teish (Black). With women like these, the loneliness of writing and the sense of powerlessness can be dispelled. We can walk among each other talking of our writing, reading to each other. And more and more when I'm alone, though still in communion with each other, the writing possesses me and propels me to leap into a timeless, spaceless no-place where I forget myself and feel I am the universe. *This* is power.

It's not on paper that you create but in your innards, in the gut and out of living tissue—*organic writing* I call it. A poem works for me *not* when it says what I want it to say and *not* when it evokes what I want it to. It works when the subject I started out with metamorphoses alchemically into a different one, one that has been discovered, or uncovered, by the poem. It works when it surprises me, when it says something I have repressed or pretended not to know. The meaning and worth of my writing is measured by how much *I* put myself on the line and how much nakedness I achieve.

> *Audre said we need to speak up. Speak loud, speak unsettling things and be dangerous and just fuck, hell, let it out and let everybody hear whether they want to or not.*[8]
>
> Kathy Kendall

I say mujer magica, empty yourself. Shock yourself into new ways of perceiving the world, shock your readers into the same. Stop the chatter inside their heads.

Your skin must be sensitive enough for the lightest kiss and thick enough to ward off the sneers. If you are going to spit in the eye of the world, make sure your back is to the wind. Write of what most links us with life, the sensation of the body, the images seen by the eye, the expansion of the psyche in tranquility: moments of high intensity, its movement, sounds, thoughts. *Even though we go hungry we are not impoverished of experiences.*

> *I think many of us have been fooled by the mass media, by society's conditioning that our lives must be lived in great explosions, by "falling in love," by being "swept off our feet," and by the sorcery of magic genies that will fulfill our every wish, our every childhood longing. Wishes, dreams, and fantasies are important parts of our creative lives. They are the steps a writer integrates into her craft. They are the spectrum of resources to reach the truth, the heart of things, the immediacy and the impact of human conflict.[9]*
>
> *Nellie Wong*

Many have a way with words. They label themselves seers but they will not see. Many have the gift of tongue but nothing to say. Do not listen to them. Many who have words and tongue have no ear, they cannot listen and they will not hear.

There is no need for words to fester in our minds. They germinate in the open mouth of the barefoot child in the midst of restive crowds. They wither in ivory towers and in college classrooms.

Throw away abstraction and the academic learning, the rules, the map and compass. Feel your way without blinders. To touch more people, the personal realities and the social must be evoked—not through rhetoric but through blood and pus and sweat.

Write with your eyes like painters, with your ears like musicians, with your feet like dancers. You are the truthsayer with quill and torch. Write with your tongues of fire. Don't let the pen banish you from yourself. Don't let the ink coagulate in your pens.

Don't let the censor snuff out the spark, nor the gags muffle your voice. Put your shit on the paper.

We are not reconciled to the oppressors who whet their howl on our grief. We are not reconciled.

Find the muse within you. The voice that lies buried under you, dig it up. Do not fake it, try to sell it for a handclap or your name in print.

Love,
Gloria

ENDNOTES

1. Cherríe Moraga's poem, "It's the Poverty" from *Loving In The War Years*, an unpublished book of poems.
2. Alice Walker, editor, "What White Publishers Won't Print," *I Love Myself When I am Laughing—A Zora Neale Hurston Reader*, (New York: The Feminist Press, 1979), p. 169.
3. Moraga, *Ibid*.
4. Naomi Littlebear, *The Dark of the Moon*, (Portland: Olive Press, 1977) p. 36.
5. Cherríe Moraga's essay, see "La Güera."
6. Nellie Wong, "Flows from the Dark of Monsters and Demons: Notes on Writing," *Radical Woman Pamphlet*, (San Francisco, 1979).
7. Alice Walker, "In Search of Our Mothers' Gardens: The Creativity of Black Women in the South," *MS*, May, 1974, p. 60.
8. Letter from Kathy Kendall, March 10, 1980, concerning a writer's workshop given by Audre Lorde, Adrienne Rich, and Meridel LeSeur.
9. Nellie Wong, *Ibid*.

DISCUSSION QUESTIONS
AND WRITING ASSIGNMENTS

On the Reading by Anzaldúa

1. Identify three or four of the key claims made by Anzaldúa or the writers she quotes—for example, her idea that "the dangers we face as women writers of color are not the same as those of white women." Explore the importance of these to her letter as a whole, and discuss any claims you consider controversial.

2. What are Anzaldúa's goals in terms of her named audience of Third World women writers? In addition, what message(s) might Anzaldúa have for those of us who are not Third World women writers?

3. Review the features of *écriture féminine* as summarized in What Would a "Feminine" Rhetoric Look Like? Which of the listed characteristics can you find in Anzaldúa's letter? (Give specific examples.) Discuss the effects these have on you as a reader. Which of these strategies, if any, do you think you could use in your own writing?

4. In what ways does Anzaldúa's letter assert her authority as a writer and thinker, as a voice worth listening to? Which ways are traditional (e.g., the Biblical allusion in her title) and which are untraditional (e.g., using more than one language)? Would you read Anzaldúa's text differently if you had found it in a book published by a small feminist press rather than in a textbook from a major academic publisher?

On Chapter 5

5. Write a journal entry or short paper in response to one or two of the quotations included in this chapter. Possible approaches include the following:

  • Explain the meaning of the quotation. For example, what might it mean to call the pen a "metaphorical penis"?
  • Use the quotation as a starting point for your own reflections or experience relating to the topic. For example, assess Christa Wolf's claim that men and women experience a different reality.
  • Amplify on the quotation: develop it, provide examples.
  • Explain why you agree or disagree with the quotation.
  • Compare and contrast two or more quotations.

6. To heighten your awareness of your own verbal idiosyncrasies, spend a week or more jotting down whatever unusual expressions you can think of. Then, write a narrative or dialogue using as many of these as you can. The phrases may be comic or straight, current or archaic; may reflect regional or other dialects; or may be clichés. They may prove obscure to classmates, so explain any they don't understand. Some examples from my

own experience: I knew you when you were just a gleam in your mother's eye (or when you were knee-high to a grasshopper); That and fifty cents will get you on the subway; Rich or poor, it's nice to have money.

7. Having obtained permission to do so, visit a class you are not enrolled in. Make a comprehensive list of all the ways the instructor's authority is asserted, shared, or challenged. (This might include speech, gestures, tone of voice, dress, and so on.) Analyze your observations in a journal entry or brief paper, or report them to your writing class.

8. Having obtained permission to do so, visit a class that includes student discussion. Look for evidence of differences between male and female speech. For example, does one group speak more often or at greater length? What kind of speaking is encouraged, and what is discouraged? Who interrupts more? Who listens better? Is the teacher's behavior entirely consistent with male and female students (e.g., who is asked more questions or tougher questions?)? Analyze your observations in a journal entry or brief paper, or report them to your class.

9. Working in a group, if possible, compile a list of all the sports analogies you encounter in one week of reading and listening. How many of these analogies do you consider necessary, appropriate, or useful? Explain why a few specific examples do or do not seem gender-neutral. Then write a short essay or narrative using as many sports analogies as possible—to the point that their effect is comic.

10. Analyze the two short passages below. They are the openings of two writers' essays on "paternalism" (defined below in the first passage). Compare and contrast the two writers' rhetorical strategies, their assumptions about knowledge and audience, their voices. Which writer seems more expert to you, and which passage feels more "authoritative"? Do you prefer passage A or B, and why?

> *A. This paper will define paternalism and discuss its justification. Paternalism is the action of one person interfering with another person's action or thoughts to help him. The person who interferes, called the paternalist, breaks moral rules*

of independency because he restricts the other person's freedom without that person's consent. He does it, however, in a fatherly, benevolent way, and assumes that the person being restrained will appreciate the action later.

B. *Consider the following situations:*

Situation One: Mister N, a member of a religious sect which strictly forbids blood transfusions, is involved in a serious automobile accident and loses a large amount of blood. On arriving at the hospital, he is still conscious and informs the doctor that his religion forbids blood transfusions. Immediately thereafter he faints from loss of blood. The doctor believes that if Mister N is not given a transfusion he will die. Thereupon, the doctor arranges for and carries out the blood transfusion. Is the doctor right in doing this? ... [The writer presents two more hypothetical cases or examples at this point, then proceeds as follows.]

Sometimes paternalistic actions seem justified, and sometimes not; but always, paternalism seems at least to be a bit disquieting.... The authors whose efforts will be reviewed here have undertaken the task of trying to spell out conditions which must be satisfied for paternalistic actions to be justified.... [S]o a preliminary task is that of giving an account of what are paternalistic actions; that of settling on a definition in order to gain a clearer notion of what we are talking about, and of what, if anything, has to be justified.

[NOTE: These paragraphs are taken from "Reading and Writing without Authority" by Ann M. Penrose and Cheryl Geisler, in *College Composition and Communication* 45:4 (December 1994), 505–506. Consult this essay for the "answer" to this question.]

REFERENCES

Anzaldúa, Gloria. "La conciencia de la mestiza/Towards a New Consciousness." In *Borderlands/La Frontera*. San Francisco: Aunt Lute Books, 1987.
Behar, Ruth and Deborah A. Gordon, eds. *Women Writing Culture*. Berkeley: University of California Press, 1995.

Barrington, Judith. *An Intimate Experience: Lesbian Writers on Sexuality.* Portland, OR: Eighth Mountain Press, 1991.

Belenky, Mary Field, Blythe McVicker Clinchy, Nancy Rule Goldberger and Jill Mattuck Tarule. *Women's Ways of Knowing: The Development of Self, Voice, and Mind.* New York: Basic Books, 1986.

Bizzell, Patricia. "Praising Folly: Constructing a Postmodern Rhetorical Authority as a Woman." In Louise Wetherbee Phelps and Janet Emig, eds., *Feminine Principles and Women's Experience in American Composition and Rhetoric.* Pittsburgh: University of Pittsburgh Press, 1995.

Bizzell, Patricia and Bruce Herzberg. *The Rhetorical Tradition: Readings from Classical Times to the Present.* New York: St. Martin's Press, 1990.

Bridwell-Bowles, Lillian. "Discourse and Diversity: Experimental Writing within the Academy." In Louise Wetherbee Phelps and Janet Emig, eds., *Feminine Principles and Women's Experience in American Composition and Rhetoric.* Pittsburgh: University of Pittsburgh Press, 1995.

Cazden, Courtney. *Classroom Discourse: The Language of Teaching and Learning.* Portsmouth, NH: Heineman, 1988.

Cixous, Hélène. "The Laugh of the Medusa." In Patricia Bizzell and Bruce Herzberg., *The Rhetorical Tradition.* New York: St. Martin's Press, 1990.

Coates, Jennifer. *Women, Men and Language* (2nd ed.). NY: Longman, 1993.

Connors, Robert J. "Women's Reclamation of Rhetoric in Nineteenth-Century America." In Louise Wetherbee Phelps and Janet Emig, eds., *Feminine Principles and Women's Experience in American Composition and Rhetoric.* Pittsburgh: University of Pittsburgh Press, 1995.

Finn, Janet L. "Ella Cara Deloria and Mourning Dove: Writing for Cultures, Writing against the Grain." In Ruth Behar and Deborah A. Gordon, eds., *Women Writing Culture.* Berkeley: University of California Press, 1995.

Garcia, Cristina. *Dreaming in Cuban.* New York: Ballantine Books, 1992.

Geisler, Cheryl and Ann M. Penrose. "Reading and Writing without Authority." *College Composition and Communication* 45:4 (December 1994) 505–506.

Glenn, Cheryl. "sex, lies, and manuscript: Refiguring Aspasia in the History of Rhetoric." *College Composition and Communication* 45:2 (May 1994) 180–199.

Kauffman, Linda S. *American Feminist Thought at Century's End: A Reader.* Cambridge, MA: Blackwell Publishers, 1993.

Kirsch, Gesa E. *Women Writing the Academy: Audience, Authority, and Transformation.* Carbondale: Southern Illinois University Press, 1993.

Laennec, Christine Moneera. "Christine *Antygrafe:* Authorial Ambivalence in the Works of Christine de Pizan." In Carol J. Singley and Susan Elizabeth Sweeney, *Anxious Power.* Albany, SUNY, 1993.

McCracken, Nancy Mellin and Bruce C. Appleby, eds. *Gender Issues in the Teaching of English.* Portsmouth, NH: Boynton/Cook, 1992.

Morrison, Toni. *The Bluest Eye.* New York: Simon & Schuster, 1970.

Phelps, Louise Wetherbee and Janet Emig, eds. *Feminine Principles and Women's Experience in American Composition and Rhetoric.* Pittsburgh: University of Pittsburgh Press, 1995.

Sanborn, Jean. "The Academic Essay: A Feminist View of Student Voices." In Nancy Mellin McCracken and Bruce C. Appleby, eds., *Gender Issues in the Teaching of English.* Portsmouth, NH: Boynton/Cook, 1992.

Singley, Carol J. and Susan Elizabeth Sweeney. *Anxious Power: Reading, Writing, and Ambivalence in Narrative by Women.* Albany: SUNY, 1993.

Tedlock, Barbara. "Works and Wives: On the Sexual Division of Textual Labor." In Ruth Behar and Deborah A. Gordon, eds., *Women Writing Culture.* Berkeley: University of California Press, 1995.

Tompkins, Jane. "Fighting Words: Unlearning to Write the Critical Essay." Quoted in Gesa E. Kirsch, *Women Writing the Academy.* Carbondale: Southern Illinois University Press, 1993.

Zuber, Sharon and Ann M. Reed. "The Politics of Grammar Handbooks: Generic *He* and Singular *They*." *College English* 55:5 (September 1993) 515–530.

6

Dialects and Composition

How could either of you tell what the other was
saying? He talking Louisiana, you speaking
Tennessee. The music so different, the sound
coming from a different part of the body.
—TONI MORRISON

Thinking about dialects can help you become a better writer. For one thing, what you learn about dialects in this chapter may give you a new perspective on your own language, whatever your background; moreover, the concept of dialects helps explain *all* academic learning. Chapter 6 begins with a discussion of American dialects, with a special focus on black vernacular English, also known as Ebonics, one of the most important and controversial of the dozens of United States dialects. After the discussion of Ebonics, the chapter turns to "Spanglish," another very interesting cultural and linguistic phenomenon; although writing Spanish/English essays for college is not an option for most students, the issues surrounding this combination language are enlightening even for monolingual (one-language) speakers.

With some understanding of what dialects are and why they are important, you will be in a position to think about dialects and the composition classroom. This chapter explains how assimilating into the culture of higher education in the United States is, for many students, very much like learning a new dialect. I am not speaking only of bilingual students, or bidialectal students, or students whose primary language is not English, though mastering standard academic English may include special challenges for such individuals. I am speaking of the vast majority of college undergraduates, from whatever linguistic or cultural background. I am speaking of you. To do your best in college, you will have to learn many new words *and* new ways of writing; your composition courses are just the beginning of this learning process, not the end. Indeed, the analogy comparing college study to language learning becomes even stronger as you progress in your studies and your chosen profession, whether chemistry, anthropology, business, or any other field.

Carrying through on the notion of college study and professional development as language acquisition, Chapter 6 looks at the way writers from different fields employ different dialects even when they discuss a single subject, in this case cloning. Seeing the diversity of these academic dialects may open your eyes to how professionals in diverse fields write very different versions of English. Trust me: language that strikes you as bizarre today may in a decade be your most natural dialect.

Near the end of the chapter, you will find a trio of readings about dialects and English; the authors are Eldridge Cleaver, prominent black activist and opponent of Ebonics; Fawn Vrazo, who compares the Ebonics debate to a similar controversy about dialects in Scotland; and James Baldwin, one of the twentieth century's greatest writers, who makes a powerful claim for regarding black English as a language.

☒ FEATURED PAPER TOPIC

Writing about dialects requires special knowledge that relatively few students have, so the featured paper topic for Chapter 6 asks you to write instead about a related issue, namely, education for college students whose primary language is not English. The goals are to investigate the language diversity at your school *and* to judge how well the school is accommodating this diversity. Because of its complexity, this assignment is best tackled collaboratively; it also assumes that there *is* substantial language diversity at your college or university.

Begin by establishing what questions you want to answer. Here are some examples: What percentage of students at your college or university are nonnative speakers of English? What other languages do they speak? Are some such students required to take additional or preliminary classes? Do students whose primary language is not English succeed as well overall as other students? What resources, if any (e.g., tutors, classes, computerized language programs), are available to nonnative or native speakers of English who need extra help? Adjust such questions to your particular environment.

Next, identify likely sources of information and assign pairs or small groups to do the legwork. You may find knowledgeable people—plus hard data, written reports, and so on—in several campus locations, including the President's Office, the Writing Center or Learning Lab, the English Department, and the EOP (Economic Opportunity) office. You may be able to read documents, interview faculty members and administrators, or even develop a simple survey you can give to students.

The final stage is to analyze and present the information you have found in an organized way. Naturally, I can't predict what you will discover, but one sensible objective for your writing would be to identify areas in which your school could do a better job.

WHAT IS A DIALECT?

Bob Close, who was accustomed to talking in pidgin to the natives of Northern Australia and New Caledonia, wanted a pole for some work on hand. Pointing and gesticulating to make his meaning still clearer, he gave his orders to Eliasi: "Bring one fellow stick long me two times, thick all same this arm belonga me!" Eliasi quietly replied: "Yes, I understand, Mister Bob. You want a pole twelve feet long and three inches across. I will get it at once."
—*anecdote told by Jeff Siegel, quoted in Macauley*

Please remember this for the rest of your life: you don't simply speak English, you speak a dialect of English. A lot of people have trouble understanding that no individual's or group's version of spoken English is truly standard. Even a professional TV news-caster like Dan Rather (such folks are sometimes identified with standard English) would sound funny to English-speaking people in England, Scotland, Ireland, and Australia, though they could certainly understand him. Closer to home, you will acknowledge that rural Southerners, Boston politicians, Wisconsin teenagers, and Hawaiian farm workers speak observably different versions of American English. That's all a dialect really is—the common language of some group of people.

Dialects are more alike than different. Two dialects of a single language are marked by a tremendous overlap in vocabulary and grammar and by the ability of speakers of the two dialects to understand one another well, if not always perfectly or effortlessly. Speakers of two different languages, in contrast, will either be unable to communicate or will perhaps do so with great difficulty if the languages are closely enough related, like Spanish and Italian. Of course, different dialects do, by definition, vary; the easiest variations to note are those of vocabulary (do you say "levis" or "jeans" or "blue jeans" or "dungarees"?) and pronunciation (do you rhyme *route* with *pout* or with *toot*?), though linguists can often identify grammatical and other differences. Linguists, like everyday listeners, pay most attention to the differences between dialects; it's important to remember that for the most part, different dialects of American English are really very similar.

Note also that dialects blur into one another: they do not have absolute, set boundaries, especially now that natural barriers such as rivers and mountains are so easily crossed, by car and especially by TV broadcast. In one sense, a dialect is just a convenient abstraction, like "the middle class," that imposes some order on a world that would otherwise be overwhelmingly complex. Linguists sometimes identify about thirty major American dialects, but most of these could be quite reasonably subdivided until the total number of American dialects would reach the hundreds.

> *For the first time he actually looked at me, drawn up short by the thick Oxford drawl emerging from the gypsy girl, and I reflected upon the extraordinary effect gained by speech that is incongruous with one's appearance.*
>
> —*character created by novelist Laurie R. King*

Our biggest problem with dialects is not that Americans cannot communicate with one another, but rather that we persist in making value judgments about dialects. From a linguistic point of view, no dialect is more efficient than any other, or more beautiful, or more logical, or more flexible, or better in any other way, but many Americans nevertheless make all sorts of assumptions based on the way people talk. They may consider Bostonians intellectual (or perhaps just stuck-up), African Americans unintelligent, southerners racist, Californians air-headed, midwesterners humorless, and so on, largely because of the ways they talk. The obnoxious stereotypes and the perceptions of dialects are inextricably intertwined. When people are looking to divide themselves from others (whether regionally, ethnically, economically, or educationally), ridiculing another group's language is an easy and effective strategy. Given the expanding gulf between the haves and have-nots in the United States, and given our long history of racial animosity, this may not change anytime soon, but the more people have thought about how senseless and harmful it is, the better. End of sermon.

Another vexation—and a source of confusion—is the fact that there *is* something kinda sorta roughly approaching a standard *written* dialect for formal occasions such as academic writing, with variations according to situation and audience. Rules for this language appear in your college handbook; some appear in this rhetoric; more important, they exist in many other places throughout the culture, including the editorial policies for newspapers and magazines, miscellaneous style guides for business publications, guidelines for authors of books and dissertations, and so on. Most important of all, there's a rough consensus about what constitutes appropriate writing at different cultural sites such as courtrooms, technical manuals, coffee-table books, textbooks, special-interest magazines, junk mail, and other publications. In some of these places, it's OK to use contractions, to inadvertently split infinitives, to use prepositions to end phrases with, and to make *increment* a verb; other audiences consider such choices infelicitous ("unhappy") or simply wrong. For better or worse, though, virtually none of these myriad publications would accept a black English construction such as "He be checking his stock portfolio every morning."

To succeed in college and in most careers, you will have to become (or remain!) proficient if not masterful in the "standard" written dialect of English. Depending on your field, you will be forgiven a small number of venial sins in grammar or usage, but the bulk of your writing will have to conform to your audience's expectations, and that means your writing will *not* just look like your speech written down. It's a key recognition for some college students that simply transcribing what they would say out loud does not produce prose that is as polished, controlled, and, indeed, "standard" as their professors expect.

> *Language is the tool of my trade, and I use them all—all the Englishes I grew up with.—Amy Tan*

While we're making distinctions between spoken and written language, it's important to remember that the more formal written versions are not inherently better than a spoken dialect—they are simply different. Because mastery of a formal written dialect goes hand in hand in our culture with academic and professional success, spoken dialects that vary considerably from the formal standard are sometimes judged second-rate, low-class, uneducated, and so on. Like our other prejudices, this one is likely to be around for a while, but it's essentially a bunch of hooey. If I want to call a "skunk" a "polecat," who are you to feel superior? Even as an English professor, in informal situations I can get away with saying "Sprolly in the worshing machine" when I mean "It is probably in the washing machine." Saying "worshing" doesn't make me ignorant or lazy—it just shows that my parents spoke a *dialect* of English as they raised me. As we all do. As we all do.

DIALECTS AND SCHOOLING

> *Black Language is Euro-American speech with an Afro-American meaning, nuance, tone, and gesture.—Geneva Smitherman*

Ebonics

In December 1996, the Oakland, California, school board published a resolution aimed at improving the language skills and thus, they hoped, the overall academic performance of their 28,000 African American students, whose overall G.P.A. was an alarming 1.8, or

D+. The resolution recognized "Ebonics" as a language separate from English and called for teacher training so that Ebonics could be understood and used in the classroom. Suddenly—and to their great surprise—the school board found themselves under attack from all sides: conservative California Governor Pete Wilson was predictably a foe, but the resolution was also blasted—at least initially—by prominent black leaders, including poet Maya Angelou and the Rev. Jesse Jackson.[1] One could write a book about the rhetorical events of the next couple of months, as the school board hired a PR expert and revised its resolution, public figures renegotiated their positions, talk show hosts poured gas on the fire, and Ebonics jokes flew across the Internet. An anti-Ebonics advertisement in Atlanta asked readers to imagine Martin Luther King, Jr., saying "I *has* a dream." Rarely had language issues so strongly grabbed the nation's attention. I'll summarize some of the highlights of the controversy here.

Ebonics (from "ebony phonics") is a relatively recent term[2] for what has also been called black English, or black vernacular English. Only the most stunningly ignorant call it "slang" or "ghetto talk," but there are plenty of such folks around. Until 1996, *Ebonics* was a proud, affirmative, if little-known word for a major American dialect. Use of the word was meant to recognize facts linguists have agreed on for the past thirty years—that black English is not substandard or incorrect English, but a dialect that, like many others, has distinctive vocabulary, pronunciation, and grammar. Unfortunately, differences in pronunciation or intonation can easily be disparaged as *mis*pronunciations, just as adherence to a different set of grammatical rules can be interpreted as ignorance of grammar.

Anyone who crosses a dialect border is liable to face prejudice, but speakers of black vernacular English have faced especially strong prejudice for a number of related reasons. Most obviously,

---

1. Jackson, who first called the resolution "an unacceptable surrender bordering on disgrace," soon met with Oakland school and community leaders; after issues were clarified, he voiced support for programs that use a knowledge of the language patterns students bring to school to promote better learning of standard English.

2. The term was coined in the early 1970s. Incidentally, such a word is called a "portmanteau" word; for example, *dandle*, as in dandle a baby on one's knee, came from combining *dance* and *handle*. Unfortunately, *ebonics* is easily mocked: those who scorn the term have come up with *leprechaunics* for Irish English, *autobahnics* for German English, *won-tonics* for Chinese English, and other similarly offensive jokes.

black English is linked to African American ethnicity, historically the least prestigious in the United States. All the racial stereotypes about blacks, concocted and perpetuated over the course of centuries, are interwoven into opinions about black speech. Moreover, the social and cultural distance of many African Americans from so-called mainstream America (not to mention frequent racial antagonism) has led the black English vernacular to vary further from prestigious English than does any other American dialect. (It is the only dialect that some linguists consider a separate language, and its distinctiveness may still be growing.)

> *Upward mobility is impossible for underdogs who have not learned middle-dog barking.—James Sledd*

Despite the buckets of ink spent ridiculing the Oakland resolution, I think it was mostly sensible. It must be admitted up front that the original resolution included one extremely ill-advised phrase, claiming that African language systems are "genetically based." To most readers, this implied that Ebonics is inherited biologically—a claim so stupid and repugnant that I believe the school board's explanation of what it meant to say, namely that African language systems don't come out of thin air but have their *genesis* or origins in West African and Niger-Congo languages. The resolution was revised to this effect.

As you may recall, the resolution was sharply criticized on many other fronts as well. Here are the critics' key objections to the Oakland resolution, along with my responses:

Criticism. The resolution calls Ebonics a separate language, but "black English" is actually just slang or "bad English" or "substandard English" (a phrase used by Oakland Mayor Elihu Harris, himself African American). Ebonics is gang talk.

Response. Admittedly, the resolution makes a very strong claim when it calls Ebonics a separate language, not a dialect of English. Experts disagree on the dialect-versus-language issue, with the majority calling black English vernacular a dialect. This is not to say it is *just* a dialect, though, or that it is a *mere* dialect. A dialect is a very real and important and complex thing. The gist of the resolution is "right on," to use a black English expression: Ebonics is a legitimate language system

---

☒ **WRITING BREAK**

Ebonics

Review the list of criticisms of the Oakland policy and responses to them and the Diverse Perspectives on Ebonics on pp. 262–263. Choose one or more of the ideas to generate a journal entry or to initiate a small-group or class discussion.

---

having a distinctive vocabulary and its own rules of pronunciation and grammar. To characterize these patterns as mistakes or as substandard usage misses the boat. Not incidentally, speakers of all American dialects use words and phrases of African or black English origin, including *banjo, banana, jazz, zombie, cola, gumbo,* "gimme five," "uptight and outta sight," *shades,* and many others.

Criticism. The resolution institutionalizes a lower standard of English for black students and thus sets them up to fail in higher education and in their careers. The resolution is designed to excuse failure or to help students preserve their sense of self-worth despite failure; it is not designed to help them succeed.

Response. Though the original resolution was a little murky, it seems clear now that no one is saying that students need not master standard English. The idea is to teach teachers enough about Ebonics so that they can better help students learn standard academic English as well. Some research suggests that this approach can work, though many experts think we won't really know until more research is completed. With Oakland's 28,000 African American students averaging a D+, I'd say it's time to give such an approach a try, even with scant supporting evidence of its effectiveness.

Criticism. Teaching African American students using Ebonics demeans them.

Response. It would be a mistake to assume that all black students speak Ebonics, or to imply in any way that there is some limit

text continued on page 264

DIVERSE PERSPECTIVES ON EBONICS

The key to teaching black children (or any children) is not in convincing them that they speak a foreign language, but that they are capable of mastering any material put in front of them.

—Ellis Cose
author and social commentator

If we don't do something, where these children are heading is one of the greatest industries in the state of California—and that's the prison industry.

—Toni Cook
one of the authors of the Oakland resolution

The University of California is not going to cut them any slack when they say, "I was taught in my primary language," nor is the San Francisco Police Department or the U.S. Army.

—Delaine Eastin
superintendent of California schools

Black kids are always the kids in the petri dish, in the laboratory bottle. They're always the ones that are being experimented on.

—Linda Chavez
president of the Center for Equal Opportunity

[Ebonics is] substandard grammar and nothing more.... We should not allow the street into the classroom.

—California State Senator Ray Haynes

This is a terrible commotion and everyone is very upset. But that's not as bad as what it was before, which was silence while black kids were underachieving, dropping out and getting into all kinds of trouble. Sometimes I don't think controversy is the worst thing in the world.

—William Labov
linguist specializing in black English

What's black English? You mean slang? I'm black, I speak English. What they're trying to say is we don't talk proper English. That's not true. If you got a brain in your head, you can talk any way you want to.

—student Aaron Andrews

I'm incensed. The very idea that African American language is a language separate and apart is very threatening, because it can encourage young men and women not to learn standard English.

—*poet Maya Angelou*

I be thinking that Ebonics be stupid.

—*film-maker Spike Lee*

You must correct them, my dears.

—*Marge Levy*
Los Angeles teacher

I think Ebonics is absurd. This is political correctness that has gone out of control.

—*North Carolina Senator Lauch Faircloth*

Ebonics...is nothing more than a linguistic sham that, with porcine gluttony, vacuum-sucks every verbal deformity from plantation patois to black slang, from rap to hip hop, from jive to crippled English, and serves up the resultant gumbo as "black English."

—*James E. Shaw*
consultant to Los Angeles County Office of Education

No one was concerned about the condition of African American students before this controversy. I wonder how many people will be tomorrow.

—*Sylvester Hodges*
co-chair of the African American Task Force
that drafted the district policy

Elevating black English to the status of a language is not the way to raise standards of achievement in our schools.

—*U.S. Secretary of Education Richard Riley*

Why stop with resolutions legitimizing black English? If Castlemont [High School] is to' up, why not rebuild it from the flo' up?... Today, Ebonics is the issue that has everyone up in arms. Tomorrow, it just might be the takeover of the district by a people in need of a relevant education.

—*Kevin Weston*

to what students of any particular background can achieve in language, or to set lower goals for African American students, but the resolution does not do these things. What is more likely demeaning is the message schools sometimes send kids—that their language, the language of their parents, family, and friends, is "wrong" or "slang" or "substandard." In a diverse culture, students come to school speaking varied dialects; it's silly to ignore that fact rather than try to work with it or even turn it to our advantage.

Criticism. The poor academic performance of many African American children has little to do with language; it is a result of poverty, low family stability, and other nonverbal social problems.

Response. We should be able to recognize a linguistic dimension to the problem of underachievement without underestimating other circumstances such as poverty or malnutrition. People need access to dialects associated with power.

Criticism. The resolution is basically a trick designed to siphon funding intended for bilingual and nonnative students of English to programs for African American students.

Response. It looks to me like the resolution's authors were in fact trying to jockey for position for funding; given the state of California's schools, I'm very sympathetic to that, though depriving one group to help another is an unacceptable solution. Can you imagine a society that adequately funds education for all its students, regardless of linguistic background, ethnicity, class, or gender?

Spanglish

If you really want to hurt me, talk badly about my language.
                                        —*Gloria Anzaldúa*

There is a widespread belief in the United States that we should all speak the same language. Sometimes, this belief seems to be an offshoot of unthinking prejudice against anyone who is "different"; other times, it is based on a reasoned argument about a need for cultural unity to insure a harmonious society. In its extreme form—

that is, the notion that the United States should be an "English-only" society—this idea causes substantial problems for many Americans, including recent immigrants and bilingual citizens. The consequences of maintaining a second language in an English-only atmosphere can be severe: in August 1997, two workers for a Texas insurance company were fired for speaking Spanish to each other in the workplace. Ironically, they had won their jobs in part because their knowledge of Spanish let them communicate with the company's numerous Latina/o customers.

In cases like these, in which language differences threaten to divide us from one another, people find varying ways of coping. Citizens who speak very little English may live in communities where Chinese, Vietnamese, or Spanish is the primary language. Bilingual Americans often shift from one language to another as they move from home to community to the workplace and so on. Perhaps your campus has students who communicate in English in the classroom but sometimes in another language outside it. In all of these cases, the languages themselves remain essentially separate, though talented individuals are capable of moving across their boundaries.

If you think of the border between a language and a dialect as a broad gray area, not a distinct line, Ebonics may reside in that transitional area. Where, though, does Spanglish belong? In a sense, the name says it all—Spanglish combines Spanish and English—but a hundred questions remain. For example, does the fact that English and Spanish are both languages automatically confer language status on Spanglish? Or does it perhaps mean the opposite, that it can't truly be a language because it's just an intermingling of two legitimate languages? Can the versions of Spanglish spoken in New York, Texas, and Los Angeles be called "dialects"? How much Spanish must mix in with English, or vice versa, for Spanglish to result? Could a speaker be bilingual in English and Spanglish but not Spanish, or does Spanglish require near mastery of both source languages? Could some Spanglish speakers be considered *tri*lingual?

Sometimes I write in English and sometimes in Spanish. It depends. You have to elect a language according to theme.—Tato Laviera

Whatever you think about such questions (and I've found no definitive answers), one particularly interesting thing about Spanglish is that the blending of two languages mirrors other kinds of cultural diversity within our population. I confess to an outsider's perspective—I speak no Spanish—but it seems to me that the attitude of Spanglish is hip, sophisticated, and inclusive, though not without an edge. If that's true, it could be a metaphor for how cultural diversity ought to be regarded.

For these and other reasons, I encourage you to speak and write Spanglish if you're capable of doing so, though it's clear that few if any college courses will welcome Spanglish compositions. Your audience can be wider than a classroom, and Spanglish may be very much in line with twenty-first century culture. Consider the emergence of the bilingual magazine *Latina*, for example. This is somewhat different from the addition of an all-Chinese channel to a cable-TV menu. In *Latina*, English and Spanish don't mix fully, but both are acknowledged, respected, even celebrated, as is the diversity of a culture that spans English-speaking, Spanish-speaking, and bilingual members. An August 1997 story, for example, is about *curanderas*—traditional Latina folk healers; the article, in English, is peppered with Spanish terms such as *susto* ("fright") and *yerbera* ("herbalist"); there is also an abbreviated version of the article entirely in Spanish. Some *Latina* ads are in Spanish, others in English. Letters to the editor shift unpredictably between the two languages.

Culture, then, is ahead of academia. You can even find "Cyber-Spanglish" on the Internet: Yolanda M. Rivas has compiled a list of more than 650 terms—English/Spanglish/Spanish equivalents—at http://www.actlab.utexas.edu/~seagull/spanglist.html. Whether or not you become a CyberSpanglish expert, cherish and develop all the linguistic resources you've been given. If you can use some Spanish or Mandarin or Arabic in a composition course or creative writing class, great. If your academic assignments don't accommodate languages other than English, use them in writing you do for yourself, for friends and family, for special interest magazines, or for the appropriate Internet audiences. Play with the languages. Do translations. Aside from everything else, such activities will improve your English, too.

Dialects and the College Writer

If you speak a dialect of English that differs substantially from standard academic English, you may face special challenges in composition courses or other classes such as seminars in which verbal skills are at a premium. For example, spelling can be more difficult for speakers whose dialects drop the endings of words. Similarly, making subjects and verbs agree can be challenging when the rules of your dialect differ from the rules of academic English. Occasionally, you may use a word that's unfamiliar to your classmates, or vice versa, or your pronunciations may differ markedly. Without dismissing the importance of such glitches in communication, I would like to point out that they are usually quite minor compared to the totality of your college reading, writing, speaking, and listening.

You can and should master the standard dialect, but don't overestimate the importance of occasional errors. Remember also that what looks like dozens of grammatical problems in an essay could just be repetitions of one or two unfortunate patterns; as you try to learn from your mistakes, look consciously for such patterns, and set priorities for what to master first. This is often easiest if you look at three or four papers at once; tutors and instructors should also be able to help. When revising papers, focus on one thing at a time. (All this advice is based on the assumption that dialect differences are causing some interference in communication, but not ruining it. If, on the other hand, you often find yourself unable to understand instructors or other students, or if you cannot readily make yourself understood to them, get expert help immediately from your campus learning center.)

As noted above, our society's most serious problems with dialects are attitude problems, not strictly linguistic or communications problems. The same is true, I believe, in the classroom. If you speak a distinctive dialect, you may be told in subtle or not-so-subtle ways that your language is wrong, inadequate, inferior, low-class, or comic. Expect this from ignorant people. Educate them if you have the time and energy, but in any case, resist their message. Learn the new academic lingo, but feel no shame about the dialect you speak.

> *Realizing that I was in danger of losing my relationship to black vernacular speech because I too rarely use it in the predominately white settings that I am most often in both professionally and socially, I have begun to work at integrating the particular southern black vernacular speech I grew up hearing and speaking in a variety of settings. It has been hardest to integrate black vernacular in writing, particularly for academic journals.—bell hooks*

If you *are* quite comfortable with academic language, show some understanding and consideration for classmates who are having to make bigger adjustments to a new environment. In a peer response session, for example, consider how much more valuable it might be to engage yourself with someone else's ideas rather than to circle their verb errors. Demonstrate the same patience and respect with someone learning a new dialect as you would with someone learning a new language; in some ways it can, indeed, be as hard or harder.

To end on a positive note, you may occasionally be able to take advantage of being bidialectal. As the quotation from bell hooks indicates, academe is not yet the friendliest environment for American dialects. You may nevertheless be able to put your knowledge of a dialect to work in creative writing (fiction, poetry, drama) or in some personal essays; in addition, any writing that has to do with cultural differences—whether it is literary analysis, gender studies, or sociology—may provide openings for you to use a nonacademic voice. Beyond that, it gets rather risky, especially for students, whose shifts in voice may be judged accidental rather than artful. In personal writing—journals, diaries, letters, e-mail—you may of course write however you like.

ALL LEARNING IS
LANGUAGE LEARNING

You already know a tremendous amount of English—otherwise, you couldn't read this book. Your teachers may point out errors and gaps in your knowledge, but you've mastered thousands of the most important facets of the language. It's easy to think, then, that unless you are going to major in English, you probably have most of the language skills you need and can safely concentrate on the content or subject matter of your major. Not so fast! Your learning in any field has a verbal or linguistic side to it; indeed, it's much like learning a dialect.

Academic Dialects

I can begin to draw the analogy by pointing out how much new *vocabulary* you will have to master to complete your college degree.

Next time you're in your college bookstore, take a quick look at the advanced texts in your major or anticipated major; scan the indexes of a few books and note the vocabulary there. You'll find lots and lots of new words. One of the key steps in learning a new language, or a new dialect, is simply learning enough of the words to enter into a conversation. The fact that your education will involve learning new English words rather than Dutch or Thai words doesn't really make much difference. After all, if you don't know what *hegemony* means, it may as well be Greek.

Note also that it's virtually impossible—not to mention outrageously inefficient—to learn the concepts fully without learning the vocabulary. There are often no synonyms available, and even when there are, you can't afford to use them: when everyone around you says, "Femur," you can't say, "That big bone in your leg—the one above the knee."

Just to underline that there's a lot of language learning going on, I've listed below a handful of terms for a few undergraduate majors. These are not bizarre, arcane words, but common words within the various majors:

Political Science: realist, rationalist, parameter, polis, supranational, division of labor, EU, IMF, multilateral

Criminology: competency, extradition, delusional, trace evidence, Interpol, forfeiture, three strikes, cannabis

English: intentional fallacy, Petrarchan sonnet, persona, carpe diem, metonymy, malapropism

Music: ensemble, polyphony, vibrotactile, requiem, swing, lieder, scat, notation, bebop, hip-hop, trichordal, tonal

Chemistry: titration, spectroscopy, polymer, bond lengths, hydrometer, enthalpy, Raman frequencies

The specialized vocabulary of any academic dialect is probably its most immediately visible characteristic, but speakers/writers of these dialects observe many other verbal distinctions. For example, use of the first-person pronoun *I* is accepted in many academic settings but frowned on or forbidden in others. Choosing to use *I* or not is not unlike a student of German choosing between the familiar pronoun *du* ("you") and the formal option, *Sie* (also "you"). Such choices are a matter of etiquette, really, not vocabulary. I've had many college writers ask me, "Is it OK to use *I* and *me* in my paper?" The very question shows both that such writers recognize a linguistic issue and that they are not quite familiar enough with the local dialect to feel confident about their choices. As they become more acquainted with a particular field, students get a better feel for what that dialect expects; dozens of choices must be made (sometimes unconsciously, thank heavens): Is the passive voice acceptable or even preferable? How long should my sentences and paragraphs be? How much can I quote? Can I use a snazzy title, or should I just be straightforward and descriptive? What terms must I define? May I risk a joke or pun? One could go on and on, but I hope the point is clear: along with learning the subject matter in your chosen major, you will have to learn how people write and talk about that subject matter. (Many colleges offer special writing courses to initiate students into the new dialects; if you're at such a school, take that course as soon as possible after choosing your major.)

Tips for Language Learning

If you are persuaded that lots of your college education will have a verbal dimension, here are some things you can do to learn the necessary local dialect(s):

- *Buy and use a good dictionary.* This is standard but immensely valuable advice. I know from painful experience that it's easier said than done; I arrived at college with a good vocabulary, but I confused knowing a lot of words with knowing enough words, and the right words. I resisted looking up unfamiliar terms, trusting that I could get the gist of them from context. For years, certain words confused or intimidated me (*tessellated, reticule*), when a minute's work would have taught me that a reticule was simply a particular kind of purse. Keep your dictionary nearby; assume you're going to need it. Don't be frightened by what you don't yet know—just learn it.
- *Assess your current situation and needs.* Many students enter writing courses saying things like, "I've always been a weak writer," yet have little understanding of what their strengths and weaknesses really are. Good teachers and tutors—people proficient in the standard academic dialect—will help you with

this, but you may have to take the lead yourself. Some students need to work hard on standard grammar and punctuation; others may be strong in grammar but need practice developing and organizing their ideas; still others may hope to reduce wordiness or stretch their vocabulary. The trick here is to move from abstract or overly general problems ("My writing is dull;" "I make too many mistakes") to specific aspects of your writing that you want to improve ("I need to consider possible objections to my thesis" or "an occasional metaphor would 'lively up' my prose").

- *Set specific goals.* Simply writing down goals can be a powerful motivational tool, and doing so certainly forces you to focus on what you want to achieve. For example, do you think you could learn fifty new words this semester? Write a short paper with *no* grammatical errors? Publish a letter to the editor of the school or local paper? Attend one public lecture related to your major? Write down one or two long-term goals and perhaps five or six easier, short-term goals. Draft the list right now. Post the goals where you write or study. Assess yourself at the end of the term and adjust accordingly. This should be an endless cycle, like the shampooing instructions "Wash, Rinse, Repeat."

- *Read with dual vision.* Train yourself to pay attention not only to the "content" of what you are reading, but also to its language. Until you have formed this habit, set aside five to ten minutes of each study session to focus on language. Examine the language and style of what you are reading—vocabulary; sentence and paragraph length and structure; scheme of organization and methods of signaling transitions; level of formality; use or absence of metaphor; use of quotations, statistics, or visual materials; and so on. The Diversity of Professional Dialects, found later in this chapter, undertakes this kind of analysis.

- *Find the style guide for your major.* Once you choose a major, begin using a guide designed for writers in that field. In the humanities, for example, get the *MLA Handbook for Writers of Research Papers*; many social sciences follow the *Publication Manual of the American Psychological Association*; authoritative guides for science are published by the Council of Biology Editors, the American Chemical Society, the U.S. Geological Survey, the American Mathematical Society, the American Institute of Physics, and other organizations. If in doubt, consult a professor. You won't want to spend hours reading these things, unless you have in-somnia, but they do contain much useful information, and you're going to need one as a reference tool sooner or later. If you have Internet access, see also the online guides to citation in your field; these may soon be the best tools for most writers.

- *Spy on the experts.* Do some reconnaissance of the field you're studying. Your teachers will be introducing you to their dialect, but it never hurts to look ahead a little. There are several rela-tively painless ways to do this. Take a peek each month at one or two of the leading professional journals in your field (your professors and librarians can identify these); read some ab-stracts, when they're available, and try to read at least one arti-cle each month, even if part of it goes over your head.

The Diversity of Professional Dialects

To illustrate how widely professional "dialects" can vary, I present below four passages having to do with cloning, a subject of interest to many different kinds of writers and readers. The first passage, excerpted from a piece by *Washington Post* reporters Rick Weiss and John Schwartz, describes the production of monkeys from cloned embryos. I reproduce here (pun intended) one of the story's most technical passages:

> First, researchers created several monkey embryos using a standard in-vitro fertilization method of mixing eggs from a single female with sperm in a petri dish. Once the embryos had divided into eight cells, Wolf and colleagues teased apart the embryos' cells.
>
> In the second step, the scientists took one full set of chro-mosomes from each embryo cell and inserted each batch into a fresh egg cell whose DNA had been removed.

This is a good example of science writing for a very broad gen-eral audience of newspaper readers. The writers do an admirable job of walking the line between desired accuracy and overwhelm-ing detail. Because of the scientific nature of the story, they must employ some scientific vocabulary (e.g., *in-vitro, petri dish, DNA*), but they don't bury readers in jargon. Other features of the prose also support its straightforward, explanatory, or "expository", goals:

it follows a clear chronological order, marked by lots of transitions ("First," "Once," "In the second step,"); sentences are reasonably short; the vocabulary aside from the necessary technical terms is as simple as possible.

Note, however, that while the passage sketches an outline of how to clone monkeys, it doesn't provide a recipe for doing so. Perhaps the most interesting thing about the language above is how it uses ordinary terms to stand in for technical procedures. For example, what does it mean to "tease apart" the embryos' cells? Does one do that with a scalpel? a centrifuge? fingernails? If you were going to try this experiment at home, you would want more information about this, and about how to "take" chromosomes from a cell, "remove" DNA from a cell, and "insert" chromosomes into a cell. As a set of instructions, this story would be about as helpful as this lesson on how to play the trumpet: "Blow into the mouthpiece and move the keys with your fingers." Of course most *Post* readers don't want to clone monkeys, so the prose here is well suited to its audience—educated adults whose specific knowledge of cell biology may be quite modest.

The second example comes from another newspaper, the *San Jose Mercury News*. Written by reporters Shankar Vedantam and Mary Otto, it appeared in the Perspective section of the paper March 2, 1997, a few days after the successful cloning of Dolly the sheep was announced. Here are the first five paragraphs of "When Man Tries to Play God":

> The Bible simply resonates with sheep, from the dumb beast cowering before the shearer to the triumphant lamb upon the throne. But where would Dolly, the clone, fit into the Scriptures?
>
> Once again, the boundary between religion and science has moved. A chorus of ethicists yells halt and accuses the researchers of playing God.
>
> The reality is this: The boundary is always moving. And before scientists and theologians work out what they think about such change, people have to make crucial decisions.
>
> What about parents having a baby so that they could transplant its blood cells into an ailing older child? Or family fights over the possession of a dead man's sperm? Or altering humans to make them taller, or smarter?
>
> This is uncharted territory, and there are no rules.

What can we observe about this passage? First, although it comes from a newspaper, it goes far beyond the simple reporting of facts. As befits its placement in the Perspective section of the paper, it provides a point of view and helps readers think about the issue of cloning. It is much more literary and more stylistically ambitious than a typical news story: it assumes some familiarity with biblical images; it makes bold, absolute claims ("The boundary is always moving," "There are no rules"); it poses a series of very tough ethical dilemmas. Yet, for all these nice touches, it addresses a general audience. The vocabulary is sophisticated but not specialized, the pace is quick, and the sentences are short and simply structured. If there's a universal American dialect, Vedantam and Otto know how to write it.

Despite their differences, both newspaper excerpts clearly address a general audience; the dialect they speak is one that almost all educated Americans can readily understand. In the next examples, the language will grow more specialized—the dialect more distinct— as the intended audience shrinks and becomes more specialized.

At one extreme is language for experts in genetic engineering, language that nonexperts cannot understand. Here's a brief sample from *DNA Sequencing Strategies: Automated and Advanced Approaches,* edited by Wilhelm Angorge, Hartmutt Voss, and Jürgen Zimmermann:

> Less subcloning effort is needed if walking primers are easily available. First-order subclones are obtained from cosmid restriction fragments. One set of restriction fragments, generated for example by EcoRI, is subcloned into plasmids.

It's easy to see why this is incomprehensible to most of us: Although the sentence structures are very straightforward, the passage mentions half a dozen things we've never heard of. As far as I can tell, the writing is perfectly fine; I just don't know enough to belong to its intended audience.

Challenging, perhaps, but not overwhelming is the next sample passage, by Susan Sherwin, a philosopher. Linking biology, ethics, and politics, Sherwin brings a feminist approach to the ethical questions raised by "reproductive technologies" (including but not limited to cloning). As you read these paragraphs, look for clues about Sherwin's intended audience.

Most commonly, the label of "new reproductive technologies" is applied to a variety of techniques that are employed to facilitate conception or to control the quality of fetuses that are produced, including such increasingly common practices as artificial insemination, ova and embryo donation, in vitro fertilization (IVF), gamete intrafallopian transfer (GIFT), embryo freezing, prenatal screening, and sex preselection. Included among the technologies now emerging or still on the horizon are embryo flushing for genetic inspection or transfer to another woman's womb, genetic surgery, cloning, and ectogenesis (fetal development wholly in an artificial womb)....

Complex cultural attitudes toward both technology and reproduction shape the meanings and values that the various reproductive technologies carry in our society. In evaluating a particular technology in this area, it is important to consider its place within the vast network of measures that have been designed to control human reproduction. The degree and extent of possible human manipulation of reproduction is rapidly expanding, but it is useful to remember that the desire to control reproduction is a long-standing one in human history. Therefore, it is especially significant that the new forms of reproductive technology promise a much greater scope for the direction and management of reproduction than has ever been possible before.

Although both technological and reproductive choices are usually placed in the sphere of private decision making, feminist methodology directs us to evaluate practices within the broader scheme of oppressive social structures. Therefore, the ethical evaluation of reproductive technologies requires us to ask questions about their social, political, and economic effects, in addition to questions about their place in the lives of those individuals who seek to use them. After all, reproductive practices carry profound social as well as private implications.

You don't have to be a geneticist to understand this, but clearly, Sherwin is addressing a very highly educated audience and one having more than a casual interest in reproductive technologies. She uses moderately technical language, packs a lot of information into a short space, and expects readers to understand abstractions readily. Her tight logic, straightforward sentences, and careful transitions assist the reader, but the complexity of her ideas is daunting.

Again, the style is a good match for its audience: Sherwin's topic is of interest to specialists in different fields—biology, ethics, feminism, health care—and her language reflects her ability to span these diverse disciplines and help readers see where they intersect. The gap you see between this prose and *Time* or *Newsweek* might resemble the gap you'll see when you look back from graduate school at your current writing.

DEVELOPING AN APPROPRIATE ACADEMIC STYLE

Very few students enter college "speaking" precisely the kind of language that instructors most value and reward. Instead, as they progress in their studies, students gradually acquire the academic dialect of their field of study. To some extent, students develop academic styles unconsciously, through immersion in the college environment. You can hasten your progress toward an effective style, however, and you can learn to emulate the best of your professors and texts and avoid imitating the worst of them. This section describes three keys to developing your voice for college writing—levels of diction, jargon, and the "official style."

Levels of Diction

For at least 2,000 years, rhetoricians have recognized three fuzzily defined levels of "diction," or word choice, namely high, middle, and low. The easiest way to explain this is with an example: the verb *die* is an example of middle diction; *expire* is a higher-level (and usually unnecessary) option; *croak* is a low-level choice. Please note that "high," "middle," and "low" describe choices of vocabulary, not speakers! Your dictionary may label certain words as "slang," which would put them in the low level, but otherwise, the distinctions are convenient but loose and unofficial descriptions. All speakers of English are sensitive to levels of diction, as you will recognize if you glance at these three examples:

> *Low:* "The AM were wicked bright and us a bit sick however we scored our wake ups boosting some items at a sidewalk sale in the Harvard Squar where it were warm upping and the snow coming off onnings...." (novelist David Foster Wallace)

Middle: "From the footpath that cuts through the grove on the opposite side of the road, she hears the sound of branches being thrust aside, twigs snapping underfoot." (novelist Julia Alvarez)

High: "That artless theories could and did prevail was a fact he had ended by accepting, under copious evidence, as definite and ultimate; and it consorted with common prudence, with the simplest economy of life, not to be wasteful of any odd gleaning. To haunt Eaton Square, in fine, would be to show that he had not, like his brilliant associate, a sufficiency of work in the world." (novelist Henry James)

The extreme styles James and Wallace have created for their novels would seldom be appropriate for college writing. In fact, you can do quite well for yourself by sticking to a middle level of diction on most occasions. This means using ordinary, straightforward language—language that is more controlled, varied, and ambitious than your everyday speech but not inflated, pompous, ornate, or euphemistic. As the sentence by Alvarez shows, a middle level of diction does not imply dull writing. A low level of diction can be used, sparingly, for shock effect or comedy in some college writing assignments, but, by and large, readers will find it inappropriate. The biggest challenge for most college writers in terms of diction, then, is to find the line between middle and high.

When in doubt, err on the side of ambitious word choice. A vocabulary or level of diction that strikes you as slightly pretentious or flashy may seem routine to instructors. When folks start commenting

---

⊠ WRITING BREAK
Diction

Identify each word or phrase below as high, middle, or low diction. Then, try to think of equivalent terms at the other levels of diction. You may use your dictionary.

talk	masticate	multitudinous
alleviate	recalcitrant	punch
drunk	steamed	luminous
catch some Z's	dis	

that you're relying too much on a thesaurus or that you are frequently misusing words, you can tone things down. Even if you go over the edge occasionally, this approach lets you learn something and gives you a chance to produce your best work. Playing it safe by limiting your vocabulary leads to dull writing and produces few opportunities for growth.

Jargon

Jargon is bad. Jargon is good. Though *jargon* is a slippery term, it's easy to escape the apparent contradiction. Jargon is good when it aids communication. In such circumstances, jargon may be defined as the specialized terminology of some group whose members have common interests. When sleep researchers discovered, for example, that significantly different kinds of sleeping could be distinguished by the presence or absence of rapid eye movements, they found themselves referring to these rapid eye movements over and over again. Phrases such as "rapid-eye-movement sleep" or "sleep in which rapid eye movements can be observed" don't exactly roll off the tongue, nor are they much fun to type or write dozens, hundreds, even thousands of times, so it probably took about five minutes for researchers to start using abbreviations. The abbreviation R. E. M. soon lost its periods and became an odd new word, *REM*. (Such newly coined words are called *neologisms,* a term having mildly negative connotations.) Before 1970 or so, *REM* was jargon—but good jargon. Few ordinary Americans knew the word, but for scientists studying sleep, it was a precise and efficient term, a term so useful that its counterpart *NREM* (*non-REM*) also became indispensable. *REM* soon appeared in dictionaries; by now, it is widely enough known that few would call it jargon.

There's nothing mysterious about the process of forming new words or giving them new meanings, and it's not just scholars who engage in it. Members of virtually any group that can be identified—surfers, violinists, mechanics, gardeners, rappers, dendrologists—share a somewhat distinctive vocabulary that in turn reflects their common knowledge. Defined this way, using jargon is inevitable and beneficial, whether or not the terms or special meanings enter mainstream use as *REM* did.

Things *can* go wrong, though. A writer may misjudge her audience and use language foreign to some portion of it. Only a very limited audience can understand a sentence like this intentionally exaggerated example created by Dawson Dean: "Savvy wavelet compression is the fiber signpost of the virtual chillout room." The principle of matching terminology to audience seems simple, but as you move into a career or profession, you'll see it get increasingly important and complex. In a robotics company, for example, the audience for certain documents might include electrical engineers, programmers, accountants, lawyers, sales people, and customers, a diverse group of people.

Most of us learn about misusing jargon the hard way—by using it and leaving our audience puzzled or amused. The best ways to minimize such problems are to analyze your audience carefully and to have a real reader or two from that audience check drafts whenever possible. Many writing classes build in some type of peer response to drafts of papers, but too few students carry this strategy to their other classes. Peer feedback, whose quality is often inconsistent in first-year classes, can become increasingly valuable as you undertake work in your major, for as you progress in your studies, your classmates become increasingly knowledgeable and sophisticated readers.

The "Official Style"

I've written above that you need to learn an academic style and an academic jargon that may have been quite unfamiliar to you before college. Complicating this task, unfortunately, is the abundance of mediocre and even dreadful writing all around you. You are liable to read mounds of such prose throughout your years of higher education. So, in the process of acquiring an academic dialect, you have to learn what *not* to imitate as well.

In *Revising Prose*, Richard Lanham defines the "Official Style" and teaches you how to avoid this stuffy, wordy, shapeless kind of writing. I can't recommend his short book too highly: it contains dozens of "before" and "after" examples and gives you a clear, step-by-step method for revising your prose. I'll limit myself here to a general description and just a few examples.

The Official Style shows up in bad academic writing as well as in legal, political, and bureaucratic prose. You can recognize it by the way it strings together nouns—often euphemisms or bits of jargon—using forms of the verb *to be* to hold things together, barely, in lifeless sentences. Everything has a fancy name, and the people who actually do things disappear into the verbal fog. Here's an example:

Ordinary English: "You forgot to take out the garbage."

The Official Style at work: "It seems to be the case that there has been a lapse in the dutiful performance of mutually agreed-upon postprandial chores, specifically in the garbage-removal area."

It's rarely quite this bad, but you get the idea. Ironically, much writing that is extremely hard to understand arises from an attempt to be absolutely, unmistakably *clear.* For example, you can easily understand the sentence "She entered the United States in January." But when entry into the country becomes an important legal concept, look at its definition in the 1994 United States Code:

The term "entry" means any coming of an alien into the United States, from a foreign port or place or from an outlying possession, whether voluntarily or otherwise, except that an alien having a lawful permanent residence in the United States shall not be regarded as making an entry into the United States for the purposes of the immigration laws if the alien proves to the satisfaction of the Attorney General that his departure to a foreign port or place or to an outlying possession was not voluntary: *Provided,* That no person whose departure from the United States was occasioned by deportation proceedings, extradition, or other legal process shall be held to be entitled to such exception.

Title 8, Chapter 12, Subchapter 1,
Section 1101, Definitions (a)(13)

This sentence is almost 150 words long—a typical symptom of confusing prose. Note also the incredible complexity of its logical structure; stripping away details, the logic goes something like this:

Entry means A
from x or y or z
(whether p or q)

Except not if he proves that B (to x or y or z)
was not C
Provided that l, m, or n doesn't apply.

Finally, the sentence displays related symptoms that Richard Lanham associates with the Official Style: passive verbs, linking verbs, and loads of prepositional phrases.

An example from the 1997 Federal Income Tax Guide for Individuals similarly uses a very long sentence overstuffed with details; reading becomes a kind of problem-solving exercise:

> If you are self-employed (a sole proprietor or a partner), compensation is your net earnings from your trade or business (provided your personal services are a material income-producing factor) reduced by your deduction for contributions on your behalf to retirement plans and the deduction allowed for one-half of your self-employment taxes.

Parentheses used like this will give the scheme a bad reputation: the helpful explanations interrupt the flow of thought. Moreover, following the flow of thought requires the reader to understand almost a dozen concepts in just one sentence. Again, the sentence relies on *is* and *are* and chains together monotonous prepositional phrases: *by* your deduction *for* contributions *on* your behalf *to* retirement plans."

Compounding the unfriendliness of such writing is the sad fact that readers encounter such sentences not one at a time, but by the hundreds or thousands, in long documents. The United States Code, for example, fills several dictionary-sized volumes. As Hamlet noted, sorrows come not single spies, but in battalions.

These examples from tax and immigration law are extreme, but lots of writing in other settings shares these problems to varying degrees. Long sentences, abstractions, wordiness, and monotonous structures make reading more difficult than it ought to be. Here is a final, less extreme example of such prose, this one from a U.S. Department of Labor report on the American workforce:

> The results for female-headed families when classified by education are quite dramatic, indicating that individuals in families with a female head without any college education are far more likely than any other family type, when classified by education level, to be at the bottom of the income distribution.

This isn't bad, actually, compared to a lot of documents I sampled, but compare it to this translation: "Poorly educated single mothers tend to earn little money." I grant that the translation is imprecise, but don't write like the Department of Labor until you absolutely must. Don't *aim* to sound like that.

Your instructors and tutors will presumably help you revise your own writing, and many of their revisions will reflect one or more of these guidelines:

- Minimize use of the passive voice and linking verbs.
- Use concrete vocabulary when possible.
- Vary sentence length and structure.
- Read your papers out loud, or have someone read them to you.

⊠   ⊠   ⊠

The three readings for this chapter return to the controversies surrounding black English. We begin with Eldridge Cleaver's impassioned editorial opposing Ebonics in the schools. In the second reading, Fawn Vrazo tries to shed light on Ebonics by describing how a Scots dialect is being actively taught rather than suppressed by schools. The final reading—but the one written first—is James Baldwin's response to the 1970s version of the debate, a response that still speaks powerfully today.

RESCUING KIDS FROM EBONICS

Eldridge Cleaver

There are children who go around biting other children. Should our response be to legalize and institutionalize cannibalism and hand out bottles of ketchup?

I am one of the most liberal people in the world. And I am all for black pride. I am not just a freedom talker; I am a freedom fighter. But I say "no" to Ebonics.

When I was growing up, what is now being euphemistically called Ebonics was accurately called bad English. I have the greatest respect for linguistic diversity. I speak English, Spanish and French. If I hadn't learned Spanish growing up in Los Angeles, I would not have survived my sojourn in Cuba. And I survived Algeria and France because I speak French. At the same time, I insist that as U.S. citizens, we must put English first and uphold a standard of excellence. I understand and applaud cultural and linguistic diversity, but I reject all arguments that carry political correctness to the extreme of promoting anything other than English as our official language.

I believe that schoolchildren should be required to study foreign languages, particularly Spanish, but not to the detriment of their mastery and excelling in English.

The thirst for exclusivity and recognition often is misguided, as it is in this instance. It is like Jesse Jackson running down the street naked, screaming "I am a man! I am somebody!" Thanks for telling us. We never would have noticed.

The only place for Ebonics is the streets. We don't need it in the classroom.

Begone, you "poots." And you teachers of Ebonics, get a real job teaching something with a redeeming social value. Stop flaunting your ignorance.

ENGLAND'S STRUGGLE WITH SCOTS SIMILAR TO EBONICS CONTROVERSY

Fawn Vrazo

(Queensferry, Scotland) The kids in Davie Cunningham's class say all sorts of words that to many ears sound like ignorant slang: "Dinnae" for don't, "winnae" for won't, "ken" for know, "aye" for yes.

High school English teacher Cunningham has a problem with this—but not the one you might imagine. Scottish educators have concluded that the youngsters are not speaking slang at all but a legitimate Scots language that deserves the same respect as standard English.

Cunningham's problem: Many of his students still guiltily think their Scots words are coarse slang best left on the street corner. It is now the job of Cunningham and other

Scottish teachers to convince them that it's "no sae bad" (not so bad) to be speaking Scots in the classroom, and in fact is an admirable thing.

If all this reminds you of the heated Ebonics debate in America, you're not mistaken.

Just as the United States wrestles with the idea of legitimizing black English, so Scotland has been struggling with the issue of legitimizing Scots, a language and/or dialect that has been derided for decades as a "bad" way of speaking English, out of place in the school or office.

The two struggles are so similar, in fact, that there may well be a lesson in Scotland for pro-Ebonics educators in the United States: It took more than 20 years of emotional, sometimes angry fighting, and there are still big pockets of resistance and a long way to go, but in the end, Scots won.

While it may not yet be acceptable for an African-American student in the United States to say "I be hungry," many Scottish students are now congratulated if they say things like "Who's all comin tae the jiggin?" (Who's coming to the dance?)

And perhaps not surprisingly, some of the strongest supporters of the American Ebonics movement are to be found among pro-Scots educators, who have nothing but sympathy for the black English cause.

"Good luck to them!" said Stuart McHardy, director of the Scots Language Resource Center in Perth, directing his best wishes to Ebonics fans. His advice: "Keep your cool. Just make your case. Do not create confrontational situations but do not give an inch." For both Scottish youngsters speaking Scots and Americans speaking black English, says University of Edinburgh educator Chris Robinson, it's just a matter of respect.

"In the early years of schooling, a child's home dialect should be given the respect it deserves," she said. "If you tell a child it's speaking wrong, all the time you're undermining the parents' authority. He's going to go home and say, 'Mommy, why do you speak wrong?' It's undermining the child's confidence."

Scots is one of the two indigenous languages of Great Britain's Scotland, the other being Gaelic. Unlike Gaelic, though, which is incomprehensible to most English speakers and readers, Scots is wedded to English and the two languages share many words and have many words that are just slight variations on each other. In Scots, for instance, loch means lake, tak means take, sang means song, hame means home and auld means old.

Like black English, Scots has a wide range of dialects and regional variations. "Broad Scots," the farthest removed from English, is likely to be spoken by Scotland's poorest residents and also its farmers, while more common Scots-English—the variation often used by famed Scottish poet Robert Burns—is a polyglot of both languages comparable to the "Spanglish" spoken along the U.S. border with Mexico.

Citing the similarities between Scots and English, Scottish educators over past decades have dismissed Scots as a mere slang dialect—one that had to be beaten out of students so they could learn to speak "properly." As one old Scottish educators' textbook said: "It's up to the teachers to encourage (Scottish students) even in their outside speech, but then the parents sometimes speak even worse than they do, so there's not much you can do about it."

Many of today's pro-Scots educators, including McHardy and teacher Cunningham, can well remember their own days as young students—when they were under constant threat of a whack from a "tawse" (leather strap) if they blurted out a single "aye."

But in the 1960s, jolted by a new sense of nationalistic pride, Scottish educators began seeking new respect for Scots—arguing that it was not an improper dialect but a language in its own right. While it did indeed descend from English, they argued, Scots emerged separately as a form of early English and then set off on its own path with Gaelic, French and Old Norse influences.

It took decades of arguing, but the pro-Scots movement finally succeeded beyond anyone's dreams.

For the first time this year, all public schools in Scotland have recognized Scots as a formal part of the curriculum, and there is a growing abundance of Scots dictionaries and modern literary works—most notably books from acclaimed

"Trainspotting" author Irvine Welsh, who writes in the spoken dialect of Glasgow Scots.

But the fight is far from ended. Except for the occasional "wee," Scots is never uttered by Scottish TV anchormen. And even pro-Scots educators still argue among themselves over whether it is a dialect or a language in its own right. The debate may never be resolved. McHardy and Robinson assert that a language is just a dialect with an army, and Scotland does not appear ready to take up arms to fight for independence from England.

Meanwhile, skirmishes continue over little issues like apostrophes. Some Scots writers might write comin' (for comin, meaning coming)—evoking an angry response from purists, who note that the apostrophe implies something is missing from the word when it is not.

And the biggest foes of Scots, in McHardy's opinion, remain the Scottish, particularly Scottish mothers. Like African-American mothers urging their children to "talk right," he said, Scottish mothers discourage Scots "because they feel it will limit their children's potential.... That's because the language has been so denigrated."

IF BLACK ENGLISH ISN'T A LANGUAGE, THEN TELL ME, WHAT IS?

James Baldwin

The argument concerning the use, or the status, or the reality, of black English is rooted in American history and has absolutely nothing to do with the question the argument supposes itself to be posing. The argument has nothing to do with language itself but with the *role* of language. Language, incontestably, reveals the speaker. Language, also, far more dubiously, is meant to define the other—and, in this case, the other is refusing to be defined by a language that has never been able to recognize him.

People evolve a language in order to describe and thus control their circumstances, or in order not to be submerged by a reality that they cannot articulate. (And, if they cannot articulate it, they *are* submerged.) A Frenchman living in Paris speaks a subtly and crucially different language from that of the man living in Marseilles; neither sounds very much like a man living in Quebec; and they would all have great difficulty in apprehending what the man from Guadeloupe, or Martinique, is saying, to say nothing of the man from Senegal—although the "common" language of all these areas is French. But each has paid, and is paying, a different price for this "common" language, in which, as it turns out, they are not saying, and cannot be saying, the same things: they each have very different realities to articulate, or control.

What joins all languages, and all men, is the necessity to confront life, in order, not inconceivably, to outwit death: the price for this is the acceptance, and achievement, of one's temporal identity. So that, for example, though it is not taught in the schools (and this has the potential of becoming a political issue) the south of France still clings to its ancient and musical Provençal, which resists being described as a "dialect." And much of the tension in the Basque countries, and in Wales, is due to the Basque and Welsh determination not to allow their languages to be destroyed. This determination also feeds the flames in Ireland for among the many indignities the Irish have been forced to undergo at English hands is the English contempt for their language.

It goes without saying, then, that language is also a political instrument, means, and proof of power. It is the most vivid and crucial key to identity: it reveals the private identity, and connects one with, or divorces one from, the larger, public, or communal identity. There have been, and are, times, and places, when to speak a certain language could be dangerous, even fatal. Or, one may speak the same language, but in such a way that one's antecedents are revealed, or (one hopes) hidden. This is true in France, and is absolutely true in England: the range (and reign) of accents on that damp little island make England coherent for the English and totally incomprehensible for everyone else. To open your mouth in England is (if I may use black English) to "put your business in the street": You have confessed your parents, your youth, your school, your salary, your self-esteem, and alas, your future.

Now, I do not know what white Americans would sound like if there had never been any black people in the United States, but they would not sound the way they sound. *Jazz,* for example, is a very specific sexual term, as in *jazz me, baby,* but white people purified it into the Jazz Age. *Sock it to me,* which means, roughly, the same thing, has been adopted by Nathaniel Hawthorne's descendants with no qualms or hesitations at all, along with *let it all hang out* and *right on! Beat to his socks,* which was once the black's most total and despairing image of poverty, was transformed into a thing called the Beat Generation, which phenomenon was, largely, composed of *uptight,* middle-class white people, imitating poverty, trying to *get down,* to get *with it,* doing their *thing,* doing their despairing best to be *funky,* which we, the blacks, never dreamed of doing—we *were* funky, baby, like *funk* was going out of style.

Now, no one can eat his cake, and have it, too, and it is late in the day to attempt to penalize black people for having created a language that permits the nation its only glimpse of reality, a language without which the nation would be even more *whipped* than it is.

I say that this present skirmish is rooted in American history, and it is. Black English is the creation of the black diaspora. Blacks came to the United States chained to each other, but from different tribes: neither could speak the other's language. If two black people, at that bitter hour of the world's history, had been able to speak to each other, the institution of chattel slavery could never have lasted as long as it did. Subsequently, the slave was given, under the eye, and the gun, of his master, Congo Square, and the Bible—or, in other words, and under these conditions, the slave began the formation of the black church, and it is within this unprecedented tabernacle that black English began to be formed. This was not, merely, as in the European example, the adoption of a foreign tongue, but an alchemy that transformed ancient elements into a new language: *A language comes into existence by means of brutal necessity, and the rules of the language are dictated by what the language must convey.*

There was a moment, in time, and in this place, when my brother, or my mother, or my father, or my sister, had to convey to me, for example, the danger in which I was standing from the white man standing just behind me, and to convey this with a speed, and in a language, that the white man could not possibly understand, and that, indeed, he cannot understand, until today. He cannot afford to understand it. This understanding would reveal to him too much about himself, and smash that mirror before which he has been frozen for so long.

Now, if this passion, this skill, this (to quote Toni Morrison) "sheer intelligence," this incredible music, the mighty achievement of having brought a people utterly unknown to, or despised by "history"—to have brought this people to their present, troubled, troubling, and unassailable and unanswerable place—if this absolutely unprecedented journey does not indicate that black English is a language, I am curious to know what definition of language is to be trusted.

A people at the center of the Western world, and in the midst of so hostile a population, has not endured and transcended by means of what is patronizingly called a "dialect." We, the blacks, are in trouble, certainly, but we are not doomed, and we are not inarticulate because we are not compelled to defend a morality that we know to be a lie.

The brutal truth is that the bulk of the white people in America never had any interest in educating black people, except as this could serve white purposes. It is not the black child's language that is in question, it is not his language that is despised: it is his experience. A child cannot be taught by anyone who despises him, and a child cannot afford to be fooled. A child cannot be taught by anyone whose demand, essentially, is that the child repudiate his experience, and all that gives him sustenance, and enter a limbo in which he will no longer be black, and in which he knows that he can never become white. Black people have lost too many black children that way.

And, after all, finally, in a country with standards so untrustworthy, a country that makes heroes of so many criminal mediocrities, a country unable to face why so many of the nonwhite are in prison, or on the needle, or standing, futureless, in the streets—it may very well be that both the child, and his elder, have concluded that they have nothing whatever to learn from the people of a country that has managed to learn so little.

DISCUSSION QUESTIONS AND WRITING ASSIGNMENTS

On the Readings by Cleaver, Vrazo, and Baldwin

1. Cleaver's article is approximately 250 words long, or about one double-spaced, typed page. Write your own 250-word editorial on Ebonics, expressing your own point of view; try to imitate Cleaver's forcefulness and conciseness. If possible, share your piece with classmates in small groups to begin a discussion or debate.

2. Explain the fifth paragraph of Cleaver's article. What point does the author make with his reference to Jesse Jackson?

3. Cleaver writes, "Begone, you 'poots.' " What are "poots"? What resources are available to you that might help you find out? Why do you think Cleaver uses this unusual word?

4. Discuss the claim made in the title of Vrazo's article, namely that England's struggle with Scots is similar to the Ebonics controversy. What similarities do you see in the Scots and Ebonics controversies, and what differences? How much weight would you give the Scots controversy in deciding what, if anything, American schools ought to do about Ebonics?

5. Write an imaginary dialogue between Eldridge Cleaver (author of "Rescuing Kids from Ebonics") and Davie Cunningham (the English teacher in Vrazo's article) on the topic of teachers and dialects.

6. Many discussions and debates about dialects include linguistic information like that found in this chapter or in Vrazo's article on Scots dialects. James Baldwin, however, writes that "the argument has nothing to do with language itself but with the *role* of language." What do you think this statement means, and why does Baldwin make this distinction?

7. Why, in Baldwin's opinion, is Black English a language?

8. What does Baldwin mean when he writes "it is late in the day to attempt to penalize black people for having created a language that permits the nation its only glimpse of reality, a language without which the nation would be even more *whipped* than it is"?

9. Of the three reading selections in Chapter 6, which do you think expresses the ideas that are most interesting, important, or accurate?

On Chapter 6

10. Review the Diverse Perspectives on Ebonics listed on pages 262–263. As a journal entry or a short essay, write a response to one or more of these quotations.

11. Research what has happened in the Oakland schools since the controversial resolution of 1996. Report to your class or write up what you learn in a short paper.

12. Translate several of the simple words below into jargon; that is, think up a wordier, more pretentious word or phrase. *Pain,* for example, might become *painful symptomatology.* How plausible are the examples you come up with? Could any of them turn out to be useful in the right context?

pain	up
cold	dishonesty
victory	two
big	hollow
crime	tax
traffic signal	storm
fire (as in lay off)	

13. Pick a paragraph from any convenient source that you think is written using a middle level of diction (word choice). Then, rewrite the paragraph twice, once using a high and once a low level of diction.

14. Think of an area in which you know more of the jargon than most people. (Your knowledge could come from an academic interest, a hobby, or a job.) Write a brief description or narrative using as much of the jargon as possible. The passage need not

make sense to anyone who lacks your knowledge. Here's an example written by Frank Gannon, based on the speech of certain Californian youth:

> I'm not grain-fed, but I know a gomer and they always have their theme. They act like a gork for weird on the moving mall stairs. Or they blow a hype on the pigeon tower.

15. The Diversity of Professional Dialects section reprints four passages about cloning written for four different audiences, but there are many more possibilities. Predict what kinds of discussions of cloning you would find in a legal context, in science fiction, in preaching, or in some other distinctive genre. To extend the assignment, find an interesting passage and analyze its language, or compare and contrast the differing styles of two such passages.

REFERENCES

Angorge, Wilhelm, Hartmutt Voss and Jürgen Zimmermann. *DNA Sequencing Strategies: Automated and Advanced Approaches.* New York: John Wiley and Sons, 1997.

Applebome, Peter. "English Unique to Blacks Is Officially Recognized." *New York Times* (Dec. 20, 1996) A8.

Associated Press. "Group Rewords Ebonics Proposal." *San José Mercury News* (Jan. 13, 1997) B1, B4.

"Bilingual Workers Fired for Using Spanish." Associated Press (Aug. 15, 1997).

Colvin, Richard Lee. "Education: Officials Try to Defuse Uproar over Resolution that Labeled Black Speech Patterns a Language." *Los Angeles Times* (Dec. 31, 1996) A1.

Cose, Ellis. "Why Ebonics Is Irrelevant." *Newsweek* (Jan. 13, 1997) 80.

De Witt, Karen. "Not So Separate: Ebonics, Language of Richard Nixon." *New York Times* (Dec. 29, 1996) E3.

Emmons, Ron. "Black English Has Its Place." *Los Angeles Times* (Dec. 27, 1996) B9.

Gannon, Frank. "A Portrait of the Artist as a Young Californian." *The New Yorker* (Mar. 25, 1985) 41.

Golden, Tim. "Oakland Revamps Plan to Teach Black English." *New York Times* (Jan. 14, 1997) A8.

Hale, Constance, ed. *Wired Style: Principles of English Usage in the Digital Age.* San Francisco: HardWired Books, 1996.

Harris, John F. "Ebonics Program Not Entitled to Federal Funds, Education Secretary Says." *Los Angeles Times* (Dec. 25, 1996) A18.

Holmes, Steven A. "Black English Debate: No Standard Assumptions." *New York Times* (Dec. 30, 1996) A7.

Johnson, Clarence. "Holding on to a Language of Our Own" [Interview with John Rickford]. *San Francisco Chronicle* (Feb. 16, 1997) Zone 3, p. 3.

Kleffman, Sandy. "Jackson Switches Sides in Ebonics Debate." *San José Mercury News* (Dec. 31, 1996) B1, B2.

Lacey, Marc. "U.S. Panel Grills Officials on Ebonics Policy." *Los Angeles Times* (Jan. 24, 1997) A3.

Leland, John and Nadine Joseph. "Hooked on Ebonics." *Newsweek* (Jan. 13, 1997) 78–79.

Lewis, Neil A. "Jackson Says Black English Isn't a Separate Language." *New York Times* (Dec. 23, 1996) B9.

Macauley, Ronald K. S. *The Social Art: Language and Its Uses.* New York: Oxford University Press, 1994.

McKinley, Jesse. "Board's Decision on Black English Stirs Debate." *New York Times* (Dec. 21, 1996) I8.

Pasternak, Judy. "Linguists Praise Oakland's Plan to Use Ebonics." *Los Angeles Times* (Jan. 4, 1997) A1.

Pyle, Amy. "95th Street School: Ebonics in Real Life." *Los Angeles Times* (Jan. 19, 1997) A1.

Rickford, John R. "Ebonics Succeeds Where Traditional Methods Do Not." *San José Mercury News* (Dec. 26, 1996) B8.

Shaw, James E. "Perspectives on 'Ebonics'; Don't Self-Inflict Another Obstacle." *Los Angeles Times* (Dec. 27, 1996) B9.

Sherwin, Susan. "New Reproductive Technologies." Reprinted in Dana E. Bushnell, ed., *Nagging Questions: Feminist Ethics in Everyday Life.* Lanham, MD: Rowman & Littlefield, 1995.

Weiss, Kenneth R. and Richard Lee Colvin. "Oakland Schools Drop 2 Key Points in Ebonics Stand." *Los Angeles Times* (Jan. 16, 1997) A3.

Weiss, Kenneth R. "Oakland Vote Hopes to End Ebonics Uproar." *Los Angeles Times* (Jan. 17, 1997) A23.

Weiss, Rick and John Schwartz. "Monkeys Cloned from Embryos." *San Francisco Examiner* (Mar. 2, 1997) A2.

Weston, Kevin. "Of Ebonics and the Relevance of a School's Curriculum." *Los Angeles Times* (Jan. 5, 1997) M6.

Woo, Elaine and Mary Curtius. "Oakland School District Recognizes Black English." *Los Angeles Times* (Dec. 20, 1996) A1.

Woo, Elaine and Solomon Moore. "School Decision on Black English Stirs Up a Storm of Commentary." *Los Angeles Times* (Dec. 21, 1996) A24.

Index

This page constitutes a continuation of the copyright page.

Chapter 1

José Antonio Burciaga. "What's in a Spanish Name?" from *Spilling the Beans* by José Antonio Burciaga, published by Joshua Odell Editions, Santa Barbara, California.

Roger L. Welsch. "Enter Laughing but Beware the es-ex factor." With permission from *Natural History,* July 1996. Copyright the American Museum of Natural History 1996.

Patricia Williams. "Town Hall Television." Reprinted by permission of the publisher from *The Rooster's Egg* by Patricia Williams, Cambridge, Mass.: Harvard University Press, Copyright © 1995 by the President and Fellows of Harvard College.

Chapter 2

David Guterson. "Wood Grouse on a High Promontory Overlooking Canada" from *The Country Ahead of Us, The Country Behind* by David Guterson (New York: Harper & Row, 1989) Copyright 1989 by David Guterson. Reprinted by permission of George Borchardt, Inc. for the author.

Roger von Oech. From *A Whack on the Side of the Head* by Roger von Oech. Copyright © 1983, 1990, by Roger von Oech. By permission of Warner Books.

Juanita Johnson-Bailey. "Poet Sonia Sanchez: Telling What We Must Hear" interview with Juanita Johnson-Bailey from *Flat-Footed Truths: Telling Black Women's Lives* by Patricia Bell-Scott, ed., © 1998 by Patricia Bell-Scott. Reprinted by permission of Henry Holt and Company, Inc.

Chapter 3

Jamaica Kincaid. "In History." Copyright © 1997 by Jamaica Kincaid, first printed in *Callaloo,* reprinted with permission of The Wylie Agency, Inc.

Chapter 4

Michael Kelly. "Running On." Originally published in *The New Yorker,* September 23, 1996.

Hendrik Hertzberg. "Big Talk." Reprinted by permission; © 1995. The New Yorker Magazine, Inc. All rights reserved.

Chapter 5

Gloria Anzaldúa. "Speaking in Tongues: A Letter to 3rd World Women Writers" from *This Bridge Called My Back.*

Chapter 6

Shankar Vedantam and Mary Otto. "When Man Tries to Play God" from the *San José Mercury News,* March 2, 1997. Reprinted with permission of Knight-Ridder/Tribune Information Services.

Eldridge Cleaver. "Rescuing Kids from Ebonics" by Eldridge Cleaver. Copyright, 1998, Los Angeles Times. Reprinted by permission.

Fawn Vrazo. "England's Struggle with Scots Similar to Ebonics Controversy" from *The Philadelphia Enquirer.* Copyright 1997. Reprinted with permission of Knight-Ridder/Tribune Information Services.

James Baldwin. "If Black English Isn't a Language, Then Tell Me, What Is?" Copyright © 1979/1987 by *The New York Times.* Reprinted by permission.